THE CURIOUS MIND

Twenty-Five Years of
John Quinn *Radio Programmes*

THE CURIOUS MIND

Stay Curious!
Best Wishes
John Quinn

VERITAS

First published 2009 by
Veritas Publications
7–8 Lower Abbey Street
Dublin 1
Ireland
Email publications@veritas.ie
Website www.veritas.ie

ISBN 978 1 84730 200 7

10 9 8 7 6 5 4

Designed by Lir Mac Cárthaigh
Printed in the Republic of Ireland by Hudson Killeen Ltd., Dublin

Veritas books are printed on paper made from the wood pulp of
managed forests. For every tree felled, at least one tree is planted, thereby
renewing natural resources.

DEDICATION

To all the contributors to this book – to share their experiences and ideas has been my pleasure and my privilege.

CONTENTS

FOREWORD
On Education

THERE IS A great deal of discussion in the literature on the theme of change in education. Notwithstanding the energy devoted to the issue however, the suspicion persists that much of what passes for change in education is more imagined than real – while the wine is sometimes changed, the bottles remain stubbornly familiar.

While there are many possible reasons underlying such inertia, two in particular come to mind in Ireland. First, traditionally teachers as a professional group have been wary of change. New curricula and pedagogical innovations are routinely subjected to the acid test of their application and relevance in the classroom. This is understandable. Plotting a course between order and chaos in the classroom is a highly skilled and potentially treacherous endeavour where the margin of error is sometimes very slender. It has low tolerance for failed experimentation. The fact that much that is new has tended to be generated outside of the classroom, as for instance in the relatively sanitised or even disconnected environment of the third level, adds to their scepticism.

There is however a further element to this scepticism. It arises from a widely disseminated but rarely tested view of the high quality of Irish education. Regardless of a significant body of evidence drawing attention to our shortcomings, as for instance the PISA tables, Irish education has often been characterised by a high level of complacency and a reluctance to interrogate.

In a report published earlier this year, the National Economic and Social Council (NESC) draws attention to what it considers to be the five major crises which Ireland must now address. These are the fiscal crisis; the banking crisis; the economic crisis; the social crisis; and the reputational crisis. In short, there is no room for complacency with regard to any aspect of modern Ireland. Rather, the country must now embark on a relentless process of introspection as it attempts to re-imagine and re-build itself out of the debris of the collapse of the Celtic Tiger.

It is entirely appropriate and timely that this book should emerge now as a key contributor to the rethinking process which must now begin. It is deeply ironic that so many of the thinkers and ideas which are captured in this hugely eclectic collection would have been considered by many in Irish education when they were first heard on radio to be 'interesting but not practical'. One of the great cultural lessons from the collapse of the Celtic Tiger has to be that just being practical is no longer sufficient. If the practical pre-empts the questioning, not only is a fundamental pillar of democracy removed, but the society loses its capacity to re-create itself in the light of changing circumstances.

Throughout its many years on radio, 'The Open Mind', one of the series featured prominently in this book, consistently questioned practice and the merely practical. By drawing attention to alternative views and alternative ways of doing things, it shone a light on the conventional, focusing on its shortcomings and forcing it to justify its positions and assumptions. Throughout its long radio life-span it was a source in equal measure of inspiration and discomfort. The Socratic style of questioning which John Quinn uniquely brought to the programme gently led the interviewee and the audience on a path of new discovery, new insight and ultimately new wisdom.

John has now done the immense service of bringing many of these interviews together in this extensive collection of readings. The book reads like one great summer school where ideas and perspectives float from every page and where the reader is continuously arrested and challenged by the unconventional or the unexpected.

Every generation must plan the future and lay the foundation for it. To achieve this it must have an image of the future and a coherence in pursuing it. In the current period of unprecedented upheaval, there is little in the way of a shared or optimistic vision for the future in Ireland. Such a vision will undoubtedly emerge. It can only do so in an environment where there is a profusion of ideas and an animated discussion amongst the citizenry regarding options. This book is an invaluable catalyst in triggering this process.

TOM COLLINS
Professor of Education, NUI Maynooth
August 2009

FOREWORD
On Broadcasting

JOHN QUINN AMBLES into the office at the Radio Centre. Like a hunter-gatherer, he returns from the field with a tape recorder slung on one shoulder and bag full of books, batteries and audio tapes in hand. He installs himself at the desk, clamps on the headphones, and stokes a cheroot until he's puffed up a blue haze. As the big spools of the playback machine rotate, he smiles now and then and sips industrial-strength coffee. He could be anywhere under the sun or rain – in the Punjab with the young Spike Milligan, or walking Ballivor bog, or taking a turn on Berkeley campus with Seamus Heaney.

This is how radio is made. Or at least, this is how John made it look easy. He followed his instinct – which is to say, the promptings of his uniquely curious and companionable mind. Here is a book of reflections, insights, arguments, contentions, lessons learned, emotions relived. It's also a hosting of remarkable contributors for whom John conveys respect, admiration, and – most importantly –

affection. When Frank O'Connor recalled his school teacher, Daniel Corkery, he said that Corkery so impressed him that he imitated even how his master walked. And from that experience he concluded that true learning is rooted in love.

Many of the pieces in this anthology are brief, but they are compact with the power of profound lyrics. Perhaps this is because so many of John's companions draw on their childhood memories – those vivid sounds, sights and smells that are the fabric of our first conscious encounters with the world. And to these elemental experiences of puzzlement, wonder, doubt, pain and pleasure, we all return in the never-ending effort to make sense of who we are and where we came from.

The whole trick with radio is not to make it sound like a book. Yet here is radio bound between covers. It's a risky venture. Socrates distrusted the written record. He thought that copying inevitably leads to distortion, and so it poses a threat to the integrity of the spoken word, the fresh, direct and unmediated human statement. But what would we know of Socrates if Plato had not taken notes? So think of this book as a chance to hear again, or for the first time, in your mind's ear an unrivalled series of dialogues. They were conducted over a quarter of a century and first offered as public broadcasts to enrich the experience of each private listener to RTÉ Radio. As you read, you'll find yourself in dazzling and surprisingly varied company. You may even feel a sense of elevation as you survey the many different landscapes in this particular atlas. But that's as it should be, according to Hugh Leonard who reminds us here that the purpose of reading is 'To fly, not alone, but in companionship'.

ADRIAN MOYNES
Former Director of Radio, RTÉ
August 2009

THE CURIOUS MIND

INTRODUCTION

You meet a lot of people in twenty-five years. When broadcasting is your business, you meet a lot of *interesting* people over that period of time – people who have had interesting lives, who expound interesting ideas, who are doing interesting work.

In my twenty-five years as a radio broadcaster with RTÉ, it was my privilege to meet a range of such people – writers, philosophers, entertainers, educationists, activists, politicians, business people – and to bring their experiences and ideas to a wider public through the wonderful medium of radio. These encounters featured in a range of series – *The Open Mind, Education Forum, A Portrait of the Artist as a Young Girl, My Education, Heroes and Heroines, Millennium Minds, This Place Speaks to Me, I Remember, I Remember, The Great Educators, The Mark of Man, The Rural Development School, The Tinakilly Senate, My Books, My Friends, L-Plus* – and these are just the series that are represented in this book!

It has long been a dream of mine to distil a selection from that radio archive of twenty-five years into print, simply because I felt that there were riches in that archive that would otherwise languish in the radio vaults forever ... As the sources above indicate, those riches extend far beyond the subject of education (my main area of concern) into areas such as history, the environment, music, literature, humour and personal memoir. I have also included excerpts from a number of documentaries on topics ranging from Eskimos to All-Ireland Final Day. I am cognisant of the fact that good radio does not always make good print and so some excerpts have needed judicious editing, but I have at all times remained faithful to the original source.

If I have learned anything over those twenty-five years, it is that there are many ways of knowing the world. I am deeply grateful to the many contributors who have helped enormously in opening my mind in so many ways. I hope in turn that the reader will find in these pages something to delight, to challenge, to ponder – some new way of knowing the world.

My working career has embraced education and broadcasting. I am especially honoured that two very eminent representatives from these fields – Tom Collins and Adrian Moynes – have each contributed a foreword to the book from their particular perspective.

I am deeply indebted to Veritas for their belief in this project and their commitment to it. As editor, Caitríona Clarke has been most supportive and insightful with her advice and suggestions. A special thank you to my wonderful typist, Máire Ní Fhrighil, who seeks perfection always and is no mean editor in her own right!

JOHN QUINN
October 2009

AN INDIAN BOYHOOD

SPIKE MILLIGAN *recalls growing up in India in the 1920s.*

I WAS BORN in India primarily because I wanted to be near my mother ... My father came from Sligo and like many young men of his time he found the British Army to be a way out of poverty. The regimental depot in Sligo was like an employment exchange. He was posted to India where he did well, rising to the rank of sergeant. He met my mother in church there and fell in love with her singing voice.

My first memory of school was in an army tent in the Hyderabad Desert. It was fairly primitive – when the wind rose we were sent outside to sit on the tent pegs to prevent the pegs blowing away. At the age of five I was sent to the Convent of Jesus and Mary school in Poona, where I did very well under the tutelage of Mother Fabian – a tall, red-faced nun, bursting with repression. The nuns were responsible for putting me on stage. They had a problem with scene changes in their Nativity play, so they dressed me as a clown and sent me on to jump up and down between acts. When they were ready they would say, 'That's all, Terry. You can come off now!' How strongly prophetic it was, seeing as how I would spend my life being a clown ...

India was quite an exotic place to grow up in at that time. The sights, the sounds, the scents ... I remember the lines of marching regiments – Sikhs, Gurkhas etc. – in their bright turbanned uniforms, the beating of leopardskin drums, the blare of silver bugles from the Ulster and Connaught Rifles. How lucky I was to see it all. We travelled a lot because some bureaucrat in London would justify his existence by moving regiments hither and thither. Bombay, Calcutta, Karachi – on the

Peninsular Railway – often four or five-day journeys. I remember the train pulling into some remote station at night and the vendors would call out, offering Biddy cigarettes, hot milk, oranges and bananas. Then the great hiss of steam as we moved off, with the kitehawks screaming overhead. When we passed over a great river gorge the sound changed dramatically – *ticket-a-tick, ticket-a-tick*, DUM-DUM, DUM-DUM – I loved that. I loved too the sound of the monsoon rain on the corrugated roof of our verandah when I was tucked up in bed.

And music – there was always music. My father was a good musician, as was my uncle Hughie. Hughie played the saxophone – ragtime stuff like 'Black Bottom' and 'Miss Annabel Lee'. He was a very good athlete, draughtsman, mechanic – and a lunatic! He couldn't get it together in his head. He used to dress up as Tarzan and play the saxophone while flexing his muscles.

When I was about seven years old, I got a taste for gambling. I would go down to the West Indian Turf Club in Poona with a few pence in my pocket. The Hindu bookmakers wrote out the bets on fine cigarette-paper, so that if the police came along, they could roll up the paper and swallow it. I was quite successful as a seven-year-old gambler. My ambition then was to be a jockey, but I was too tall. Myself and my friends would make paper goggles like the jockeys had, mark out a course and 'gallop' for miles until we were exhausted. At Poona racecourse I saw my first aeroplane – a Bristol fighter – and when I watched the pilot in his red leather helmet climb aboard and take off, it took my breath away. For the next fourteen years I wanted to be a fighter pilot – until I failed the exam back in England. I was heavily into jazz also – from the moment I heard my first jazz record in the army canteen – Fats Waller singing '*I'll be glad when you're dead, you rascal you*'. Amazing.

I was an only child for eight years until we moved to Rangoon where my brother Desmond was born. I hadn't a lot of access to my father in those eight years and it disturbed me – I used to wet the bed a lot. As a result I was too close to my mother. She was somewhat overpowering, so that when I was eventually let out into the world, I fell apart at the seams. When I was given responsibility, I couldn't cope. I let my first

THE CURIOUS MIND

wife down. I let my army colleagues down. I let everybody down. I became psycho-neurotic and was in and out of mental hospitals a lot. My brother was much more balanced because my father was more accessible to him. In Rangoon I went to the De La Salle Brothers school. There were a few Jesuit brothers there who were marvellous to me. They opened me up when I was at that gawky, pimply stage. I remember asking Brother Theophilus, 'Do you ever think about women?' 'Oh, all the time,' he said. I couldn't believe it.

Eventually we left Rangoon for England when I was fifteen. Even though we sailed on a troopship, it was an extraordinary voyage. It was travel on a grand scale, real *fin de siècle* stuff. Lascars scrubbing the decks with sand ... polishing up the brasses ... fine white tablecloths ... concerts at night. A marvellous experience. I remember as we sailed down the Irrawaddy river through the rain and mist, I was suddenly overcome with tears and hid myself away. I was leaving my childhood behind – my friends, the trees, rivers, lakes and animals that I knew and loved. Life would never be the same again. Many years later I wrote a poem about this.

> What happened to the boy I was?
> Why did he run away?
> And leave me old and thinking like
> There's been no yesterday?
>
> What happened then? Was I that boy
> Who laughed and swam in the bund*?
> Is there no going back? No recompense?
> Is there nothing – no refund?

* canal

THE INFLUENCE OF PARENTS

Growing up in Derry, politician JOHN HUME *learned much from the commitment and self-sacrifice of his parents.*

MY FATHER HAD beautiful copperplate handwriting and he was a highly intelligent man. A lot of people in the district used to come to him to write their letters for them, or to write letters to the local authority. So, from a very early age – as we didn't have a very big house – I was conscious of people and their problems. We had two bedrooms, one living room and a parlour, and people would queue up waiting for my father as he sat writing at the table. He was very committed to helping people solve their problems, because he had a very good knowledge of the whole system.

Without the dedication and self-sacrifice of my mother, I don't think I would have got anywhere in life. She was totally committed to rearing us in the best possible way, with very, very limited resources, and when I look back I just don't know how she did it. I am absolutely convinced that the major influence on any life is the parents and that this takes place in the early years of a child. Even though usually buried in the subconscious, these are the forces that create you and make you what you are and give you your attitude to life.

When I think back on those early days, I can see the roots of a lot of the things I later became involved in. I was founder of the first Credit Union in the North – in Derry – at the age of twenty-three. I learned about credit from my mother having to borrow to rear us and repay at a high rate. I remember thinking that if she and her sisters got together every couple of weeks and pooled their money, they would have enough to go out, instead of this borrowing. When I discovered that these organisations existed, a group of us got together and set up our own Credit Union and had our first meeting with £5 1s 9d. Today, there are fourteen thousand members in that Credit Union branch and it has a brand new building and nine million pounds in savings. I became the national president of the Credit Union movement when I was twenty-seven years old and I was president for four or five years. It is the most powerful co-operative in the history of Ireland, and if I did nothing else in my life, I would be very happy with that.

IN PRAISE OF MEANDERING

PENELOPE LEACH, *the writer on child development, extolled for me the value of meandering in a child's life.*

SOME YEARS AGO I interviewed Penelope Leach, the writer on child development. She bemoaned the fact that children today are denied the opportunity to 'meander' – the chance to pause and reflect, to stand and stare, to work things out. Instead, we hurry them through their young lives, often organising those lives out of existence.

I love the word 'meander'. Its very sound rolls musically off the tongue. Meander. It depicts a mazy, sinuous movement, winding and weaving, pausing and moving on. Like a river in fact. And of course, that is the origin of the word. Meander is the name of a river in Asia Minor. A river is a most creative force. It forges its own path and follows a natural course. It works things out – slowly, deliberately.

The eleventh commandment, Penelope would say, is 'Thou shalt not be bored'. And so we supply the children with 'things' and pursuits that will occupy their time. Albeit with the best will in the world. We want our children to have interests and – dare we say it – skills that might just give them an edge in that big competitive world out there. Fine – up to a point. But children need time just as much as skills and interests. Time to think, to wonder.

This all came back to me a long time ago when I did a study of children's leisure pursuits. The children were supplied with diaries blocked-out in half-hours. In those diaries they would record how they spent their free time. Out of the thousands of diaries I had to read, I can remember only one – from a boy who faithfully recorded that – for four successive half-hours – he was 'firing stones' ... 'firing stones' ... 'firing stones' ... 'firing stones' ...

Given that he wasn't firing stones at a neighbour's glasshouse, what dilemmas he must have wrestled with, what solutions he must have entertained!

What meandering he must have done.

IN PRAISE OF READING

HUGH LEONARD *in praise of the joys of reading and recalling the books that gave him wings.*

IT HAS LONG BEEN my personal conviction that an essential part of every Irish family is a mad aunt. In my more fanciful moments, I imagine a stud farm – probably in Kildare – where the species is bred or at least maddened to order. In my own family we never wanted for madness for not only was there my mother's sister, Mary, but also my father's Aunt Julia – an ancient creature who dressed in layers of dusty black bombazine and had hands like old leather. One day, when I was perhaps eight, she came to our house and gave me a halfpenny – accompanying the gift with the unassailable observation that as long as I possessed it, I would always have money. She had another gift for me – a copy of *Great Expectations.* Great-aunt Julia was a miser and before a day had passed, repented of her prodigality and demanded the return of both gifts.

By then it was too late. I had met Pip and the terrifying Magwitch and Joe Gargery and had reached the point where Uncle Pumplechook drank the tarwater in mistake for Mrs Joe's Christmas brandy. By then the harm was done. I was a reader of books. Many years later, in a book of my own, I mentioned that incident – for there are not many moments in life that one can point to as a turning point. Perhaps that is why we go to plays. It makes the world tidy, with an exciting bit in Act Two and a turning point every five minutes. In time I not only finished reading *Great Expectations* but also adapted it for television.

Recently I have turned to books that were part of my growing up – rather as one suddenly craves to see again a friend of one's youth. There is one book in particular that I have revisited with pleasure. It is Neville Cardus's autobiography. He so vividly recalls that beacon of light in his early life which was the yellow glow that shone through the windows of Manchester Public Library. I have only to open the pages of this very great book to go pounding once again up the granite steps of the Carnegie Library in Dún Laoghaire, to feel the gentle sigh of warm air, to go through the wicket gate at the counter and ransack the shelves of the newly returned books. In those days, I acquired a nickname – Go-by-the-Wall – because I invariably read as I walked along and brushed the nearest wall with my elbow as a guide to navigation. I read everywhere – at street corners, on trams and buses, while waiting for the pictures to begin. I can remember my chagrin at losing Jack London's *The Call of the Wild* in the Carlton cinema and my joy when it was found (my address was on the flyleaf) in the same cinema, two years later.

Who did I read? Dennis Wheatley, whose thrillers often threw in a history lesson for good measure. Dornford Yates, whose novels we thought the last thing in humour with their allusions to wops and dagos – which to modern eyes are rabidly fascistic. I read *The Good Companions* and *Angel Pavement*, filled with Priestley's brand of common sense and solid as roast beef. I read *If Winter Comes, Love on the Dole* and *The Citadel*, and there was *The Story of San Michele* – evidence of either a remarkable life or a remarkable liar. There were travel books such as Halliburton's *The Magic Carpet* – which was exactly that and transported me through Keats's charmed magic casements, opening on the foam of perilled seas in fairy lands forlorn. And there were the travel books of H.V. Morton, who did not roam so very far away but could bring the reader into the very soul of a city.

We lived after all on an island and for much of my youth it was wartime and so we travelled with the aid of books. I remember a passage from Morton's *The Year in London*, in which he brilliantly evokes a November afternoon with the fog outside crowding at the windows and buttered muffins to eat and the firelight – I remember the phrase exactly – 'glinting on a pair of silk-clad knees opposite'. I discovered too the Irish novels of L.A.G. Strong – an unglamorous journeyman writer who never wrote a bestseller, but depicted the passing of an age. His books and stories showed me that I could find material in the most seemingly dull and unlikely places, for they were set in Glasthule and Dún Laoghaire. To Strong these were places of romance. To myself – who grew up there – they were the prison from which I longed to escape.

Reading was not always regarded during my lifetime as a good thing. It was feared and detested by some. There were those who saw it not as a means of enlightenment and aesthetic pleasure but rather as a source of possible corruption, as a weapon of degenerates, as a means by which the devil's helpers would lead us to perdition. It is now perhaps not so well remembered that the list of banned books comprised twelve thousand publications at one time. It seems like a bad dream at this distance – the idea of a society where one could not read freely. The authors whose works were deemed indecent or obscene included – among Irish writers alone – O'Casey, Joyce, Kate O'Brien, Liam O'Flaherty, Benedict Kiely, Frank O'Connor and Seán Ó Faoláin. I remember when as an amateur actor I asked a middle-aged man to direct our choice of play, he returned the script to me on the basis of one line of dialogue and said it was the dirtiest play he had ever read. The offending line was – 'You have the clammy touch of a sex-starved cobra', from *The Man Who Came to Dinner*.

A book is a personal experience between reader and author – an actual relationship. These 'friendships' – as I call them – have been part of my life and have been all the more delightful when unexpected. In the Book Exchange in Dalkey a few years ago, I found a volume with the unwieldy name *W. Somerset Maugham's Introduction to English and American Literature*. It turned out to be a personal anthology of stories, poems and *belles lettres* intended for service men and women during World War II. Each section was introduced at length and lovingly by the old party himself. It's a treasure-house of the unexpected and valued above rubies.

And so too is a book I found on an otherwise empty shelf in a hotel on an island at what seemed to be the end of the world. It was *Anna Karenina*. The last thing I wanted to read about was the story of a love goddess. Then I read the opening lines – 'All happy families are alike but an unhappy family is unhappy after its own fashion'. Good heavens! It was actually readable! And Anna Karenina was not a heroine at all but a silly, self-serving woman, blinded by her all-sacrificing need to be a romantic. I had discovered what to me is the greatest novel ever written.

I recall being in a garden in Taormina, riotous with flowers and within sight of Mount Etna. It was there that I opened *The Path to Rome* by Hilaire Belloc. I never finished it, because I shall do so – or not at all – in the same garden, for the book and the setting became one.

The person who opens a book acquires wings, and the better that book the higher he flies. He does not travel alone. The writer bears him company, and together they go hand in hand. And that is the purpose of – and the justification for – not only reading but for writing as well. To fly, not alone, but in companionship.

A POLITICAL EDUCATION

For twenty-five years, GERRY FITT *was embroiled in the cauldron of Northern Ireland politics.*

AFTER I CAME home from sea, I used to go to classes at the Workers' Education Association, run by the trade union movement. I went there and learned a wee bit about economics. And then there was the International Correspondence School. They sent a book and the work was all done by correspondence – you did the work and then you sent it back to them for marking. It cost seven quid at the time. I think I did three different papers and I passed them all, but by this time I was rearing a family and I couldn't afford to give up another seven quid. Also, I belonged to the library in Belfast and I read whatever I could get my hands on. I became very interested in economics, but I never had any great urge to go to university. I was too busy doing other things.

Those three years between 1958 and 1961 were the most important years in my political life. I didn't get paid for being a councillor. I had no money and I was rearing a small family. But I was absolutely obsessed with being in politics and being able to help people. I read all the National Insurance Acts and I used to go down to the local tribunals representing people. I became known as the Perry Mason of the local tribunals!

When I was elected, I deliberately set out to prove that I wasn't a Catholic representative but that I was a non-sectarian representative. I remember Protestants coming to my door in 1958 and they would start, 'Councillor Fitt, I'm a Protestant', and I would say, 'Look, I don't care whether you're a Protestant or not ...'. Those people were living in exactly the same conditions as the Catholics and they were having the same problems. There was massive unemployment at the time and a whole lot of them were on the dole or on sickness benefit. I began to represent them and news of this travelled like wildfire all over the place. The more I helped them, the more they sent their relations to see me. It took a lot out of me. I had to neglect my own home and family, going to local tribunals and then going to city council meetings. I made a lot of friends in those three years.

In 1961 I defended the seat and I won it with a big, big majority. And then in 1962 the parliamentary seat came up for re-election. I went out and fought the seat and won. That gave me some sort of economic wherewithal to stay in politics. I had seven hundred quid a year and I thought I was a millionaire, but at least I was able to look after my wife and kids. In 1965 Terence O'Neill had taken over from Lord Brookeborough as prime minister and he called an election for November. I was very, very apprehensive about this election, because the history of Dock up until then had been that no political party had held the seat at successive elections. Here I was, the second time around, fighting against history, but I fought like hell and I won with an even bigger majority.

In 1968 the civil rights movement began and I played a reasonably prominent part in that. I was interested in bringing in legislation which would help the underdog living in the Catholic ghettoes in Northern Ireland. I went to Derry in October for the famous civil rights march. I had taken the precaution of bringing Labour MPs over, because I knew what was going to happen. I knew they were going to beat the hell out of us, and so I got some photographers over as well. I was grabbed by the police and they beat me over the head with a baton. The blood ran down my face and the cameras were there to see. It caused a great big furore. When I returned to Westminster, I made speech after speech, saying, 'I got this beating for asking for the same rights for my constituents as you have for yours'.

The civil rights movement was totally justified, but it scared the life out of the Protestants, because they saw it as an attack on their privileges, which it actually wasn't. And that began the trouble. The Unionist underdog began to rebel against what he saw as concessions being given. There was awful fear in West Belfast. The Catholics thought that they were going to get slaughtered in their beds. I telephoned Jim Callaghan, who was the Home Secretary, and pleaded with him to send the army in, because there was a real fear that a pogrom could have broken out in Northern Ireland. I remember what Jim Callaghan said to me. 'Gerry,' he said, 'I can get the army in, but it's going to be a devil of a job getting it out.' And how right he proved to be.

I had a very nasty election in West Belfast, because the IRA were coming to the fore and they were beginning to attack me as being pro-Brit and so on. I won that election again in 1970. Then, in 1971, the IRA started shooting. When this happened, it changed my whole political life, because I could never understand how the IRA could be guilty of some of the terrible atrocities that they committed. Internment came in in August 1971 and that just tore the whole community asunder; the Catholic population were totally opposed to it.

In 1969 John Hume, Ivan Cooper, Paddy O'Hanlon and Paddy Devlin had been elected because of the civil rights agitation that was then taking place. There was great pressure on them to form a new political party. I had reservations about it, because I was from Belfast. I knew Belfast, I knew Protestants, but the others who were elected didn't have that same sort of political experience. They were Catholic representatives, as such. I formed with the rest of them the SDLP, the Social Democratic and Labour Party.

Bloody Sunday, in 1972, was a big watershed in politics in Northern Ireland. Because of that and our agitation, Stormont was abolished and then we came under direct rule. In 1973, we went to Sunningdale and we had the Sunningdale Conference.

I thought then and I think now – and I will continue to think – that Sunningdale was by far the most hopeful development that we ever had politically in Northern Ireland since its creation. There were two tangents to it. One was the setting up of a Northern Ireland executive, composed of both Catholics and Protestants. I thought that was a tremendous advance. In that executive, I was the deputy Prime Minister – the deputy chief executive – John Hume was the Minister for Commerce, Austin Currie was the Minister for Development, Paddy Devlin was the Minister for Health and Social Services, Ivan Cooper was the Minister for Community Relations. They were four of the most important offices in any government. The second part of the Sunningdale Agreement was the part which actually killed Sunningdale. A provision was made for a Council of Ireland which would involve the ministers in the Republic sitting with us. And that scared the living daylights out of the Unionists. When the executive fell in May of 1974, it caused great bitterness. People then realised that we should have done more to hold on to it.

Paddy Devlin was a socialist like myself, with a trade union background, and the Belfast wing of the SDLP were the Labour men. We were the socialists; the ones outside were the Catholics and the Nationalists. So there was always this conflict within the party. And then Paddy Devlin left in 1977, which left me isolated with a few others from Belfast, and I was becoming increasingly despairing of anything ever happening.

The IRA were trying to kill me and they broke into my house in 1976. I will never forget the job I had getting them out. I had a licensed weapon at the time. Had I not had that, they would have beaten the hell out of me with iron bars. I felt particularly incensed because I was a Catholic and these people were doing things allegedly in my name and in the name of Ireland. Whenever I appeared on television I would make my position clear – that I detested them and everything they stood for. I charged them with dragging the name of Ireland through the gutter and said they were not speaking on behalf of the Irish people.

But there were some of my colleagues in the SDLP who – when the IRA committed some terrible atrocity – would keep their heads down. It got to such a stage in 1979 that I left the party, because I felt I was on my own. In 1981, the hunger strike took place and that was a really big disaster for Northern Ireland. It tore the heart and soul out of the Catholic community and the Unionist community. The Unionists saw those hunger strikers as people who had murdered their friends; the Catholics saw them as patriots or just some misguided young Irishmen, and it just tore them all apart.

I had an awful time during that period around my home on the Antrim Road. They used to gather outside my house every night and throw stones and petrol bombs. They would stand outside the door and shout 'Gerry Fitt is a Brit'. It was the worst word they could have thrown. I was no more a Brit then than I had ever been. I didn't go into politics as a Catholic or a Protestant or a Republican or a Unionist. I went in as a working-class candidate to try to help people, but the whole thing was going awry.

In 1983 I had to defend my West Belfast seat. The SDLP was under the leadership of John Hume. Gerry Adams, the Sinn Féin candidate, came into the field and the SDLP deliberately put up a candidate. Again it was a nasty election. I couldn't send out my election addresses, because the IRA wouldn't let the postman deliver them. Gerry Adams got 16,000 votes, Joe Hendron, who was the SDLP candidate, got 10,900 votes and I got 10,400. The SDLP got that result with a pretty good election machine. I had no election machine at all. I only fought that election to prove to myself that I had done no wrong. Nobody ever said that I was a bad MP or a bad candidate or that I didn't represent them. Even in defeat, half of my votes had still come from across the political and religious divide.

THE POWER OF UNCERTAINTY

One of the most compelling talks I was fortunate enough to record was WALTER MCGINITIE's *'The Power of Uncertainty': I made no apologies for repeating it several times on radio.*

MOST OF US like to embrace certainty. We like to be sure that we are taking the right course of action, to know that we are saying the right thing. We tend to steer clear of uncertainty. Yet there is a great power in uncertainty. That was the theme of Professor Walter McGinitie's closing address at the 1982 World Reading Congress, held in Dublin. Yes, uncertainty is frightening, McGinitie conceded, but it is also liberating. We link uncertainty with fear, but it is the foundation of hope. We link certainty with security, but it is the womb of indifference and the precondition for despair.

Uncertainty does not mean indecisiveness. It permits a rational basis for decisions. Uncertainty does not mean lack of planning or lack of action. It means planning based on reasonable alternatives and action based on current evidence.

Perhaps, McGinitie argues, it is the nature of our job as teachers – in which we plan the lives of others – that makes it so tempting to be certain about what we do. He saw the teacher's dilemma as similar to that of the child psychiatrist in Peter Shaffer's play *Equus*. At the end of that play, the psychiatrist despairs:

'In an ultimate sense I cannot know what I do in this place – yet I do ultimate things. Essentially I cannot know – yet I do essential things ... Irreversible, terminal things. I need – more desperately than my children need me – a way of seeing in the dark.'

Teachers equally need a way of seeing in the dark, McGinitie argued. We naturally feel the need to be certain to know that what we do is right ... We inflict our certainties on students in so many ways. We regard test scores as absolutes. We are too positive about our judgements ... we expect behaviour that fits our stereotypes of students.

But the good teacher must have doubts. The good teacher knows that he or she will always have much to learn. It is that lack of certainty that

THE CURIOUS MIND

enables a teacher to be effective. For only a person who is willing to be uncertain can learn; only an uncertain person can show how learning is done. That for Walter McGinitie is the power of uncertainty. Another point of view is always possible.

THIS PLACE SPEAKS TO ME
(THREE SCENES)

Excerpts from the series in which a guest brings to life a particular place that 'speaks' to him.
Scene One: MICHAEL COADY *in the Protestant graveyard,*
Carrick-on-Suir, Co. Tipperary.

IN THE EARLY 1980s I came to this site when it was an overgrown wilderness with a friend – Hugh Ryan, a local historian – and we systematically combed through this place. It was exciting for me because here I was in the heart of my native town discovering its history on its gravestone inscriptions. I love graveyards. To me they are not morbid places. They can be quite sensuous places in the summertime. Graveyards commemorate lives, not death, and as I worked here I came to know these lives. One stone simply recorded the brief life of Sally Edmonds, born 1744 died 1747. The mystery of that brief life intrigued me and I wrote a poem about it.

> All of human anguish
> is told upon this stone,
> sorrow's tale is chiselled
> down to barest bone.
>
> Did water fire or fever take
> this three year child away?
> Little Sally Edmonds
> is two hundred years in clay.

Love that sparked her making
in darkness of the past
whispered on white willows
or smiled in summer grass

Hairs on head are numbered
and sparrows count they say,
little Sally Edmonds
is two hundred years in clay.

Scene Two: DON BAKER *revisits the now derelict Daingean Reformatory in Co. Offaly, where he was committed as a thirteen-year-old.*

HERE AT THE bottom of the stairs is where they used to flog us. If you did anything wrong, you were in for a serious flogging. 'Wrong' might mean a fight with another boy, but the rules were so strict, it wouldn't take much for something to be considered 'wrong' ...

Listen (*he claps his hands and the sound echoes through the staircase*). You knelt here at the bottom and stretched your hands to the third step. One of the brothers – a big, big man as I recall – stood on your outstretched fingers, so that you couldn't move away. Another brother stood in the doorway – he was a 'medic', but he never intervened. A third brother administered the punishment. That's what I called it, in my innocence, thinking I had done wrong. It was a beating with a leather strap, from your knees up to your back. The mark of the leather came out on your back, like lines on a blackboard. Tiny pinpricks of blood appeared on your legs. The beating might take half an hour. Your body went into spasm after each blow. The brother would wait for you to relax before the leather came again. In between there was dead silence, except for the shivering sound of trying to get your breath back. I went into therapy for years afterwards as a result of this. My big mistake was in not crying. I was trying to be the tough guy. Most other lads would scream and of course (*he claps again*) their cries were heard in the dormitories above, terrifying the boys in their beds. It was quite an ordeal for thirteen-year-olds.

That night I was told not to get into bed. I was too sore, so I just knelt up on the bed for a while. A nightwatchman sat at a desk in the dormitory all night. He was a local man, employed to supervise us. I remember the night of the beating he came up to me offering me a piece of liver on a fork. I suppose it was his way of saying he didn't approve of what was going on. In the morning a brother woke us and if you didn't hop out smartly you got the stick across your legs. 'Out! Out! Back-street curs!' he would call. It was prison for young boys. Little Auschwitz, I used to call it.

Scene Three: PADDY GRAHAM *returns to Monaghanstown Bog in Co. Westmeath.*

I ALWAYS HAD a great sense of religion about this place. I would sit here as a boy and have a primal experience of this deep, rich, luscious bogland. I had a sense of being rooted in it. I would look up at the sky, with the larks hanging there, and then back down to earth in a great circular sweep. I understood nature and God like that for years. It found echo in latter years when I was recovering from alcoholism and I would have philosophical discussions with my friend Fr Raphael. He introduced me to the Kierkegaardian notion of 'thrownness'. When he said that word I was back in this exact place. This is where I was 'thrown' back and out of myself. Being who I am, obsessed with myself, this is where I get relief from myself and find a sense of otherness. I had my own trinity: the physicality of myself, the sky which was the 'throwness'; the notion of what God-ness might be; and then the pure, beautiful sensuality of the bog. I used to strip off and lie on the bog, feeling a sensual belonging to it. That meeting of earth and sky – that horizon appears in all my paintings, locking everything together.

As a child everything was at eye-level – the wonderful browns and purples, the flies and midges hovering above. I could almost taste the sensuality of it all. This was the exotic – here in the heart of the midlands. You didn't need to travel in search of it. It was here, in the wonderful sense of elation of moving out of yourself. And then there was the great silence – which isn't silence at all, of course. If you slow down and listen, you will hear that choir of noises, an orchestra of beautiful sounds – buzzing, chirping, flitting. It 'earths' you. You belong to it and you know you're going back to it. It's your home. I live near the sea in Dún Laoghaire, but *this* is my home. I love the 'thatch' on top of it and the rich female sensual earth underneath.

This is where I pray. I don't say words. I just look and listen. It's a prayer of wonder about nature.

THE ART OF IMPROVISATION

Sometimes learning and advancement come about by quick thinking – by improvising. Barrister and politician PATRICK LINDSAY *excelled at this particular art …*

I HAD READ an awful lot before I went to boarding school – Charles Kickham, Canon Sheehan and virtually all of Dickens. I read Lord Macaulay's essays and I had come across poetry too, mainly the works of Oliver Goldsmith.

When I went to St Muredach's College in Ballina, that reading was both an advantage and a disadvantage. It allowed me to doss but, there again, mischief is largely built on ingenuity – how to get into trouble and, better still – as the old LDF books used to say – how to retreat from it. There were two notable examples in Ballina.

On wet days, there was very little to occupy people's minds and we had to invent our own fun. We used to congregate in the second and third-year classrooms and somebody would do his party-piece. Mine was imitating the then bishop, Dr James Naughton, on prize day before the Christmas holidays, and I could do his accent perfectly. One day I noticed a considerable lack of appreciation for my performance and something prompted me to look round. Behind me were the bishop and the president of the college. The president sent me up to his room – which meant at least twenty strokes – but the bishop said a better punishment would be to make me do my impersonation again. I did and it wasn't a bad performance!

The second incident is well-known to many people. There were two prizes that I won every year in Ballina. One was – and this will surprise many people – first prize in catechism and apologetics. My real interest in it was that it wasn't a book prize nor was it any kind of religious token – it was a full-sized, genuine five pound note. There was another prize of five pounds on the annual school sports day for the bicycle race, which I had won the four years prior to my final year.

When sports day arrived in my last year, I went to ask permission to go into town and borrow a bicycle. However, I was *persona non grata* with the authorities and I was told by the president – who later became Bishop of Killala – that I couldn't go into town that day or any other day, for that or any other purpose, and he banged the door in my face. As I was going downstairs – a little hurt but not beaten – I saw the reflector of a bicycle sticking out of a little alcove near the oratory door, so I went over and took it. It was a huge, three-geared green Raleigh, not the racing type, but I was a fairly strong fellow and I knew I could win on it. I did win the race and then had to go over and stand with the bicycle between myself and the president, who was giving out the brown envelope with the fiver in it. He was a great gentleman, because he never adverted to the fact that it was his own bicycle ...

As a politician, I never wrote a speech. I would be travelling from one chapel to another on the political scene and I would make a different speech at each chapel, because I would make it up as I went along in the car, talking aloud to myself. I did the same thing with law later. I always had a tendency to speechifying and declaiming. Our professor at St Muredach's – the late Father John Murphy – was a brilliant man who inculcated a love of language in us by the way he read poetry to us and the way he got us to read to him. He never corrected an essay – you had to stand up and read it out to him.

In February of my Leaving Cert year, he had given us a freelance essay. We could choose any literary or historical character and write about him or her. I chose, for better or worse – worse as it happened – Catherine the Great of Russia. What my attraction to her was I don't know, because she wasn't very attractive, but I stood up and said my little piece. He told me to read the last sentence again. I repeated it, but it was obvious that I had changed it, so he said, 'Show me that – it's not the same as the first time'. I handed him the copybook and there it was, the only thing I had written in it – '*Patrick J. Lindsay, 4 September 1927*'. I had never written an essay – I had spoken them all.

Father Murphy went mad, but he apologised years later when I was addressing a meeting in his parish in Lacken, north of Killala. He said he had been quite wrong not to have given me full credit for having performed so well for nearly five years!

THE COUNTRY GIRL

Edna O'Brien *remembers growing up in Co. Clare.*

We lived in a quiet farming area where nothing much happened to disturb the passage of the seasons. Strangely enough, I remember only two seasons from my childhood. In summer, I remember picking wild flowers on (what seemed then) the very long and very precarious journey to the village school. In winter, I remember the tall, frosted grass, like plumes of ostrich, and the trees, fields – everything fixed in that bejewelled frost-like limbo.

Life was fervid, enclosed, catastrophic. It was religiously very fervid – religion permeated every aspect of one's life. My mind was never not on the question – was I or was I not committing sin? We said the rosary every night, of course, but along with that I was getting in and out of bed every five minutes to say more prayers and ejaculations. The fear of hell – and indeed of purgatory – was outlandish and it was pervasive. I remember reading in St Adamnan, I think, a version of the after-life which makes Dante's *Inferno* jocular. It described waiting for hell in the next world in an utter, utter wilderness. There were different bridges leading to banishment. If you weren't an utter sinner you crossed on a bridge that was fairly level; but if you had been dissolute in your life, you began on a wider bridge that grew narrower and narrower until you were sucked into the flames. The description of your tongue turning into flame and then the flame inhabiting your brain was terrifying. It was a totally destructive attitude to the after-life. I hope there isn't one.

Life was enclosed in the way that any village is enclosed. Everybody knew our life and we knew everyone else's life. If somebody had shingles, if somebody got consumption, if somebody brought a cow to the fair and didn't sell – you always knew. I remember the great confusion and upset that ensued when we sold a cow in calf and about three days later the purchaser came back, outraged, to say that the cow was not in calf. In fact, the cow had calved without anyone knowing it and the calf was later found stillborn in some bushes. But such was our world that the whole countryside knew about the row.

Life was catastrophic. The sense of catastrophe is peculiar to a lot of Irish people. I was always nervous of something that would befall one. It was a sense of not being physically at ease in one's body and feeling that one would fall or drown or come to grief. As a result I am ashamed to say that I don't drive a car – and I wouldn't call myself a wonderful bicycle-rider either!

I had fears of animals – which is a great handicap when you live in the country. I was frightened by the people around me. I identify very much with Kafka in that respect. Dogs were a source of terror to me. They were so unpredictable. They would take fits, and I remember being badly bitten on the neck by a dog, trying desperately to escape and thinking I never would.

Also, of course, there was the fact of our own history – what one was taught and what one read at school was dinned into one as the catastrophic story of what had happened to our country.

I remember the travelling players coming to our village. When the Shannon Players came it was a great event, because they brought that much-sought and much-valued word 'glamour' to the village. Their coming was always announced with great ceremony beforehand, but in fact the repertoire was usually the same – *East Lynne* and *Murder in the Red Barn*. There would be a comedy sketch first, then a raffle and then a play. I can still see the village hall, with black curtains over the windows and six paraffin lamps which served as footlights at the front of the stage. And on the stage those characters looked so real in their pancake make-up. I think that no theatre I ever attended in my grown-up life could assume the awe and the magic that I felt then in that little village hall.

Living as we did a bit 'over the fields', my brothers and sisters and I were always longing for people to come. One regular occasion for meeting people was threshing day, when workmen from all around came to help out. We children were not really included – except to butter the bread and bring up tea to the men every ten minutes (or so it seemed), but it was still a great and exciting event for us.

The other great event was Christmas and I connect it very much with things my mother would be doing. She was a very generous woman, and she was forever making Christmas cakes for various people, especially for the nuns. When it came to icing the cakes she did it with such a flourish that I felt she was Leonardo da Vinci. She would do boiled icing and then work on it with great pride, with a spatula, making dents and elevations and finally decorating it with little silver balls.

When we killed a pig, which was about twice a year – a pretty gory event – my mother would give away fillets of pork and we loved going to each house because we got lots of praise – and maybe even sixpence.

There were no books at all in our house. My mother was extremely suspicious of literature because she thought it was bad and could lead to sin. My father wasn't interested in books. His reading was confined to the *Irish Field* and bloodstock manuals. There was no travelling library in our locality then. There were simply no books. Once, when someone in the village actually got a copy of *Rebecca*, there was such an avidity for it that it was loaned by the page. Unfortunately you would get page 84 and then page 103. As a result, I did not grasp the story of *Rebecca* for ages. But however restricted the diet may have been, reading was and

THE CURIOUS MIND

still is my great prop against reality. As Mr Eliot says, humankind cannot bear too much reality!

When I left national school I went to a convent boarding school in Loughrea, Co. Galway. A lot of my life there was as portrayed in *The Country Girls* – certainly the actual bleakness of the convent and the regimented life found their way into that book. But the narrative is not true – I was not expelled. I was a good student and keen on learning. I suppose I did have the inevitable thoughts of a vocation – most convent girls do. You fall in love with nuns and you think how beautiful it would be to devote your life to the service of God. Looking back on it, though, it was just a whim – there was nothing serious in it. When *The Country Girls* was published, the head nun wrote me a rather crisp letter about my 'wicked book'. 'I give credence an open mind until I read it,' she said. I never heard what she made of it when she did read it – that is, if ever she did.

THANK YOU VERY MUCH, MR HITLER!

PETER USTINOV *was an interviewer's delight – full of humour, anecdotes and accents, but also a man of great insight into the human condition. I was privileged to interview him twice. The second time was a delightful two-hour session in the Westbury Hotel, Dublin. Here he recalls some wartime experiences.*

MY DRAMATIC CAREER was interrupted somewhat by Mr Hitler and the war. That was the longest run I've ever been in – the worst parts and very underpaid. I hated every moment of it. However, I knew that it would be wonderful material when it was all over and that I'd be laughing about it. I had every intention of surviving. But I must say – as a worm's eye view of human nature – there's nothing like the army to awaken your absolute aversion to and hatred of certain things. I never got into the 'real' action, but anybody who lived in London got into the action enough without wanting to. I saw much more action in London fire-watching on the roof of Wyndham's Theatre with a stirrup pump and a tin hat than I ever did in the army.

I was later attached to the Directorate of Army Psychiatry – not as a client, but as a consultant on the techniques of morale-building. Britain needed that very badly at that time – the armies were going backwards everywhere. The Far East was lost and it was a pretty grim show all round. The psychiatrists were given opened letters by the censors and had to try to find out what men wanted from their letters to home, which was probably the most intimate exposition of their feelings about all sorts of matters. It was a fascinating time, but vaguely absurd as all those things are. I couldn't take it terribly seriously.

I wrote a play, which was highly praised – over-praised, I should imagine – by James Agate, and this was actually performed while I was a private in the army. Naturally, the papers gave that wide diffusion. *The Daily Mail* had a photograph of me in uniform, looking pathetic, with the caption 'The Play of the Year'. So that – although I was A1 physically – I was not sent anywhere else but was given willingly to the psychiatrists or to write film scripts, or to do anything, even at my tender age.

When we first went into the army, we had to report to Canterbury and I sat there miserably with my kit-bag, in my civilian clothes, in front of a fire. Nobody had yet decided what to do with us and there was an old soldier – an old sweat, a regular – sitting in front of the fire too, casting his mind back to his own first day. He said, 'I see you're going into the army. I find it difficult to remember the time when I first went in. I'm a volunteer, you see, a peace-time soldier, and I never moved up from private. I like it like that. But there was a story I heard when I first went in which might help explain the army to you.

'There were two soldiers, you see, on latrine duty. It was autumn and one was sweeping up and a sudden gust of wind caught up a piece of used toilet paper. Like an autumn leaf it floated in the air. They couldn't reach it and – before they could prevent it – it floated in through the colonel's window. Now what were they to do? One of them said, "Look, you go on working here. If anybody asks where I am, I've been taken short, right? And meanwhile I'll go up and see if the old man's in and try and recuperate that piece of paper". So the man went off and came back five minutes later and the first one, who was still sweeping, said, "Did you get it?" and the other one said, "No, I was too late. He'd already signed it".'

THE DEATH OF LANGUAGES

Linguistic expert DAVID CRYSTAL *warns of the dangers of monolingualism.*

I GREW UP in Holyhead in the 1940s and was intrigued by living in a multilingual society – English in my home, Welsh among my neighbours and Irish at a social level. There was quite a large Irish community in the town. Later, at secondary school in Liverpool, I learned Latin, Greek, French, German – and Scouse, of course, for survival! I did an English degree in the University of London and became interested in linguistics.

Language is forever growing and changing. Each new technology – each new development in society – brings a new dimension to language. Think back to pre-radio and television days. There was no sports commentary, no weather forecasting, no documentary etc. Broadcasting brought a whole new variation in language. The internet comes along – newer styles of language emerge. Similarly with television advertising – language is constantly being enriched by new styles, dialects, tones of voice. When we hear greetings exchanged on American streets like 'Wassup?', it simply gives us an insight into language in another part of the world. For me it is like saying, 'You've got some nice flowers in your garden, but have you seen this one?' Some people might see the new flower as a weed, but one man's weed is another man's flower!

The problem is that flowers are dying off in the garden of languages! There are reckoned to be about six thousand languages in use in the world at present. Half of them are thought to be in danger and will die out in the next hundred years. On average a language will die every two weeks. This poses serious problems for language diversity. These endangered languages are spoken by less than a hundred thousand people – mostly in Central Africa and South-East Asia. The last speaker of a language is an amazing and dramatic concept. On 5 November 1995, the last speaker of a language in West Africa died, and – because no one had ever written it down or recorded it – it simply disappeared. It is so important to record language, but what is happening at the moment is not that the people but that the languages are dying.

People want to speak their language but globalisation is preventing that from happening. Language is a nation's heart and identity and when a dominant language squeezes it out as the language of business and commerce, it becomes endangered. Natural disasters such as earthquakes and tsunamis can also kill a language, as can disease such as AIDS. In some parts antagonism to minority languages can be a major threat. Nigeria is a case in point – where there are 450 different languages.

A sensitive policy of multilingualism based on mutual respect can lead to a peaceful society, however. Examples are Switzerland and Finland. If there are enough speakers of a language around, we need the following for its survival:

1. Bottom-up goodwill towards the language – demonstrated by speaking it in the home.
2. Top-down interest from the local government.
3. Investment of money – to encourage publication, recording and teaching of the language.

Just imagine if you woke up one morning and your language had disappeared. What would you have lost? Your favourite novelist, poet, TV programme. Language gives you a sense of identity, tradition and community. Without it you will be an anonymous blob facing the steamroller of the dominant culture that is coming towards you – American English in the case of most of us! The internet is the great hope for language survival. At least a quarter of the world's languages now feature on websites. This is giving minority languages a presence on the world stage they might not have experienced heretofore. So there is more than a glimmer of hope with the expansion of the net.

GRANDMA, MR YEATS AND GBS

ANNE *and* CATHERINE GREGORY *recall an idyllic childhood at Coole,*
Co. Galway, with their grandmother, Lady Gregory.

GRANDMA WAS THE centre of our lives here in Coole, where we were born
and bred. She wasn't just Grandma – she was really our mother. She
could be quite a disciplinarian, but for her the important things were
'always be on time' and 'manners maketh man'. She had incredible
friendliness. Class or creed meant nothing to her. If, in the middle of a
day's work, someone came to the door looking for apples or sticks, it
didn't matter to her. She would come down and have a chat. The
extraordinary thing was while we were having this wonderful life here,
she was writing, running the Abbey, going up and down to Dublin and
over to London to fight for the Lane Pictures – but she would always
have time for us. She might be in the middle of writing a play when we
would rush in to tell her of a bird's nest we had found. She would drop
everything at once to hear our story.

She was our teacher – and a slightly easy-going one too. She taught
us our tables and simple arithmetic, some French also, but her
pronunciation was appalling. We had to read a chapter of the Bible to
her every morning. She would read to us every evening, anything from
Brer Rabbit to James Fenimore Cooper. *Swiss Family Robinson* was our
favourite book. We used to act it out, pretending our pony was an ostrich
on a desert island.

When you look at photographs of Grandma, she looks like Queen
Victoria – all in black – but she actually had a great sense of humour.
She was never a prude. We had a general knowledge book full of
questions like, 'Why in public places does water at drinking troughs
always come out of the mouth of a lion?' Grandma said, 'Well, it would
look awful coming out the other end!' and then exploded into laughter.
She just couldn't stop. I can still see her with her hankie up to her eyes,
the tears streaming down her cheeks ...

She also made us learn poetry by heart, although – strangely – never
any poems by Mr Yeats. He was the worst reader of his own stuff – like

a bad clergyman with an artificial 'pulpit' voice! When he wasn't writing, he would go around humming to himself. Grandma said that was why his poetry was so good to recite aloud – because Mr Yeats used to hum it to get a rhythm on it before he wrote it. He wasn't interested in children – why should he be? We were just children. His son Michael used to tell how Mr Yeats didn't recognise him when they passed on the stairs once!

We had no idea Grandma's visitors were important people. To us they were just adults (often boring) who happened to be Grandma's friends. Mr Yeats did tell us once that he came across a badger in the nut wood – which allowed him to stroke its head! Of course if it had been a real badger it would still be holding Mr Yeats' hand! It was our little dog Taddy, which had a head like a badger ...

When I (*Anne*) was somewhat older, Mr Yeats sent for me one evening and read me a poem he had written about my hair ...

> Never shall a young man
> Thrown into despair
> By those great honey-coloured
> Ramparts at your ear
> Love you for yourself alone
> And not your yellow hair ...
>
> But I can get a hair dye
> And set such colour there
> Brown or black or carrot
> That young men in despair
> Shall love me for myself alone
> And not my yellow hair.

I was very embarrassed. I thought it was awful but of course I said, 'Read it again'. Soon afterwards he read it on a radio broadcast. Next morning there was a letter for me from my then boyfriend. It said:

THE CURIOUS MIND

If I was alone on an island
And only Anne with me there
I'd make myself cushions and bolsters
By stuffing her skin with her hair!

That was the end of that romance!

Of all the visitors to Coole, GBS (*George Bernard Shaw*) was our favourite. He was a natural with children. Mind you, he was always cheating. During the Great War we couldn't have jam *and* butter on our bread. It had to be one or the other. GBS held up a dry slice of bread and asked for jam, but we had seen him butter the other side. We were horrified – and of course raging that we hadn't thought of his trick. We also found him peeping though his fingers when we played 'Hunt the Thimble'! It was so embarrassing to see a grown-up cheating and we said this to Grandma. She was very hurt and told us we must send some of his favourite apples to him in London to make up. We did that and then got this marvellous poem from him, written on five postcards ...

Two ladies of Galway, called Catherine and Anna
Whom some call Acushla and some call Alanna
On finding the gate of the front garden undone
Stole Grandmama's apples and sent them to London.

And Grandmama said that the poor village schoolchildren
Were better behaved than the well-brought-up Coole children
And threatened them with the most merciless whippings
If ever again they laid hands on her pippins ...

When Grandma died, we were desolate. It was like the end of the world to us. Coole had always been our home, even though we were grown up by then. We never felt we needed anything but what we had, which was the woods and our ponies and Grandma. It was a perfect life.

FROM BELFAST TO BERKELEY

SEAMUS HEANEY *recalls formative influences as an emerging poet.*

AFTER LEAVING QUEEN'S, there was a gradual process of linking in to a more specifically literary and writing life, which culminated with my joining the group founded by Philip Hobsbaum in 1963 in Belfast. Round about that time too, there was an anthology came out called *Six Irish Poets* and that was very important reading to me. I also got wakened up when I got the loan of Kavanagh's *A Soul for Sale* from Michael McLaverty. All that started me off, and I had some poems published in the *Kilkenny Magazine* by James Delahanty, and by Terence de Vere White in the *Irish Times*. It is very, very important for a young writer to get the stuff that he sends out accepted. I had no contacts. I had no literary milieu. I was just testing. I was sending out the messages and the message I got back was that these things were publishable – which was enormously confidence-building.

Immediately after that, Philip Hobsbaum – poet and academic – came to Queen's. He had run workshops in Cambridge and in London and he started one in Belfast. That was another very good stage of confirmation and another ripple outwards. It was at that group that I got to know Michael and Edna Longley and various other people. Through them I got to know Derek Mahon, so that was an opening out beyond the Belfast thing into the Dublin thing, since they had been to Trinity.

Encountering Kavanagh's poetry was enormously important. It was like a woman discovering women writers. I was converted and empowered and released into parts of myself through reading him. You encountered in his work that which you thought was secret to yourself. He raised the sub-cultural life to cultural status and that is extremely enabling. The older I get the more I realise that Kavanagh's great power is in 'The lines that speak the passionate heart / The spirit that lives alone.'

There's a wonderful force and vigour, a mixture of solitude and courage, in Kavanagh, a mixture of complete psychic impulse and honesty that whooshes through his poetry.

THE CURIOUS MIND

I only taught for one year in a school. I found it agonising. I found discipline a problem. I found I wasn't quite sure how to proceed, afraid of drying up in the course of a lesson. I managed, but it takes a long time to learn to teach. It takes a long time to learn the mixture of freedom within yourself and attention to the student in front of you that makes for good teaching. One of the things I really valued about getting into Harvard in the 1980s was the freedom to sit with groups of twelve students. One of the difficulties I had when I moved to the teacher-training college in Belfast – and then later in Carysfort – was having to deal with very large numbers and the frustration of not having a closer and more nurturing relationship with individuals. It was conveyor-belt teaching, really – dealing with crowds of people.

When you begin teaching, you are your own pupil. I learned a lot through simply having to prepare courses. I widened my knowledge. When you do lectures, you get to first principles – you get clarifications. I still come back to the image of the ripple which moves outwards but in some way is still the same ripple. It contains other things, other experiences, other ripples, but there is a concentric element to it – as there is to human growth. Within yourself there is always the little self who was there from the beginning. I suppose the purpose of the writing I have done has been to make a wholeness out of all those moves and differences, to get the first place and the ultimate place into some kind of alignment.

In 1970, Marie and myself and our two boys – who were just babies then – set out for a year in California. It was possibly the most important year of my life. Marie and I had lived in Belfast and had been married for five years. We had never lived outside Ireland and this was a great time to go to the West Coast of America, when the Beat Movement was at its height. There was a tremendous sense of glamour about Berkeley – the free speech movement had started there, Ginsberg was still in full flight over the bay. It was a kind of a world centre. Another very important thing was that – for the first time in my life – I had enough money to live on. We had a wonderful year, great refreshment of the spirit, a sense that you were learning something.

It was very important to me also at that time to meet Tom Flanagan, whose book, *The Irish Novelists, 1800–1850*, is one of the great founding texts for Irish studies in this century. Tom Flanagan is a man with an intense intellectual life who is also a great raconteur. His whole thinking is Hiberno-centric. In Queen's I had been used to academics whose thinking was always Anglo-centric – the points of reference were Shakespeare, Wordsworth, Dickens and so on. Tom's conversation and his mental universe were wide-ranging, but the normative thing at the centre of it was Joyce, Yeats, the sense of Ireland. This was a wonderful thing to encounter at that point because 1970–71 was a very political moment in Ireland, so I count that year of re-orientation in Berkeley an important one. It wasn't an escape from Ireland – it was a re-orienting towards it.

Poetically also, I got a lot out of being there. I read William Carlos Williams' poems and that influenced my third book – *Wintering Out* – little poems about my most intimate places like Broagh, Anahorish, Toome and so on. A lot of those came out of reading William Carlos Williams. I don't mean the themes came out of it, but the form – the tentative, short-lined stanzas.

> Anahorish, soft gradient
> of consonant, vowel-meadow,
>
> after-image of lamps
> swung through the yards
> on winter evenings.

(FROM 'ANAHORISH')

THE CURIOUS MIND

LORENZO THE MAGNIFICENT

CHARLES HANDY *nominates Lorenzo de Medici as his 'Millennium Mind'.*

I HAVE PICKED Lorenzo as my choice for a Millennium Mind because he presided over – and to some extent promoted – an extraordinary generation of people in an extraordinary time and place – Florence in the last third of the 1400s, the height of the Italian Renaissance. It was a time whose echoes are with us still, whose beauties are there to see and marvel at today, and whose philosophy of life gave a new meaning to the dignity of man and the purpose of life.

One businessman – not normally the most optimistic breed of people – spoke of it thus: 'May every thoughtful spirit thank God it has been given to him to be born in this new age, so filled with hope and promise, which already enjoys a greater array of gifted persons than the world has seen in the past thousand years.' He was thinking of the gentle art of Botticelli and Fra Angelico, the first signs of the towering genius of Michelangelo and of the young Leonardo, of Brunelleschi and his architectural marvels – not least the great dome of the Cathedral – which are still there for all to see, of Marsilio Ficino who was developing the philosophy of humanism and of Machiavelli with his politics of pragmatism. This had to be a special time to be alive, particularly since this was – for a few short years – a time of peace and plenty for Florence, with fun and festivals for all, as well as work in abundance, and new glorious buildings galore. It was so special that it even got its own name – the Laurentian Age – after Lorenzo, of course!

Lorenzo, however, was only twenty when his father died in 1469 and he found himself head of the Medici bank and potentially the most influential man in Florence, because of all the family connections. He was not only very young for his big responsibilities, he was also extremely ugly, had a high rasping voice and was a dunce at banking – none of which boded well for his future career or for what was to be the Laurentian Age. But personality, ambition and a taste for power – and Lorenzo had all three in abundance – have always been more potent than good looks. And more sexy too – Lorenzo had no shortage of love affairs before, during and after his marriage.

Lorenzo turned out to be a consummate politician. He had to be, because – as he said – it is essential for a rich man to get involved in politics. He also, however, loved it and all the intricacies of influence, which was just as well because Florence was a republic and had a special dislike of anyone who tried to lord it over them. Lorenzo, therefore, had to work behind the scenes all the time and was always careful to remind everyone that he was just an ordinary citizen with no special office – although 'ordinary' in his case was hardly the right word. However, by making sure that it was only friends of the Medici family who ever got any hold on the various jobs that mattered, Lorenzo – rather like his grandfather, Cosimo – saw to it that things worked out the way he wanted. He was the Harold Wilson of his day.

He had a bit of Margaret Thatcher too, using a little war against his neighbours – the Genoese – to promote the image of his patriotism and courage, making sure that he was seen with the soldiers in the hour of their victory. On his triumphant return, a historian of the time could say that 'Florence remained free of all troubles, to the great reputation of Lorenzo. Florence altogether gave herself up to the arts and pleasures of peace, seeking to attract thither men of letters, to accumulate books, to adorn the city, to make the countryside frutiful. In short she devoted herself to all those arts and pursuits which caused men to esteem that age so happy'.

Lorenzo would see that time of peace and stability as the justification for all his conniving and even for his cruelty – for he wasn't exactly a 'nice' man. He was quite happy to see a group of conspirators flogged, stripped and hung from the windows of the town hall – but then again, they *had* just murdered his brother in the cathedral, and had almost done the same to him.

Renaissance humanism sought to combine religious tradition with the messages from the philosophies of Greece and Rome, which had just been rediscovered. God's grace was necessary – they would admit – but man was God's supreme creation and had an intellectual duty to improve the world. That doesn't seem such a radical idea these days, but in the fifteenth century it was a blow aimed at the Church who could no longer be regarded as the only source of wisdom and authority. Confined to a debating group in Lorenzo's villas, this sort of thinking might have had little impact on the world, but at this time Gutenberg's invention of moveable type was just catching on and some ten million books were published in Europe in the last forty years of the century. Suddenly everybody – not just the rich and religious – could read stuff for themselves and make up their own minds. It was as if television had suddenly hit the world and was looking for programme material, and Lorenzo's boys were ready and waiting.

Actually, Lorenzo did far more than hold little talking parties. He revived Pisa's old and renowned university and contributed handsomely to the University of Florence – then one of Europe's best. Thomas Linacre went back from there to help found the Royal College of Physicians in London, William Grocyn founded the Professorship of Greek at Oxford after studying there, and John Colet started St Paul's school in London. And others went to other parts of Europe to spread the message of humanism in practice.

Lorenzo was himself a poet as well as a banker, a great politician and patron of the arts and learning. His poetry dwelt on devotional themes – which would have pleased his religious mother – but also included hunting songs and salacious ditties more suited to the bar than the drawing room. Best known is a poem he wrote two years before his death, when he was already ill. It starts:

> How beautiful is youth
> That flees so fleetingly by.
> Let him be, who chases joy,
> For tomorrow there is no certainty.

Combine that poetic skill with his interest in young artists. He was the first to spot the talents of the young Michelangelo and the even younger Leonardo and brought them to live and work on his estates. Add his architectural expertise, his love for literature and all learning, and you begin to see something of what we came to call a Renaissance man.

What did that Renaissance idea add up to? A significant touch of power politics – or the ability to make things happen and to keep things together, in the common interest – was one vital part of it. Renaissance men weren't idle dreamers; in fact they could be quite devious – Machiavellian in fact – in pursuit of what they thought was best. Add to that, however, an interest in the more cultured side of life – art, architecture and literature, as well as good food, good wine and entertainment – and you get that element of the all-round expert which can both daunt and impress us today. But most importantly, Renaissance man, at his best, had a philosophy which dominated all – namely that life had a purpose, that ability (particularly intellectual ability) had to be nurtured and nourished so that life for all could be enhanced. If this led to a touch of arrogance – even to a form of intellectual dictatorship – well, so be it. As men said of Lorenzo, 'If Florence was to have a tyrant, she could never have found a better or more delightful one'.

A CHILD OF STRUMPET CITY

JAMES PLUNKETT *recalls a Dublin childhood.*

MY EARLIEST MEMORY is of being woken up, terrified, at the sound of shooting near our house in Stella Gardens, Irishtown. It was during the Civil War. The Dublin I grew up in had been saturated with war – the Great War, 1916, the Civil War. My father and his brothers had served in the Great War. I remember him marching around St Stephen's Green on Remembrance Day 1925. It was very moving to see those war veterans but the city was very divided between the Remembrance Day 'poppies' and the anti-Treaty 'lilies'. Even at school there would be fights between Poppy and Lily factions.

The strand at Ringsend was our playground. It was there that we would re-enact the Tom Mix movies that we had seen earlier in the Assembly Rooms for twopence. We would pinch a few potatoes at home, dig cockles out of the strand, gather charcoal and light a fire, roast the potatoes and boil the cockles in an old can. A royal feast! Afterwards we would play rounders or follow the fishermen who were at that time catching salmon in the Liffey. If they caught any other fish they threw it to us children and we would bring it home. I was very close to my grandfather who was a carpenter. We would wander the beach collecting wood from which he would model a ship for me. He could even make a violin. He came originally from Donegal and spoke Irish, especially when he had taken a few drinks.

Between the Coastguard Station and the Pigeon House there was a building that scared me. It was a TB sanatorium. Anyone that went in there inevitably died. TB and other infectious diseases were rampant then. I remember two of my school pals – two brothers who always wore white ganseys – disappeared from the street one day and the next thing we heard was that they had died from TB.

There was great life on the cobbled streets. The rag and bone man would come in his cart. If you had any old rags or bottles you might get a balloon from him. Then on misty November evenings, the coalman came, ringing his bell and calling out 'Coal blocks, Coal blocks'. We would call out, 'What do you feed your mother on?' and he would reply, 'Coal blocks'!

There was great neighbourliness on the street – there were very few cars, of course. A big treat was to get a tram into Nelson's Pillar, buy some sweets or a toy in Woolworths and then be taken to Bewley's for coffee and cakes. There would be a trio there, playing melodies like 'The Swan' or 'On Wings of Song'.

Ours was a musical family. On Sunday afternoons aunts and uncles would visit for a musical *soirée* in the parlour with songs like 'Sweet and Low', 'I'll Take You Home Again, Kathleen' and 'When You and I Were Young, Maggie'. There would be tea and cake for the ladies and stout for the men. I wanted to learn the banjo (I had been very impressed by Dixie Minstrels) but I was sent to study the violin instead in the School of Music. Playing with the school orchestra later was a great thrill.

I read a lot – mostly boys' adventure stories, although stories like 'Bulldog Drummond' were frowned on at school. Too colonial! We devoured comics like *Rover*, *The Gem* and *The Magnet*. I had an aunt in America who would occasionally send me 'the funnies' from newspapers. I wrote to thank her – in verse! I was conscious of words and their power at an early age. I would write descriptions of places but had no notion at all of plot. The RDS held a nationwide competition for an essay on the Spring Show in 1932. I entered and won but in the same year my father died. I was twelve and it knocked the whole bottom out of my life. The RDS medal was not awarded until the following year and I was heartbroken when I realised I couldn't show it to my father. His death left a permanent mark on me. He had brought me everywhere with him. He was a very kind man who only raised his hand to me once – when I had given lip to my mother.

There was in fact a succession of deaths – my grandfather, my father, my aunts, and I grieved for them because I loved them all greatly. Apart from the trauma of their deaths, my memories of childhood are of utter protection, tolerance and goodness all the way along.

FINDING A VOICE

BERNADETTE GREEVY *remembers the world of music that influenced her singing career.*

MY FIRST MAJOR breakthrough on the international scene came about when I was working here in Dublin with Tibor Paul – learning all the Mahler that has served me so well throughout my life. I was also making records, although I had no reputation at all: I recorded the Handel arias for Decca. At that time I auditioned for Sir John Barbarolli and he took a shine to me. I always come in at the end of people's lives, sadly, but in two years I did an enormous amount of work with him. When he came here in 1970, I was his last Angel in *The Dream of Gerontius*. It was my first Angel, but it was his last one. He taught me the Verdi *Requiem*. I did several Halle *Messiahs* with him and I did my first *Mahler Three* with him, so he was a huge influence in my life at that stage.

I did an audition for the BBC and they failed me the first time and I never got over that! They said I was to come back in six months, but I said I'd never sing for them again. Six months and a day later, I was back and got accepted the second time and I have worked for them ever since. In the recent past I have recorded most of the Herbert Hughes material and all the Anglo-Irish songs – Stanford, Hamilton Harty, Moeran – for their archives, which is very nice.

If Barbarolli was a big influence as a conductor, then I suppose as a composer Mahler was my great musical mentor throughout my entire life. For about eight years, I sang with the Royal Ballet at Covent Garden whenever they did the *Song of the Earth* – which was fantastically choreographed by MacMillan. I had learned Mahler earlier on in my life and then suddenly he became very fashionable. Now everybody is an expert on Mahler. If Mahler is performed, you get a full house – they absolutely adore him.

Dietrich Fischer-Dieskau was a great influence as a singer. He was a wonderful singer in his great days. I always listened to him for the German language, because his diction is so magnificent, and he was a very elegant performer. It wasn't a huge voice. I heard him live lots of times, but he was a wonderful recording artist. Of the others, I loved Victoria de los Angeles, because she was like a breath of fresh air, even on record – a wonderful performer. There was also nobody like the young John McCormack. At his best he really was the best – just heaven.

I was always attracted to the German school of singing. It's a very disciplined school – a school that really cares for the voice. It's very thorough – nothing slipshod at all. The sound is clean, there are no huge *vibrato* things, which are terrible. It treats the voice with great respect.

I was also a great fan of Karen Carpenter. She had a real alto voice – if you sing along with her, it is pitched very low. She had a lovely easy way of putting a song over.

The great influence in my life was my late husband, Peter. Sadly, we were separated a lot throughout our marriage because of my work. But the separations were never too long and I feel that it enhanced our life together. There was always great rapport between the two of us. We used to be fascinated when we went out to dinner and saw people sitting silently staring at each other, whereas we never shut up talking. When Peter died, our son Hugh said he didn't know what I was going to do on my own – his memory of his dad and me was that we sat every night talking for ages. We never shut up – we were always talking and planning.

Peter had a major heart attack in 1980, but he had two very good years after that. He left his job and decided he couldn't hang around doing nothing, so he took on my management. He turned out to be a fantastic manager. I was doing the work he got me for about five years after his death. We were very different people. He gave the impression of being light-hearted, but that concealed a person who absorbed stress and worry. When I got a write-up in the paper that wasn't very generous or very nice, it absolutely floored him. He couldn't cope with that at all, to such an extent that – three years before he died – we agreed that we would never buy another newspaper ever again. I find it hard to find any kindness in my heart towards those newspapers because if they were trying to get at me, all they did in fact was get at him.

I didn't sing for nearly a year after his death. I couldn't even go outside my door. It was terrible. I had to pull myself together for Hugh then, because he also was grieving. He was very close to his father – he was always with him. In fourteen years, he had more of his father than a lot of guys ever have in their whole life. A year later, when I went to New Zealand, I brought him with me. I said to Hugh, 'I don't know if I can ever walk out on the stage again, but let's have a go in New Zealand. If I can't do it, it doesn't matter, especially at the other end of the world'. I don't think I could have gone if he hadn't come with me. Although I have a most loving family – without whom I couldn't have had my career – I really felt he had to be with me at that particular stage. He had lost his father and if his mother were to suddenly go off – even though it was to earn a living for the pair of us – it would never do for a child of nearly fifteen. So I took him with me and then we went to China the following year. A bond was established then. That was another thing I did right in my life. It was absolutely the right thing to do, and I have benefited from it ever since.

THE CURIOUS MIND

HAILING THE LIBERATOR

Joe Lee *chooses Daniel O'Connell as his 'Millennium Mind'.*

ONE OF THE reasons I find O'Connell interesting is that he is a representative of 'culture contact'. Many of the problems that beset us today arise from our inability to cope with other cultures, with difference, with the unknown.

O'Connell came from Gaelic stock. He came from what was in 1775 a battered Irish tradition to adjust to the two most vigorous and most imperial cultures of that time – the English and the French. He managed this so successfully that in his later years he bestrode the English-speaking world as one of the acknowledged *colossi* of Westminster politics. Beyond that, his name was known across Europe as that of the best-known public figure in the United Kingdom of the time. I think it was an extraordinary life's journey to come from the most remote part of Ireland – geographically, and in many respects culturally – and adapt so apparently effortlessly to very alien cultures, while never jettisoning his own culture. He lamented the decline of the Irish language. He may have regarded its death as inevitable but he did not dismiss it disdainfully. He was never ashamed of his roots.

O'Connell was by no means an overnight success. While he entered politics to oppose the Act of Union, he faced a long twenty-five-year struggle to find the organisational mechanism to achieve ascendancy over Catholic Ireland. When the Catholic Emancipation Act was passed in 1829, O'Connell was then fifty-four years old. He showed great resilience, enduring many setbacks. There was a bulldog in him. The 1798 Rebellion horrified him – not so much its objectives but its methods. He believed that revolt would always be crushed by superior British forces. He was in a way as close to being a pacifist as anyone in these islands has been. He is often referred to as the 'Gandhi of Europe'. He believed in very extreme democracy, by the standards of his time. In terms of mobilising the masses, probably only General Andrew Jackson in the United States of the 1820s could be mentioned in the same breath as O'Connell, who had to develop a consciousness of their political potential in the mass of the Irish people and then channel that into some form of secure representation in parliament.

His first goal was Catholic Emancipation. Land-owning Catholics got the vote in 1793 but they could not sit in parliament. If parliament was to be the forum in which he would pursue his objectives, it was essential for O'Connell that Catholics be allowed sit in parliament. He is often criticised today for making his first big issue a Catholic one, but I would argue that he had no choice in the matter. He began to mobilise the masses by setting up the Catholic Association and instituting the Catholic Rent. This was a groundbreaking move in European politics, not just Irish politics. Any leader who mobilises 'pre-political' people anywhere in the world today is following in footsteps hewn out by O'Connell in very unpromising circumstances. It took a long time to make his name known, to build up a 'media profile' at a time when there was not the media we have today, when half the population was illiterate and word of mouth was the strongest medium. O'Connell also built his reputation as 'Counsellor O'Connell', defending Catholics in court. A sort of folk image of him developed as 'our defender against unjust laws'. He projected himself as the personification of the idea of a just society for that time, culminating in the 'monster meetings' which no leader since has approached. The Catholic Rent gave the people a sense of ownership of a common crusade. It was a brilliant psychological ploy as well as being a useful fundraiser.

Westminster viewed all this with consternation. They had experienced nothing like it before. There was indignation, then bewilderment, at the numbers involved. Even though the Catholic Emancipation Act allowed only thirty or so Catholic members of parliament, it did mark a formal shift in British political culture. Psychologically, it was like black people getting into an all-white parliament. O'Connell's great achievement then was his transformation from a great political orator into a brilliant parliamentarian. He became the pioneer of democracy in the nineteenth century world.

For the next ten years O'Connell weaved and bobbed in getting practical reforms for Ireland, 'putting Repeal in storage', in winning specific reforms from a sympathetic Whig government – municipal reforms, the appointment of Catholic magistrates, and the commuting of tithes. When the Tories came into power, O'Connell decided to go for Repeal of the Act of Union. I suspect he did not think he would win Repeal but he used a return to Grattan's Parliament as a rhetorical ploy. Being a lawyer, he made a great deal out of the illegality of the Union. Once again he achieved a visible mobilisation of the masses through the 'monster meetings', which would require a four or five-day walk for many to attend. It failed ultimately when the government threatened to suppress it by force. O'Connell, mindful of the brutal events of 1798, would not inflict a repeat of those measures on the Irish people and so he backed down.

The Repeal movement waned partly because his bluff had been called, partly because of attacks on O'Connell by Young Ireland who had a more romantic concept of liberation and most of all because of the Famine which came a year after the suppression of the Clontarf meeting. O'Connell pleaded for policies that would help people survive but he was turned down. The tragedy of the Famine was personified by O'Connell's last appearance in parliament as a mumbling, incoherent figure – he was dying from a brain disease. One of the great paradoxes is that the Irish who emigrated to America – destitute and broken – would within a generation rise to great political heights in governing the cities of the New World. This must in part be attributed to their initiation into mass politics by O'Connell in Ireland.

Another reason I have chosen O'Connell as a 'Millennium Mind' is that he was at the cutting edge of liberal Catholicism and the separation of Church and State. He was also a strong supporter of the abolition of slavery and of the emancipation of the Jews. He held a consistent ideological position in terms of world developments in the attitudes he adopted. For me, it is not exaggerated to see him as a prototype Gandhian figure of the nineteenth century – long ahead of his time in this country or anywhere else at that time.

THE SECRETS OF TEACHING

Writer MAEVE BINCHY *recalls her early tentative attempts at teaching.*

I KNEW A great bossy teacher once who told me firmly that teaching was 'all a matter of confidence'. It came as a very refreshing and almost illicit change from everything else I had been told ... that teaching was a vocation, that it was all tied up with the word *'educare'* ... to lead out ... we should be leading things out of the hidden depths of the pupils' minds. Other people had told me that teaching was communicating, and winning confidence, and sharing, and encouraging ... and though I believed it all in my head and in some of my heart, it was very hard sometimes to realise it in the classroom.

I was teaching Latin to a group of girls who were four years younger than I was. They were doing their Honours Leaving Certificate; my standard of Latin was First Arts Pass, which is slightly lower, I think, than they had already achieved. I used to be up at night for hours with the *North and Hillard* ... much, much more thorough work than I had ever done on my own behalf, when it might have advanced my own career, it must be said. Anyway, no matter what I did, there were obviously great chunks where I was ignorant. To this day I remember where there were some damn verbs in the fourth conjugation with irregular futures ... some odd forms of the third person plural in *Virgil* where he left letters out so that the whole line would scan.

That's where I heard about teaching being a matter of confidence.

She was always a marvellous teacher herself, a woman who had become a nun late in life, who was often impatient with petty restrictions – either those imposed by the Department of Education or I suspect even her religious order ... I told her one autumn day as we were walking down a road covered with leaves. I remember kicking the leaves and feeling it was like being at confession.

'I don't know enough Latin to be teaching it,' I said, as if confessing to murder.

'Oh I know *that*,' she said airily. 'But I thought you'd be able to get by, you know, stop them trying to catch you out.'

The shame was almost unbearable. *How* did she know that some demon evil pupils were trying to catch me out? And anyway, if they could catch me out, shouldn't I pack up the whole thing and forget it and try some other job?

She told me that autumn day as we walked through the red and gold leaves, that once I had the courage to say that I didn't know the future tense of one of those awkward fourth conjugation verbs so let's all look it up ... there would be no reason to try and catch me out. I listened glumly. I still thought it was a poor kind of advice. Wouldn't those kids who were relying on me to teach them Latin feel desperately short-changed? No, she thought now. I mean after all I was so very old, I was twenty-one. They'd have to respect someone as old as that. And anyway if I said it with such cheerful lack of concern, then they would assume I knew Latin like the back of my hand and was only stuck for a word or a grammatical form as anyone might be in English.

My mind went back to the subject she had taught me at school and I wondered sneakily had she been as hopeless as I now suspect.

She read my mind. 'As I said, it's all a matter of confidence,' she said.

TOOLS FOR THINKING

A Dublin hotel. Eight o'clock in the morning. 'You can have fifteen minutes to talk with Mr de Bono.' EDWARD DE BONO has been thinking, writing and talking about creative thinking for twenty-five years and I have fifteen minutes to explore this field with him. Time for some serious creativity here.

CREATIVITY, EDWARD DE BONO argues, is all about changing concepts, perceptions, ideas. One of the misconceptions about it is that you need to have artistic talent to be creative. Not true. Another misconception is that one must be free and uninhibited to be creative. Not true. Creativity is not a natural gift. It goes against the normal behaviour of the mind which is to form routine patterns for dealing with a stable world. It is quite simply a thinking skill and various tools or processes have been developed to help people acquire that skill ...

And some of those tools are ... ?

The best known tool is, I suppose, the 'Six Thinking Hats'. This allows us to get away from *argument* – a crude method of thinking that has dominated western tradition for nearly two and a half thousand years. Adopting the Six Hats allows us to have much more productive discussions. It is very simple, *parallel* thinking. At any moment everyone is looking in one direction ...

> THE WHITE HAT deals with data and information ...
> THE RED HAT has to do with feelings, intuition, emotions. We put forward our feelings without apology or explanation ...
> THE BLACK HAT is the 'caution' hat. It points out when something cannot be done and prevents us from making mistakes ...
> THE YELLOW HAT is for optimism. It looks for feasibility and how something can be done ...
> THE GREEN HAT is for new ideas, different ways, alternatives, creative thinking ...
> THE BLUE HAT is for thinking about thinking. It asks for summaries, conclusions and decisions.

Everyone is thinking in parallel with this system. The hats are just a perceptual symbol to change our mode of thinking ...

Another tool?

Well, there's the CREATIVE PAUSE, which we have used successfully with violent young people. Instead of lashing out impulsively, they were taught to take a Creative Pause, take time out to think ... Then there's CHALLENGE – the notion that 'this is not wrong but is this the only way?' And PROVOCATION – the ability to say something which is not valuable in itself, but which distances you and leads you on to another idea.

There are many other tools but the important thing is that we need creativity because the world is changing and we must make better use of the assets we have.

My time is up but Edward de Bono leaves me with a salutary thought – a provocative thought:

> Traditional education wastes about two-thirds of the talent of society. Many youngsters are not good at the academic game and their self-esteem is low. What we found is that a lot of them are very good THINKERS, if given the chance.

I take my leave, wearing a green hat ...

THE CHALLENGE OF POSTMODERNITY

'We need to come out of the egg-box' is a statement that stays with me from a 1994 interview with ANDY HARGREAVES *from the Ontario Institute for Studies in Education. In his book* Changing Teachers, Changing Times, *Hargreaves examined teachers' work and culture in the postmodern age. It is a thoughtful and challenging examination.*

TEACHERS' WORK IS caught in a powerful struggle, Hargreaves argues. The struggle is between the forces of modernity and postmodernity. 'On the one hand is an increasingly post-industrial postmodern world, characterised by accelerating changes, intense compression of time and space, cultural diversity, technological complexity, national insecurity and scientific uncertainty. Against this stands a modernistic, monolithic school system that continues to pursue deeply anachronistic purposes within obstructive and inflexible structures ... '

One of those structures is the 'egg-box' design of schools which contributes to the individualism and isolation of teachers' work culture. Once upon a time, maybe, 'the wonder grew that one small head could carry all he knew'. Not any more, especially in primary schools.

'With the much-widened knowledge base of the present primary years, along with more sophisticated understandings of the special and different learning needs of many children, primary teachers can no longer know, plan and teach everything to all students, without experiencing intolerable overload or unbearable guilt about their own shortcomings.'

At secondary level there are egg-box classrooms also, compounded by organisation, curriculum and decision-making being based on the sub-grouping of subject departments. More isolation of teachers, what Hargreaves calls 'balkanised' teacher cultures, insulation of the sub-groups, little interchange of ideas and experiences, little movement of teachers between sub-groups. Territorial defensiveness, under-utilisation of human resources and excessive burdens on leadership tend to be the outcome of balkanised cultures of teaching.

Collaboration is now proposed as a solution to the problem of contemporary schooling. Its proponents claim that collaboration offers greater moral support to teachers. It also increases efficiency by eliminating duplication and sharing responsibilities. Collaboration improves the quality of teaching by encouraging diversity in teaching strategies. It reduces overload and offers greater opportunities for reflection, for learning, for ongoing professional improvement. Collaboration is *not* a panacea for all the ills of modern schooling, Hargreaves stresses. It carries dangers too – complacency, conformism and 'contrived collegiality', among others.

Nonetheless, 'the key challenge for schools, administration and teachers is whether they can live with or even actively encourage full-blown cooperative classrooms, collaborative staffrooms and self-managing schools that are charged with spontaneity, unpredictability, danger and desire; or whether they will opt for safe simulations of these things that are controlled, contrived and ultimately superficial in character ... '

ANOTHER TIME, ANOTHER PLACE

'Saving the Waifs and Strays' was a documentary based on JANE BARNES' *study of Irish Industrial schools. The Industrial School system was set up in the late nineteenth century as a state response to the very urgent needs of many thousands of destitute, orphaned and unwanted children. In this extract, Jane Barnes tells how, in daily life in an industrial school, order and discipline governed every activity.*

SILENCE WAS IMPOSED at mealtimes and in dormitories. In most boys' schools the day was punctuated by bugle calls which replaced all bells. Instruction in military drill was a feature of all boys' schools, contributing to a barrack-like atmosphere. The children's day was very long and very exhausting as a sample timetable for Artane School in the nineteenth century illustrates:

5.15 A.M.	OFFICERS RISE
5.30 A.M.	BOYS RISE, WASH AND DRESS
6.00 – 7.00 A.M.	SCHOOL
7.00 – 7.30 A.M.	SENIORS' DUTIES
	JUNIORS CONTINUE SCHOOL
7.55 A.M.	BREAKFAST
8.45 A.M.	SCHOOL INSPECTION
9.00 A.M.	INDUSTRIAL EDUCATION
11.40 A.M.	RECESS
12.15 P.M.	INDUSTRIAL EDUCATION
1.55 P.M.	DINNER
AFTER DINNER	INDUSTRIAL EDUCATION
5.00 P.M.	SENIORS' AND JUNIORS' SCHOOL SUPPER / NIGHT PRAYERS
8.00 P.M.	RETIRE TO BED

Within this overall structure, regular times were allocated each day for devotion, recreation and outdoor sports.

In order to enforce such regimes, discipline had to be implemented. Many reports from the Inspectors of Industrial Schools maintained that discipline was 'mild' and 'parental'. Various schemes of rewards and punishments were introduced and in boys' schools corporal punishment was certainly a feature. One study of a School Punishment Book has reported that in 1896 misdemeanours such as 'leaving playground without permission', 'unruly behaviour in refectory', 'talking at night in dormitory' and 'disorderly conduct in playground' merited a whipping. The most severe punishment recorded in this book arose from an incident when one boy 'went to another's bed at about 12 o'clock at night':

> Six strokes of the little scourge, composed of four narrow strips of leather, thirteen inches long, administered in the presence of Mr O'Donnell, assistant teacher. He was put on bread and water for one day and was obliged to take his meals on his knees for six days in the refectory but got the usual supply of food.

In girls' schools, the sisters in charge made use of alternative punishments such as the withdrawal of privileges and treats and indeed of food. Cutting off hair and whipping were reserved for the most serious offences. Generally the punishments for girls were milder – though often humiliating – as these entries from the punishment book for St George's School in Limerick indicate:

18 JULY 1893   OFFENCE: COMING TO CLASS NOT TIDY.
               PUNISHMENT: HAD THEIR PINAFORES PUT OVER THEIR HEADS FOR HALF AN HOUR.

24 JULY 1893   OFFENCE: FOR TELLING A LIE.
               PUNISHMENT: HAD PEPPER PUT ON HER TONGUE.

25 July 1893	OFFENCE:	IDLENESS DURING LESSONS.
	PUNISHMENT:	HAD TO DO THEIR LESSONS AT RECREATION.
27 July 1893	OFFENCE:	FOR INSOLENCE.
	PUNISHMENT:	HAD A BAND PUT OVER HER MOUTH FOR HALF AN HOUR.
25 August 1893	OFFENCE:	FOR SCRIBBLING IN HER COPYBOOK.
	PUNISHMENT:	HAD TO WEAR IT ON HER HEAD FOR QUARTER OF AN HOUR.
29 August 1893	OFFENCE:	NOT DOING THEIR WORK OR MURMURING AGAINST IT.
	PUNISHMENT:	WERE OBLIGED TO RISE AN HOUR EARLIER NEXT MORNING TO DO IT.

FINDING FORGIVENESS

GORDON WILSON, *an 'ordinary wee draper from Enniskillen', found himself in the worldwide media spotlight when he was interviewed immediately after the 1987 Enniskillen bombing which killed his daughter, Marie. Here, from 'My Education', he gives the background to that story.*

I BLUSH WHEN people say I'm famous. I'm not famous – I'm an ordinary guy. Nevertheless, the fact remains that my face and the words I used made page one in every newspaper in the world and item one on every radio and television broadcast. When the interviewer, without warning, asked, 'How do you feel about the guys who planted the bomb?', I said what I said, which, although I didn't use the word 'forgiveness', had to be forgiveness. That seemed to catch people's attention. Here was a guy in the midst of grief, who that day had lost his daughter, forgiving the people who had killed her.

I didn't say those words because they were the words people would expect me to say, or because it was a nice thing to say. I said them because I believed them. I went on to say that I would pray for those guys that night and every night, and I still do. I haven't changed my views on that since then. People say, 'The man's potty, how could he, now that he has lost his daughter, how could he?' I don't claim any personal credit. I thank God that he gave me the grace to say those words. I believe there is a God and that God loves me. I try to love him and I accept his word when he said, 'A new commandment I give unto you, that you love one another'. I accept his word when he taught us the Lord's Prayer with the words 'Forgive us our trespasses as we forgive those who trespass against us'. You either believe that or you don't. And I do.

The response was enormous by any standards – letters and flowers and the media. I even had to go ex-directory. Six weeks later, I lost my memory. Something had to give.

There is no formula, there is no list of rules that you can throw to people who are grieving and say, follow these rules and you'll be alright. Everybody has to make their own reconciliation, find their own way forward. I know this for sure because my wife Joan, and Peter and Julianne and myself, got through it in different ways. Of course, we ask ourselves 'why?' and of course the loss is there. I wouldn't be honest if I didn't say that we have times when we miss Marie very much. Of course we will never forget. People say time is a healer. Time helps one to cope a little better. Life goes on, life goes on. There is no point in sitting at home feeling sorry for oneself. One has to get on with it, and this is no disrespect to the dead.

I have the assurance that if it is the will of God, I will meet Marie again. I will again hold her hand. That is one of the things that keeps me going. I am now retired from business – to be frank, after the bomb I didn't really want to know about business. Retirement is something that doesn't just happen. One has to apply oneself. Thankfully, I have had the wit to get out, meet friends, play some golf, stay involved. There are lots of days when I could be alone in the house and that to me would be a death-trap.

I have the highest regard for the New England poet, John Greenleaf Whittier. Very often I try, unsuccessfully, to find words to talk about forgiveness and reconciliation, and above all, to talk about love, because to me the bottom line is loving my neighbour. So I ask myself the question, 'Who is my neighbour?' and the answer I get is that my neighbour is not just my Protestant neighbour nor is it just my Catholic neighbour. I must include my terrorist neighbour if I believe what I am trying to say. It is true to say that Christ died for them too, and they are the children of God just as I am, and they must repent if they are going to get God's forgiveness, just as I must. That is why I like these words of Whittier:

Follow with reverent steps the great example
of him whose holy work was 'doing good';
So shall the wide earth seem our Father's temple,
each loving life a psalm of gratitude.

Then shall all shackles fall; the stormy clangour
of wild war music o'er the earth shall cease;
Love shall tread out the baleful fire of anger
and in its ashes plant the tree of peace!

LISTEN!

FEARGAL QUINN *spent most of his adult life as a supermarket boss. He learned most about his business by listening ...*

MY FATHER AND his father before him had been in the grocery business, so I would have been the third generation except that my father had left the grocery business in the mid-1940s and opened Red Island holiday camp. In 1960, I opened the first shop in Dundalk. There was the excitement of opening a new business in a town which I didn't know, but also of a new way of doing business. Self-service was not very well known then. One of the principal rules I learned very early on was – if you listen to your colleagues, if you listen to your staff, if you listen to your own people, you learn a great deal. I think most of my education has come about from just listening to my own colleagues and people who may be even much junior to me in the company.

Being able to get close to the customer, to listen to the customer, is actually another form of education, because you learn so much from them – the customer who says: 'I'll tell you what I hate ...' or 'If only you could ...' or 'I'd come here more often if ...' That is more education than you get from any book or school or headmaster. Of course, market research is important, but not nearly as important as one-to-one contact with the customer who says: 'I'm not coming here again because ...' Even when they are things you don't want to hear – 'Your prices are too high'; 'Your quality is not good enough'; 'Your shop is not clean enough'; 'Your service isn't friendly enough' – it is very important that you do hear them. There's nothing as bad as a customer not telling you why it is they have decided to shop elsewhere.

So an important objective is to encourage your customer to complain and I don't think we're very good in Ireland at doing that. We're much happier if we don't get complaints and we sometimes judge success by thinking that the fewer complaints there are, the better things are. We've learned a huge amount from customer panels, whereby customers sit down and tell us what they like, what they dislike, what they'd like to see improved. I certainly think I have been far more educated by listening to customers than I have been by reading books.

SHAPED BY A LANDSCAPE

POLLY DEVLIN *remembers growing up by the shore of Lough Neagh.*

THE LANDSCSAPE THAT I grew up in was both ordinary and quite extraordinary. It had two very striking features. On one side was a vast expanse of water, twenty-five miles long by ten miles wide – Lough Neagh. And when you turned your back on this great silvery plain there was another plain – an aerodrome which had been blitzed into an intimate landscape of trees and bushes (Co. Tyrone is often referred to as 'Tyrone among the bushes', and never more so than in Ardboe, my native place).

We lived in the little peninsula between the two places, with one tiny road leading out to the nearest small village and then on to the bigger town of Cookstown. The farms were very small and it was a poor district, but very beautiful. Very few families lived in this rural area and while the rest of the century moved on, we stayed in this very flat, hidden byplace – a place bypassed by almost everything else. We were effectively lodged in an Edwardian time-warp. My father did have a car (my mother was a school teacher and needed a car) but that was, I think, except for the parish priest's car, the only one in the district for a very long time.

Lough Neagh played such an enormous role in our childhood that we never analysed it. It was like our parents, being there all the time. It dominated the whole landscape. Wherever you went you could hear the sough and hiss of the lough – without hearing it, as it were. If it stopped then the world would have come to an end. You only really heard it when you had been away for a while and had come back to realise how loud it was.

It was a magical place. The great cross of Ardboe stood on the only piece of high ground, surrounded by a graveyard. That was our playground, where we lay on the tombstones and climbed the walls of the old ruined abbey, keeping an eye out for King, the water bailiff. At that time the fishing rights were owned by a London firm, so all the local fishermen were classified as poachers. If the water bailiff was spotted, a bonfire was lit on the lough shore and the boats turned for home. It was exciting and hair-raising to watch King in his huge motor boat come racing towards the small boats. If he caught them it was disaster because he confiscated their lines and fined them heavily. For people who were struggling to make a living it was a nightmarish existence.

Eels were the chief crop of the lough. Every day during the season eels were caught and kept in tanks which were just slightly submerged below the water. We would lie, fascinated, looking down at those extraordinary pewter lengths combing in and out of themselves. We learned to skin eels when we were quite young – also to gut and clean them, something which invariably brought a shudder from people who didn't come from the lough shore. There is a prejudice against eels but in fact they are a great delicacy.

We learned to swim in the lough. The water was always cold and being fresh water it was not at all buoyant, so you had to work quite hard to swim. We were in and out of the boats all the time but we didn't get out on the lough in boats often, because we would be in the way of working men and also because of a superstition that the lough claimed one victim every year. I suppose the fishermen didn't want to be tempting the lough with nice fresh young bait like us, but the days when you did get out on the lough were astonishing. As you went further out and watched the landscape recede from view, the lough became the world.

It was a unique way to grow up, living between those two great flat spaces of aerodrome and lough. Caught between them, we were moulded and shaped into something, I think, which was entirely different than if we had grown up in any other part of Europe.

Our lives were so much enmeshed in each others, so netted together, that there was – it seemed to me – no way to extricate myself. The whole metaphor of enmeshment and of nets has to do with the lough, of course, but for each of us it was a great struggle to get free of our sisters because we were so close. We all loved each other but it was also easy to be passionately angry with our sisters, even to loathe them. When you have sisters, the sister has done what you want to do, she has already been where you hope to go. For each of us, therefore – except for the oldest, who had the difficult job of being the pioneer – there was always a sister ahead who appeared to be more glamorous, more clever, more successful or who appeared to have more love from our parents. It happens in every family, I suppose, but it was heightened in our case because there were so many of us with only a twelve-year span among us. We sisters all had the same pursuits, we all read the same books, we all did the same things.

The arrival of a brother in our midst was traumatic in a way. He became a focal point for all of us. We admired him and loved him, and we derived a lot of our feelings and stance about men from observing his behaviour. It had been absolutely bred into us that man was superior to woman and suddenly this male arrived in our midst – somebody who was on the same level of living as we were, but who was masculine and therefore on a higher level in another sense.

EDUCATION FOR FREEDOM

FRANK FLANAGAN *examines the educational ideas of Paulo Freire.*

PAULO FREIRE WAS born in Recife, Brazil in 1921 and was the son of a well-to-do banker who suffered a fateful reversal of fortunes as a result of the Wall Street crash in 1929. The family circumstances changed radically and they were forced to move to the countryside where they witnessed the predicament of the impoverished peasantry.

The young Paulo saw at close quarters that the ignorance and lethargy of the peasants was rooted in their political, economic and social powerlessness. They were not architects of their own fate but victims of systemic oppression. They were submerged in what he came to call a 'culture of silence', accepting their situation as part of the natural order and lacking a voice to speak out against the injustices which dominated their daily lives. By internalising their oppressor's image of them, they came to share a view of themselves as good for nothing, ignorant, idle, lazy and unproductive. Once convinced of their own worthlessness, they never realised that 'they too know things that they have learned in their relations with the world and with other men'. These kinds of self-evaluations are true of any group that is the object of prejudice and that has allowed such prejudice to dominate them.

Freire learned an unforgettable lesson about the inescapably political nature of education and its role in the process of oppression.

Education is never neutral. Every educational system has the effect of transforming the people who pass through it in certain ways. In the case of the oppressed, Freire has no doubt that the educational transformation is deliberately contrived by dominant groups that use education to encourage others to be passive and to accept oppression, to develop a 'submerged' state of consciousness. The oppressive groups exploit the passivity to 'fill that consciousness with slogans which create ... fear of freedom'.

By looking at education in this way, Freire highlights its ideological or political function – generally, education is used to make the oppressed see their oppression as natural and necessary, to see it as a function of the 'natural' or 'unchangeable' order of things and of their own lack of worth.

The fatalism which is induced by fear of freedom and lack of worth is not a natural characteristic of the behaviour of the people affected, even though they themselves attribute it to 'the power of destiny or fate or fortune ... or to a distorted view of God'. They interpret their subservience and suffering, this 'organised disorder' – in reality the effect of exploitation – as the will of God.

Who are the oppressed? What is oppression? An oppressive situation is any situation 'in which A objectively exploits B or hinders his self-affirmation as a responsible person'. Oppression requires control. The most effective and efficient means of control is not physical force or coercion, or even the threat of them. It is control of the consciousness of the oppressed: the most effective control makes people's own minds the instrument of the control – the most effective control is mind control.

The oppressed are fatalistic about their situation because they fail to see that the interests of the *status quo* are not their interests. Convinced of their own lack of worth as individuals, they deprecate their own knowledge and experience. Emotionally dependent on the oppressor, they look to the oppressor for validation of their existence. They aspire to share the way of life of the oppressor – that is, to become oppressors themselves. They aspire to be human in the fullest sense, but to them the fullest sense – the highest form of achievement – is to be an oppressor. 'Their ideal is to be men, but for them to be a man is to be an oppressor. This is their model of humanity.'

Pedagogy of the Oppressed – Freire's major and most influential educational work – can be read as a manual of resistance to the kind of mind control that keeps oppressed people in a state of submission. What is a pedagogy of the oppressed?

Humanisation is the vocation of human beings – their most important task is to maximise their humanity. Developing an education for people – no matter how well-intentioned or inspired – simply reinforces helplessness and dependency. If educators are to help the oppressed to achieve their humanity they must do so in partnership with them. The resulting pedagogy would make the phenomenon of oppression – its causes and the subjective experience of oppression – matters to be studied by learners themselves. Engagement with, as it were, the theory and practice of oppression would be a first necessary step in liberation. A pedagogy of the oppressed is a process of enabling – of empowering – oppressed people to see the realities which are keeping them in a state of subordination.

The oppressed must first of all see their condition and alternatives to it. Education empowers the oppressed to discover alternatives in situations which have been taken as natural, necessary and unchangeable. It is only when they see alternatives that they can begin to transform their own world and experience. From the educator's point of view this is a process of humanisation. From the point of view of the dominant group – the oppressor – it is 'subversion', for it challenges their control and their power.

Conventional schooling systems illustrate the process of oppressive domination. They embody what Freire calls the 'banking' concept of education.

Education is suffering from what Freire calls 'narration sickness'. The teacher-student relationship at any level – elementary, secondary or tertiary – whether inside or outside the school – is largely a *narrative* relationship. It comprises 'a narrating subject' (the teacher), and patient, listening 'objects' (the students). The teachers' function is to fill students with the contents of their narration – the teacher speaks, the students listen. Knowledge is bestowed by those considered knowledgeable upon those considered ignorant. The more teachers can accomplish the narrative task – the more completely they fill the students' minds – the more successful they are. For their part students are judged on their capacity to be filled with, and retain, the relevant material – it is largely a memory exercise.

Whatever the subject, the experience of learning loses vitality and relevance in the narrative process for two reasons. First, irrespective of whether the subject contents are values or facts, the process of narration itself renders them 'lifeless and petrified'. 'The teacher talks about reality as if it were motionless, static, compartmentalised and predictable.' The contents of the narration have become disconnected from the human experience that engendered them and gave them their original significance. Real experience has been replaced by words, and the words in turn have been 'emptied of their concreteness and become a hollow, alienated and alienating verbosity'. Second, teachers' narration expounds on topics which are removed from the students' lived experience. By being excluded from students' learning programmes, their lived experience is devalued and alienated. As a consequence, students accept the knowledge that is bestowed upon them passively – it never becomes their knowledge because it has no immediacy to their lived experience.

In a metaphor which echoes Dickens in *Hard Times*, Freire describes the work of the conventional teacher as filling learners full of knowledge, as we would fill jugs. The entire process reduces the learner to nothing more than a container to be filled.

In the banking concept of education only the teacher takes an active role – the teacher thinks, chooses, talks, disciplines etc. – while the students' participation is passive. Students do not determine their own learning experiences. Their life experience is set at nought, diminished and trivialised by the imposition of the belief that *only* what the schools teach is worthwhile knowledge.

Education then, in the banking metaphor, becomes 'an act of depositing'. The students are the depositories into which the teacher lodges instalments of learning. Students' participation extends only as far as submissively 'receiving, filing and storing the deposits'.

DUBLIN MADE ME

Humorous writer JOHN D. SHERIDAN *recalls a Dublin childhood.*

THE DUBLIN I grew up in was smaller than the sprawling complex it has since become. Moreover, it was made even smaller by the fact that the Liffey was then a great dividing line. You were either a Northsider or a Southsider. We of the Northside spoke scathingly of the Southsiders as 'Spats and no Breakfast' people; and they looked down on us as 'below the salt'.

I lived in Hollybank Road, Drumcondra. Also living there at the time were Seamus Clandillon, the first director of 2RN (as Radio Éireann was known then), and J.M. Kerrigan, the Abbey actor.

The next road to ours was Botanic Avenue, alongside which the Tolka then flowed (it has since been diverted), at the end of which were the low-lying, unhygienic Tolka Cottages, which were always flooded when the river was swollen by heavy rains. On these occasions the Corporation brought supplies of food to the Cottages and moved elderly people to safety in punts. The Lord Mayor, Alfie Byrne, was always there too, and he gave money to the homeless. Some said that this was vote-catching. Maybe it was, but Alfie always gave generously to those in need, and he died a comparatively poor man.

I was a pupil at St Patrick's National School and one day – without any of the other boys hearing – I recited for the teacher a poem that I had written:

> The sun is slowly sinking
> Behind yonder hill,
> The mist is slowly creeping
> This weary world to fill.
> The fisherman is steering
> His little craft to land
> Where his children are awaiting him
> Upon the silver strand.

Not magnificent perhaps, but it shows that I was bitten by the 'writing bug' early in play.

I have still vivid memories of the 1916 Insurrection, though I was too young at the time to know what it was all about. I had been picnicking with some other boys at St John's Castle and as we walked home in the heel of the evening we heard a countrywoman saying, 'There's murder in the city!' We thought she was referring to the usual Bank Holiday rows, but when we got nearer to the city we heard of the seizing of the GPO. Later in the week we got quite used to the rattle of musketry, the boom of the big guns, and the red glow over burning buildings in Sackville Street (as O'Connell Street was then called). One evening, as my father stood at our hall door, he was struck in the leg by a spent bullet. It was red-hot when he picked it up and it barely drew blood.

Stories were plentiful. One was about the 'oul wan' who went looting and filled an old pram with booty. When she went back for yet another fur coat, someone stole the pram. 'Dublin's a nest of robbers,' she was heard to say. 'They would take the eye outa yer head and tell you you looked better without it!'

When the regiment of British soldiers marched through Drumcondra (they had landed, I think, at Drogheda and taken the train to Malahide) the women from the Cottages – many of whom had husbands serving in France – rushed out with cups of tea. I heard one soldier say as he lowered his tea, 'We'll soon finish off these blasted Shine Finers'.

(My father, I should have mentioned, had the spent bullet mounted in gold, and wore it ever afterwards on his watchchain. I said, many years later, that if he had played his cards properly he would have got an IRA pension.)

Two places, Dublin and Donegal – for I remember little about Glasgow – have helped to make me, for better or worse, the man I am. But for that matter the majority of Dubliners have county loyalties, and a third-generation Jackeen is hard to come by. Most of us, I have found, are not more than a couple of generations from the title deeds of a farm.

JOHN D. WAS FOUND DEAD – SLUMPED OVER HIS TYPEWRITER – IN 1980. THESE WERE HIS LAST WORDS, PREPARED FOR 'EDUCATION FORUM'.

THE LITTLE COLLABORATOR

Silvana Montanaro *advises parents on the importance of taking the very young child into their trust.*

As soon as the child is walking – about twelve months old – he likes to do all the practical chores that *we* don't like – washing, cleaning, preparing food, setting the table. We usually try to distract them from these activities. We want them to play with toys which don't necessarily provide intelligent activity. If you have a two-step staircase which you put in front of the sink, you can prepare a meal while you give something real to the child to do. For instance he may cut a banana or wash the cups. It is real activity which has a result, and through that activity the child becomes a collaborator, participating in the social life of the house. He is not just a user, but a producer, which is very different.

Children are naturally obedient. If you have patience, they will respond to you in a way you cannot imagine. Parents should talk to the child as an intelligent human being from the very beginning. The child's brain has all the cells ready from the seventh month of pregnancy. A newborn child has a small body but a big mind. He will absorb good language from the parents and reproduce it as soon as possible. He may ask you to read the same story twenty times because he is looking for the meaning of the words, so read to him with patience. And talk to him as you would to an educated person, and not in a childish way. If you use good, rich language, he will absorb it. He is attending to your voice even when you are not speaking directly to him. His absorbent mind is listening and learning continuously.

All the time it is a matter of collaboration. We do things not just for the child, but with him. When we dress him we ask him to help, explain what we are doing and he learns very quickly. A child of three is to me a very 'old' child! He should be able to do so much for himself with your guidance. When I talk of the child as a practical collaborator, I am talking of the child from eighteen months onwards. For instance, if you buy a dozen eggs at the market, you should trust the child to put them in the refrigerator. He can do it. You ask him to do it as you would ask an adult.

He may well drop one or two eggs, but how expensive is that compared to buying him a comfort toy, which will not give him the same experience? Nowadays we tend to keep children too dependent and at a lower stage of development than that which is possible. This can lead to frustration and aggression in some children, passivity in others. Both situations are wrong.

The three-year-old child who has had the trust of his parents will speak perfectly and richly. He will know his environment and thus will be capable of doing any task within that environment. He will have a very good social relationship, will be attentive to others. He will be a complete human being, ready now for a higher level of education and culture.

BABIES NEED BOOKS

It is Parents' Day at the World Reading Congress, Dublin 1982.
Patricia Koppman – the feisty daughter of a Baptist preacher
from the Deep South of the USA – is doing her own bit of evangelising on
the importance of books in the child's life. A mother in the audience
tentatively asks Patricia a question. 'At what stage do I start reading to my
child?' Patricia looks her straight in the eye. 'Well, honey, I'll spare you the
delivery room. But on the way back ...' DOROTHY BUTLER *would totally*
endorse Patricia's answer.

A MOTHER OF eight from New Zealand, Dorothy has been a teacher, a bookshop-owner and a writer during her busy life. She has written the acclaimed *Babies Need Books* – a practical guide for parents – and when I met Dorothy in Dublin in 1995, the obvious starting question was, 'Why (do babies need books)?' The following is a summary of Dorothy's extended answer ...

The fact is we all need books to meet our varied needs – emotional, empathetic, entertainment; it is just so important that we start to meet those needs at the earliest possible age. Despite the seduction of the electronic media we must convince the young child that books are worthwhile. The electronic media can never do what books do for the child. There is intimacy. There is relatedness. There is enchantment. So there should be a pile of books awaiting the new-born child (makes life easy for doting grandparents, uncles, aunts!). The child's emotional needs are met superbly when he/she is cuddled on an adult lap and the simplest story unfolds from the pages of a book. The basic design of a book has never changed. A baby will very quickly realise that something magic happens when a page is turned. A new vista opens. A story continues. That magic will stay with the child for all of his/her days.

So we surround the young child with books – all around the house and especially in the bedroom. Books are often a major source of 'colour' in children's lives. They will sit for a surprising length of time poring over a book or listening to a story. The writer Joan Aiken has said that 'any parent who isn't prepared to read to a child for an hour a day doesn't deserve to have a child'! Bedtime stories are grand, but bedtime may not always be the best time. Either party may be over-tired and other children (or adults) may be making demands ... Morning is often a good time, even in the 'middle of the muddle' as I call it. And the 'after-school story' is a good idea too.

I am not in favour of 'teaching' books or 'early reading' books. Just expose the child to books for the sheer enjoyment of them. Let them own their own books, just to handle them and be familiar with them. They will never be lonely with an old friend ...

AND SO DO BIG BABIES ...

Adapted from ANNE FINE's *1996 'Open Mind' Guest Lecture.*

THE JOY OF reading and the need for reading can and should continue into older childhood. Why? The writer Anne Fine quotes a line from the film *Shadowlands* – 'We read to know that we are not alone'. In Anne

Fine's own novel, *Goggle Eyes*, a teacher says: 'Living your life is a long and doggy business, and stories and books help. Some help you with the living itself, some help you just take a break, and the best do both at the same time.'

So we all – and particularly children – read for enchantment but for enlightenment and empathy too. Who, Anne Fine asks, has not put down a book with a sigh of recognition, a sense of *Yes! That is exactly how I feel! That is exactly how things are for me* – a sense of no longer being on one's own. C.S. Lewis says, 'In reading I become a thousand men, and yet remain myself ...'

Anne Fine also reminds us that it does *have* to be a book. 'Television and film just won't do. Books can explore emotion. They can be reflective, they can expose conscience and motivation, morals and inner concern. They do not simply show you what happened next at the producer's speed – they show you how and why at your own ... Readers can test themselves against lives they might have to live – when Dad leaves ... when the bomb drops ... when plague strikes ... when the hard men take over ... when they fail all their exams ...

Frank Flanagan – a lecturer in the University of Limerick – observes that it is 'unfortunately common for adults to ignore the child's need for a voice to structure the experience of childhood. This is what good writers do. They structure, explain and evaluate the experience of childhood and empower the child to come to terms with it. They enable the child to lead a full life ...'

A full life – from a mere book? A mere piece of 'old technology'. Anne Fine recalls the words of Jane Austen: 'Oh, it's only a novel, only some work in which the greatest powers of the mind are displayed, in which the most thorough knowledge of human nature, the happiest delineations of its varieties ... are conveyed to the world in the best chosen language ...'

Or the words of a modern writer, Naomi Lewis: 'A book is a private friend, speaking to us alone, telling us whatever we long to know. Every book makes its reader a welcome and honoured guest, free from all harm in the wildest and strangest places in the world. A book can dissolve the walls of the dullest room in the dullest town and no-one seeing you sitting there can have any idea how far you have escaped ...'

ON THE DEATH OF PIAGET

JEROME BRUNER *gives an evaluation of Piaget, on hearing of the great Swiss psychologist's death.*

JEAN PIAGET IS dead. He was the leading figure in our search for the development of mind. His influence stretches from the 1930s to the present day. His contribution is enormous and his reputation is worldwide and well-deserved.

He was a man who dedicated his life to his work to a degree that can only be described as a kind of purity. He worked all the time – even when you went walking with him, as I did on many occasions in the mountains across the lake from Geneva. In his single-mindedness there was an almost childlike possession. His desk would be piled high with manuscript upon manuscript. He would be working on a new book while two or three more manuscripts were at different stages of development. He published an enormous number of volumes in his lifetime.

Piaget set himself a classic task early in his career – to find out the way human beings grow in the direction of being able to sense what it is that is *invariant* – what is constant in the world – even though it changes its appearance. The child lives in the world of appearance. He acquires a representation of the world that is based upon his action towards the world. He moves from a sensori-motor stage to the stage of concrete operations. Then he moves into formal operations where he can deal not only with the world as it exists but also with the world of the possible. It is a highly intellectualised theory, making Piaget a sacred figure for many educationalists. The conversion of his theory into one of *readiness* is to my mind a bad influence i.e. you don't teach a child maths of a certain kind until he is 'ready'. I have to confess that I stand on the opposite side of this argument, by claiming that almost any subject can be taught to any child in some form that is honest.

In the main, what Piaget has been interested in was taking epistemology i.e. the philosophy of knowledge, and seeing whether you could ask basic questions about the nature of knowledge and track them through the child's developmental stages. Piaget called himself a genetic epistemologist rather than a psychologist and – so far as I know – never considered himself to be an educator. His interests were of a philosophical kind and the purity of those interests were plain to see. Piaget is not easy to read – it takes hard work to understand him. He is so single-minded in his work. The question of *invariance* comes up again and again and always with a new twist and a new turn.

I had a letter from a former student of mine at Oxford in which he commented that he was actually reading some of Piaget's work when he heard the death of Piaget announced on the radio. He went back to the reading, feeling a sense of great loss but also of gratitude that Piaget had set down his life's work in writing.

It will take some time to evaluate the impact of Piaget. In some ways it is like the impact of Immanuel Kant on philosophy in his time. Everyone had to start off relating themselves to Kant and I think that is the way it will be with Piaget. He has forced us to look at the underlying logic of the child's mind, to look at it structurally, because Piaget represents the high point of structuralism in the field of developmental psychology. He constantly talked about the fact that you could not ever understand any one function by itself – i.e. memory or reasoning or perception – without understanding where it fitted into the structure of operations in the child's mind – what he called the *structure d'ensemble*, the structure of the whole.

I have to end by coming back to one important point. I think the place where Piaget felt there was not a problem is in the context in which learning takes place – the nature of the materials, the child's view of reality. For Piaget, action of any kind was good enough – if the child operated on the environment, he automatically built his world. We now know that it makes a difference what it is that one is engaged in. There are ways in which you can enable a mind better by following certain tracks, starting at the intuitive level and moving up to the more formal level.

What Piaget has done is to give us a sense of the orderliness and the power of children's minds. Where we carry on from here is to understand the nature of the culture in which the child operates, the way in which education can provide a set of prosthetic devices which will make the mind run and leap and sing rather than plod its way through a kind of development. Piaget started us on our way, made us aware that the child has to discover the world anew, has to assimilate it. We are enormously in his debt. He has made a tremendous contribution to his generation and he shall be missed, although his work will go on reverberating for many decades to come.

IT TAKES A VILLAGE

There is a saying – 'It takes a village to raise a child'. JIM DEENY'S *education was a clear validation of that saying. Jim Deeny was a doctor who became a devoted public servant and architect of much of Ireland's health legislation in the 1940s and 1950s. His father was a GP in Lurgan, Co. Armagh – the 'village' that raised young Jim ...*

MY FATHER AND mother and my sister, brother and I lived next door to my grandfather, my grandmother, two aunts and an uncle. We were a bit like a commune. In addition, we were reared with a governess – a remarkable woman, Miss Finnegan. We would walk along the street with her and stop to look at a shop window. Twenty yards further on Miss Finnegan would ask, 'And what did you see in that shop window?' We would tell her as many things as we could remember and then she would take us back again to see how many things we had missed! We also had a big farmyard and paddocks right in the middle of the town and there were a couple of men working there. They all took care of us and minded us.

My other grandfather lived up at Dungiven. He was a contractor, a farmer and a mill-owner. One of my uncles ran the contracting business. He was also the local head of the St Vincent de Paul Society. As he went from one building to another, some old lady in a pony and trap might meet him and he would have a wee chat with her about getting help from the St Vincent de Paul Society. In this way I learned from him. The grandfather took me for a walk every Sunday. Because he was a builder, he could tell me all about the ruins at Dungiven or he would take me up to *Poll na Péiste* – the Dragon's Pool – which is now flooded for the waterworks for Derry.

I used to run wild through the countryside. I had friends like the canal lock-keeper, who built me a boat for two pounds and I used sail it on the canal. Then there was Herbie Andrews, who was head of the waterworks. He showed me how to run the waterworks, which valves to turn, what to do when the filter-beds got clogged. And Hughie McAlinden took me fishing in his boat.

I used to be sent to get shoes soled at Lavery's the shoemakers. I would sit there for half the morning talking about shoemaking. Then Mr Lavery would go to feed his pigs and I would help him and forget to come home. I really was a dreadful child! I had a wonderful childhood – running wild one minute and then strapped down and taught to play the piano next ...

MINDING OUR MINDS

From the introductory programme to the series 'Millennium Minds', diplomat and broadcaster ERSKINE CHILDERS *takes a panoramic view of the second millennium and warns that while amazing progress has been made in the transmission of ideas, there may be problems ahead ...*

AS EUROPE BEGAN to recover from its 'Dark Age', merchants needed better records and students at the new universities needed textbooks. But virtually the only available textbooks were in Arabic, so two things happened. A veritable industry of translating Arabic into Latin sprang up in Italy and Spain. Between 1130 and 1150 Archbishop Raimond founded an entire college of translators in Toledo in Spain to work on the Arabs' studies of Greek philosophy. And by no coincidence, by 1150 the Arabs were making paper in Spain.

A century later European scholars were still frantically translating from Arabic into Latin. Paper was in more and more demand to make copies of the new books for the universities, because those irritatingly advanced Arabs had everything Europe needed – documented and built upon by their own scholarship. All the great Greek philosophers, political scientists and physical scientists – from Aristotle to Archimedes – had to be translated, and all the knowledge in every discipline which the Arabs had also assembled from Persia and India and China and Africa and Meso-America. Even in limited hand-scribed copies all this intellectual treasure provoked a ferment of enquiry and unlocked untold numbers of minds all over Europe.

It was now that big things happened in Germany, where a new metal technology had developed. In Mainz in 1448, the son of a goldsmith named Gutenberg responded to the clamour for books, the pressure from the clergy for bibles for the faithful, and the needs of business, and went into partnership with a banker named Fust to develop a metal-based printing press. It was running fairly well by the year 1457, and Gutenberg's apprentices spread out across Europe, finding a huge demand for printing presses. In 1470 there were only twelve operating printing presses in the whole of Europe; by 1498 there were 110; by 1500 there were over 200. Europe, and over time the world, would never be the same again.

It was a veritable explosion of communication. At one dimension, card games were suddenly being played all over Europe; at the other, 45,000 different books were published in less than fifty years, and we can estimate there were twenty million copies of them. Think of it. There had never been *twenty million* texts of anything, anywhere before. By the end of the 1500s it was 200 million copies of at least 200,000 individual books, and there was no turning back. Newspapers followed, and off in

America a man named Samuel Morse perfected an electric pulse carried over wire, and in 1844 the telegraph arrived. By 1882 the Honourable Joseph Cowen was telling the House of Commons at Westminster:

> Information that was once the exclusive possession of a favoured few is now the common property of all. News of events that transpire at the other side of the globe and in our most distant dependencies is flashed here in a few hours. The world has become a vast whispering gallery.

And before we knew it we were in the age of cinema and then of radio, and then of television and the computer and satellite communication and all the refinements that burst pell-mell today at ever lower cost into our lives.

But let us slow down for a moment. Shall all this sheer speed in the transmission of ideas and images and technical knowledge end up *diluting the quality* of the human intellectual and artistic product? In 2996, will another series on the minds of that millennium have as rich a treasure to distil?

The Informatics Age is very seductive, but aspects of it may also be very destructive of the long and arduous intellectual and social advancement in which the great minds this series will recall were so involved. When this Age burst upon us thirty odd years ago, we were told that a 'global village' was being rapidly created; that when all of us had instant real-time access to events anywhere in the world on one hand, and to the great libraries of the world on the other, the level of public discourse would be significantly raised and the substance of politics vastly improved; and world peace would be within our grasp. Well ... perhaps it has only been a few hiccups on this road to paradise, but I doubt it.

I think we do have to 'mind our minds'. Technology can indeed now compress onto a single silicon chip information that only thirty-five years ago needed a medium-sized roomful of computers. But technology *has not* found a way to mutate our cortices in thirty-five years to speed up our thought processes to keep pace with the silicon chip. It takes thousands of years of genetic evolution to do that to us.

So we are confronted with a problem. A recorded Yeats poem simply does not sound like a Yeats poem if the sound-track is accelerated; it sounds like gabble. A child can certainly absorb something from a Vermeer painting flashed for a second on a television screen, but not what that painting really is, and why it is beautiful. And no politician alive can convey to us in a fifteen-second 'sound-bite' policy proposals that he himself cannot understand in less than fifteen minutes of careful consideration. But they're trying to. In America it's down to eight seconds.

Shall our children and their children find ways to overcome these dangers? Not only of public discourse reduced to shallow catchphrases, but of education itself, and intellectual enquiry, deteriorating into a blur of shallow 'mind-bites'? These are already well worthwhile questions for the future. Certain it is that we must take care to carry into the next millennium all the riches of all humankind's experience in this closing one – the unalloyed triumphs and marvels of the human genius everywhere in all cultures ... and the lessons of what happens when it goes astray.

In the year 1633 Fulke Greville, a little-known English poet and politician, penned a verse that tells us minds were even then opening to the world:

> The mind of man is this world's true dimension
> And knowledge is the measure of the mind;
> And as the mind in her vast comprehension
> Contains more worlds than all the world can find,
> So knowledge doth itself far more extend
> Than all the minds of men can comprehend.

JUDGING JOYCE

DENIS DONOGHUE *offers an assessment of James Joyce.*

THE GREAT AMERICAN critic, Kenneth Burke, had a little theory. He said that a major writer's career tends to go in three phases. The first phase is always confessional or autobiographical – however disguised it may be. The young writer can only write out of his or her own experience, however limited that is. The crucial moment in a major writer's career is at the beginning of the second phase, where he imagines people other than himself and experiences other than his own. The really major writers can go through that second phase – which we might call simply communication – and discover further possibilities and they develop them to the end of the line.

If we think of Joyce in this regard, of course his early rather fragile and not terribly good poems obviously issue from his own experiences, limited and lyrical as they are. You could argue that the stories in *Dubliners* do show his power to imagine beings other than himself, but there is a kind of equivocation between *Dubliners* and the first version of *A Portrait of the Artist* – which was published as *Stephen Hero* – because most of the *Portrait of the Artist* is still lyrical and autobiographical. However, there is then the marvellous leap by which he imagines Leopold Bloom in *Ulysses*.

The comprehensiveness of this imagining does represent a new possibility – that of transcending Stephen's own narrow lyrical experience. That is clarified by the fact that Stephen is only a relatively minor character in *Ulysses*, in comparison with Leopold Bloom. What you get throughout *Ulysses* is the imagining of other beings, major and minor. What is then strange and difficult to cope with is that it is quite clear that in the later chapters of *Ulysses* – especially in the Nighttown chapter – Joyce is coming upon possibilities which he discovers not in life but in literature, not in Dublin but in language. These are internal possibilities which he subsequently carries to the end of the line in *Finnegans Wake*. He is developing a kind of language that brings with it – word by word – all its historical and etymological associations.

Of course it is still English, but it is an English in which no word has forgotten its ancestors. Every word carries with it the whole freight of its etymology, sometimes activated in the form of puns and other equivocations. Joyce is gathering up – through the etymology and the syllabic value of individual words and through the encrustations of the barnacles of other languages – these extraordinary compacted possibilities – often at considerable cost to the story, it has to be said.

What is really extraordinary about Joyce is his sense of the ordinary. Many of the things we remember and enjoy so much in Joyce's writings are little everyday events or local conversations. Sometimes he will weave them elaborately into linguistic extravagance – for example, the long disquisition on Shakespeare and paternity in the National Library scene in *Ulysses* – but many of the things that we love and cherish in Joyce are the tiny details that obviously started out as little more than anecdotes. He never lost his sense of ordinary personal social life.

T.S. Eliot had a theory that Milton and Joyce were alike in one respect. Due to failing eyesight, they both developed what Eliot called 'the auditory imagination'. I think the theory could be shown to be true. According as Joyce's eyesight failed, he depended more on memory, particularly on acoustic memory. That is why we meet so many old songs and phrases and bits of Victorian ballads and opera. The auditory imagination thus predominates over the visual imagination in Joyce's later writings. It is as if his sense of hearing developed not just in intensity but to the point where it became indistinguishable from his memory.

THE YOUNG ENTREPRENEUR

ALICE LEAHY is a tireless worker for the homeless. She is a co-founder of TRUST, an organisation which offers practical care and rehabilitation to homeless people. She traces her commitment to the homeless to her upbringing in Co. Tipperary, where she was always made to feel confident in her world.

SECONDARY SCHOOL WAS something I just passed through. It was the first time I noticed any kind of class distinction in our society. We didn't play tennis and we didn't play music. Some of that could have been due to the fact that – geographically – we were so far out from the town, but money was also a factor. I didn't find any great challenge at secondary school, although credit is due to my teachers for helping me to get through my exams.

A lot of my real education was taking place outside the school anyway. Olivia Hughes played the cello with the opera society in Clonmel and she always took us to the opera – something a lot of people would have been excluded from, even in those times. There was also an amateur dramatic group in Fethard and my parents would take us to that. We were also involved in *Macra na Tuaithe*, and the Hughes family gave us part of their house to do up as a youth club. It was a very active youth club, where we had debates, question times and visiting speakers. We did weaving, collected sheep's wool from the ditches and carded it and made long ropes. We knitted squares for the refugees. We also ran the youth club ourselves, with Olivia's help and encouragement, with a chairman, a secretary and a treasurer, and I learned about taking minutes at a very young age.

At one time, we had to think of a project for the Young Farmer of the Year contest. My project was rearing guinea pigs and I was allowed to keep the hutches under the Hughes' apple trees and rear them there. It was a very interesting experience, because I had to document every penny I spent and every penny I made. My father and mother were great believers in keeping diaries and accounts, so I had learned all of that at a very young age. I had a contract with Professor Stewart of Trinity College and he bought the guinea pigs from me for research. When they were ready for sale I had to pack them in a special box and take them on the back of a bicycle to the railway station. Then I would go into the local post office and get the postmistress to send off a telegram to Professor Stewart in Trinity. He would send someone to pick up the guinea pigs at Kingsbridge – as it was then – and that went on for years. In fact, I was awarded the runner-up in the Young Farmer of the Year contest. I couldn't become the Young Farmer of the Year because we didn't own land.

THE ART OF POSSIBILITY

'You should interview BEN ZANDER,*' a friend advised. 'He's in town to conduct the National Symphony Orchestra.' 'Why? I'm no music expert,' I countered. 'No,' she persisted. 'There's a whole other side to him. Talk to him about Possibility.' I did, for ninety riveting minutes.*

BEN ZANDER IS English-born but lives in the USA where he is conductor of the Boston Philharmonic Orchestra and a professor of the New England Conservatory of Music. With his wife, Rosamund, he has written a book entitled *The Art of Possibility*, based on their teaching experience. One unusual practice they have developed is that of 'giving an A'. At the beginning of the academic year, Zander informs his students that each of them will get an A for their course of studies. There is of course one major requirement that the student must fulfil to earn that grade.

'Sometime during the next two weeks you must write me a letter dated next May, which begins with the words *Dear Mr Zander, I got my A because ...* '

The students must place themselves in the future, looking back on all the insights and milestones they have attained during the year. Everything must be written in the past tense. Ben Zander is interested in the person that each student will have become – in their attitudes, feelings and worldview. Each student must 'fall passionately in love' with the person described in that letter. It is all a matter of possibility.

Giving the A is a very subtle and a very liberating approach. It is *not* – Zander claims – falsely building up students, but speaking to them in a way that enables them to be the best they can be. It is not about boasting of your achievements but about raising your self-esteem. It enables you to see all of who you are and be all of who you are without having to resist or deny any part of yourself. It avoids what Zander calls the 'downward spiral' – the negative thinking that says things are not possible, thus breeding cynicism and extinguishing passion.

Ben Zander draws inspiration from Michelangelo's concept that inside each block of stone or marble there dwells a beautiful statue. 'If we were to apply this visionary concept to education,' he says, 'it would be pointless to compare one child to another. Instead, all the energy would be focused on chipping away at the stone, getting rid of whatever is in the way of each child's developing skills, mastery and self-expression.' For the teacher, this innovative approach 'transports your relationship from the world of measurement into the universe of possibility'.

Giving an A can be applied in any relationship or any walk of life. It is *not* restricted to an elite of gifted students of music. 'The A is *not* an expectation to live up to but a possibility to live into ...' It is about keeping that door of enthusiasm open (remembering that enthusiasm means 'full of God') – enthusiasm that each of us had as children. We need to come from the power of children, Zander argues. He illustrates his point with an anecdote about the great cellist Jacqueline Dupré. As a five-year-old, she entered her first cello competition. When the doorman saw her come skipping down the hallway, he said to her, 'Well, it's obvious you did very well in your competition!' 'No! No!' the five-year-old replied. 'I'm just going in to play now ...'

THE CURIOUS MIND

A POLITICAL HERO

TONY O'REILLY *nominates* Winston Churchill *as one of his great heroes.*

I CHOSE WINSTON Churchill because he has had such an epic effect on the world in which we live. I think he mirrors Kipling's notion of meeting with triumph and disaster and coming through. His life was a series of ups and downs. He was cast into exterior darkness on at least two occasions and he had the intestinal fortitude to come back. There were many qualities about him which I think were peculiarly Irish – a certain gallantry, a love of words, a man of action. The central *rationale* for his whole life was the way in which he rallied the forces of world democracy in 1939 against totalitarianism – which essentially led to the great post-war world which we have enjoyed for fifty years plus now.

I became interested in him at college. It intrigued me that he could be perceived as both ogre and hero. He actually lived in Ireland for four years as a child – in the Vice-Regal Lodge, now Áras an Uachtaráin (his father had essentially been sent into exile by Queen Victoria). In later years he had great rapport with Michael Collins. They were very similar – men of action who believed in valour and a certain code of conduct. Although Stanley Baldwin once described him as having a 'one hundred and fifty horse-power mind', Churchill's teachers would not have agreed. He was a dunce at Harrow – never passed a single examination. He got into Sandhurst largely on the relationship which his mother had with the Secretary for War. He then became an instant folk hero – fighting in the Afghan wars, visiting Cuba for the *Daily Telegraph* and being twice recommended for the Victoria Cross as a journalist – heady stuff for a twenty-one-year-old! He had the great fortune to be captured in the Boer War and became a national hero when he escaped. By 1906 he had switched from the Conservatives to the Liberal Party and was a minister in the Liberal government. Of course he later went back to the Conservatives and became their leader. As he said himself, 'Anyone can rat, but it takes a real man to re-rat!'

He was a prolific writer. A lot of his writing is a form of justification of his father, whom he adored and who died at the age of forty-seven (unlamented by his wife I might add ...). Winston felt that his father had been hard done by and wrote largely to justify his achievements. His *History of the English-Speaking Peoples* is a classic piece of work. It must be remembered that he won the Nobel Prize for Literature in 1953. His book *The Gathering Storm* shows he was almost alone in Europe in perceiving the real threat of Hitler in the 1930s. That was the extraordinary thing about Churchill – when his perceptions were right, they were magnificently right and when they were wrong, they were almost criminally wrong. In sending troops into the Dardanelles, he participated in one of Britain's greatest military disasters, for example. Likewise his words and actions during the Great Strike of 1926 were wholly insensitive. In the 1930s he was very much out of favour – a derided figure – but his analysis of events in Germany and his prophecies of what would happen were chillingly accurate and led to his ultimate elevation to Prime Minister when Chamberlain failed.

He was a very self-absorbed man, given to quick decisions, relying as much on instinct as on a measured intellectual process, which of course often made him glaringly wrong. His greatest hour was the War Period. That pulled together the dissonant strands in his personality and showed him at his best. The lion-like courage, the capacity to stand in isolation, the capacity not to yield an inch and to rally his people both with his rhetoric and his bulldog determination to stand against the total enemy of totalitarianism – these were the things that made Winston Churchill great and make him one of my heroes.

BLUE REMEMBERED HILLS

ROSEMARY SUTCLIFF – *prolific and award-winning author of historical novels for children – recalls the early life that shaped her as a writer.*

I WAS AN only child. There had been a sister before me but she died aged a few months in the great influenza outbreak of 1918. My father was in the British navy, so he was away a lot. That meant a great burden for my mother who was quite wonderful to me when I got ill. She would stay up all night with me. As a result she had no social life and therefore she decided that I should be forever grateful to her and not really have an opinion of my own. She was capable of great love, but at a price.

When I was three, I contracted Still's Disease – a form of juvenile arthritis. It hits you with a wham and burns out after a few years, leaving all the disability behind – in my case joints that don't work as they should do. Luckily, I find the physical act of writing very easy and quite enjoy the feeling of a fountain pen gliding over a smooth page. Still's Disease for me meant a childhood of fever, pain and many operations. My mother and I were very close, but there was a constant battle of wills between us. I had a very spartan 'little boy' upbringing – I think she had always wanted a boy.

When I was about three we moved to Malta where my father was stationed. It was felt that the sun would help me. I couldn't walk very well and spent most of the time in a pushchair. I remember lots of goats and lots of bells in Malta. Back home again, we moved around a lot, depending on where Father was stationed. We lived near Margate in Kent when I was seven.

By this time I was in a spinal carriage. I made friends with a boy called Giles who was also in a spinal carriage due to TB glands. The carriage was horrific – like a wicker coffin. It was very boring as you lay flat on your back and saw nothing but the trees overhead when you were taken for a walk. You were also frozen, as the wind whipped through the wicker-work. On top of that we had a very cruel Swedish *masseuse* – Miss Axelin – to whom I went twice a week. She was a religious maniac, telling us we were wicked children and that God would punish us for our wickedness. I was terrified of her. To my mother's credit she took me away from Miss Axelin when she realised how cruel that woman was.

My mother read a lot to me – and she read beautifully. She read Dickens, Hans Andersen, A.A. Milne and especially Kipling, whose wonderful stories of Roman Britain aroused my own interest in that subject and subsequently influenced my writing. She also read the Celtic myths and legends and later I would write about heroes like Fionn MacCumhaill. Because my mother read to me so much and so well, I never learned to read until I was nine. Why should I bother? My hero Kipling never learned to read until he was nine also. I went to school eventually in Chatham – to Miss Amelia Beck's Academy. It was a tiny school and Miss Amelia was – believe it or not – eighty-six years old! She had no qualifications but was an excellent natural teacher. We learned poems, heard stories, did our sums on squeaky slates, learned to read (at last!) and were taught deportment.

My father retired from the navy and we moved to North Devon, where he had come from. He was a gentle man, but stern and rigid and absolutely devoid of imagination. In Devon I was the only disabled child at the school – I usually had a leg in plaster. I am glad it wasn't a special school. I prefer the integrated approach – the disabled are going to have to live in the normal world so why should they be segregated at school? I was into painting at that time and when I left school at fourteen I went to art school for three years and became a professional miniature painter.

I started to write in my mid-teens just for my own pleasure. My first efforts were dreadful – pastiches of books I had been reading. I eventually just fell into writing for children. It may be a way of living an unlived childhood. In my late teens I became very, very lonely. We lived three miles from the nearest village and I was never allowed have friends come home. I wrote therefore as a form of escape.

I had a happy childhood but it wasn't a normal childhood, by any means. I eventually fell in love, just after the war, with Rupert who had been a bomber pilot and came to live in our village. He had this ramshackle ancient car and we drove all around the countryside at frightening speeds. We had a wonderful two years until it all came to an end. My family were dead set against our romance (Rupert was awaiting a divorce) and he went away and subsequently remarried.

But if I had to choose one memory from my life it would be of a lovely summer afternoon with Rupert. The cuckoo was calling, the heavily-scented elder trees in flower. We didn't do anything but sit on the river-bank, hold hands and talk. Rupert caught a tiny frog and released it again. There was something about that afternoon that was absolutely magic and I never experienced anything like it before or since.

THE HEDGE SCHOOL

In a documentary commemorating the setting up of the National School system in 1831, tribute was paid to the irregular system which preceded it – the hedge schools.

BRIAN FRIEL'S PLAY *Translations* – set in Co. Donegal in 1833 – opens in a hedge school. This particular school is located in a disused barn but hedge schools could be found in even more primitive locations in nineteenth-century Ireland, often – as the name implied – in the shelter of the hedge. They were irregular centres of learning where students of all ages came of an evening to sit at the feet of a local man of learning – to acquire rudiments of literacy and numeracy, yes, but in many cases they acquired a classical education too.

Hedge schoolmasters carried with them a tradition and a reverence for Greek and Latin and liked to share it with their students. When one student, Máire, arrives (with her can of milk as payment) tired from a day's harvesting, she is greeted by Jimmy:

> JIMMY: *Esne fatigata? (Are you tired?)*
> MÁIRE: *Sum fatigatissima (I am exhausted)*
> JIMMY: *Bene! Optime! (Good! Excellent!)*

Jimmy is known to the locals as the Infant Prodigy (even though he is in his sixties!) and is 'fluent in Latin and Greek, but in no way pedantic – to him it is perfectly normal to speak these tongues'. Another student, Bridget, is attempting to write on a crude slate the headline set by the master, Hugh – 'It is easier to stamp out learning than to recall it' – which Jimmy readily identifies as coming from 'Book Three, the Agricola of Tacitus'.

The hedge schools were a testament to a people's craving for learning in penal times when those in authority bore witness to Tacitus's words. Learning was prized and a basic schooling would give many future emigrants a head start in the new world. Manus, the son of Hugh – and his assistant – is invited to start a hedge school on an island to the south. He is offered 'A free house, free turf and free milk, a rood of standing corn, twelve drills of potatoes and forty-two pounds a year'.

By 1833, however, the hedge school's days were numbered. A new system of national education had been introduced in 1831. As Bridget informs her fellow students:

> In the new national school, you have to stick at it until you're twelve at least – no matter how smart you are or how much you know – and every child from every house has to go all day, every day, summer or winter. That's the law ... and every subject will be taught through English and everyone will end up as cute as the Buncrana people.

THE TWENTIETH-CENTURY HEDGE SCHOOL

I look on us as a hedge school, a twentieth-century hedge school. I'm proud of that. We're not big but we're here – and if we weren't here there would be no school here. We did something for this area that no-one else did ...
(AIDAN MULCAHY, 1984)

IN 1961 AIDAN Mulcahy and his wife Síle returned to Co. Kerry from Nigeria where they had managed and taught in a school in an isolated area. Aidan initially found employment in Tralee CBS but the enthusiastic young couple had a dream. They saw parallels between their home parish of Cloghane and Badagry in Nigeria – isolated rural areas, poorly served by second-level education. Cloghane is twenty-four miles from Tralee and Dingle is 'the other side of the mountains'. This was pre-Donogh O'Malley and 'Free Education'. Why not set up their own secondary school to meet the local need? Between them, Aidan and Síle had enough subjects to make a start. So they made a start with the unusually titled Meánscoil an Leith-Triúigh i.e. the northern half of the Dingle Peninsula. 'That was the name of our locality, so no one else could have that name.'

The Mulcahys made a start in Castlegregory, eight miles from their home, hiring a draughty dance hall for £16 per annum. 'We kept the wind out by filling ladies' stockings with sand and putting them around the doors.' Aidan and Síle were the entire staff. They canvassed local parents for support and started with two classes, comprising thirty-eight students. The Department of Education gave them two years to find permanent premises. The Mulcahys had very low salaries (their service in Nigeria was not recognised for salary purposes). They could not afford to buy a site, but they had a big house in Cappagh in the shadow of Mount Brandon. Why not move the school back there?

This was done and they started with a first year class and grew by a class each year. Aidan bought a minibus and set off at seven o'clock every morning to collect his dispersed pupils, returning them on the same circuit every evening. As the school grew, the Mulcahys erected pre-fabricated classrooms at their own expense. They sought a permanent building but were turned down because the school was too small and 'not viable'. In 1966 they were threatened with closure, but with the support of Bishop Casey and a dynamic young priest – An tAthair O Laochdha (who revitalised Irish language and culture in the area) – they survived. Sheer grit and perseverance pulled them through. 'This was not a prosperous area in those days. It was disadvantaged and it was a challenge to us, but we rose to it because it was our area.' By 1984 the school had six full-time and a number of part-time teachers, offering a good range of subjects including Accounting, Art, Physics, Chemistry, French and Applied Maths.

'We did things on a modest scale. The students play football and camogie on the strand when the tide is out. On the other strand they study the seashore. The students are like our extended family. The second generation of students are coming now. We deliver the school reports personally. We have a cup of tea, a slice of apple pie and a chat ...'

Though the setting for the Meánscoil (perched on a slope overlooking Brandon Bay) was idyllic, keeping it going was far from an idyll. It was unrelenting struggle and sacrifice for the Mulcahys. They never sought contributions from the parents and the attitude of the Department of Education shocked them. They were true pioneers and patriots who left a huge legacy to generations of An Leith-Triúigh. One of their past pupils, poet Mícheál Ó Ruairc, pays tribute:

> Do thógadar scoil ar charraig
> Agus bhronnadar orainn eochair an eolais.
> Ar bharr na haille móire
> Atá Meán-Scoil an Leith-Triúigh
> Ansiúd os cionn na farraige
> Mar theach solais don dúthaigh ...

In an extraordinary irony, Aidan Mulcahy died suddenly on 6 October 2006, only hours after the new school – Meánscoil Nua An Leith-Triúigh – was officially opened in Castlegregory.

THE GREAT DANE

The distinguished scholar and scientist FRANK MITCHELL *recalls a number of mentors in his life, especially the 'great Dane' – the archaeologist Jessen.*

THROUGHOUT MY LONG career, there were a number of mentors who came into my life and influenced me greatly. One was Arthur Stelfox. He was a very curious man, who had come from Cheshire to Belfast. He trained as an architect, but was always deeply interested in natural history, and his wife too was a botanist of distinction. After various wanderings, he ended up as an assistant in the natural history department of the National Museum in Dublin. I used to go in to look at mounted groups of birds and that sort of thing and he used to wander through the museum and chat with any interested youngsters. It was in this way that he got to chatting with me and arranged for me to go out on excursions with friends of his and it was really through him that my interest in natural history was greatly fostered.

An important member of the Dublin Naturalist Field Club was Mr Brunker, who worked for Guinness. He had a passion for the flora of Co. Wicklow and indeed, before his death, succeeded in publishing a very valuable *Flora of County Wicklow*. He took to taking me out with him on Saturday afternoons. He had an old bull-nosed Morris car in which we would go down to Kilcoole and he would look out for rare clovers and identify the various birds that we saw. Brunker was unmarried and lived with several of his sisters. He was meticulous in his time-keeping at the brewery, but he looked forward to his Saturday afternoons and Sundays. He would be out in some part of his beloved Wicklow every weekend.

Both Stelfox and Brunker were very formative influences for me, but they paled into insignificance compared with the Danish man, Jessen. That was another of those chance occurrences. It was a time coming up to the war when peat-cutting was greatly emphasised and enormous quantities of peat were cut by hand. Marr, who had recently arrived as director of the National Museum, was faced with a flood of bronze implements and other things being brought in from the bogs. Tony Farrington of the Royal Irish Academy was interested in how Ireland's climate had developed after the Ice Age and Praeger was interested in anything that would throw light on the history of Irish flora, so they combined and got generous government support, largely due to Mr de Valera's personal interest in the matter. Jessen was brought with his assistant to Ireland for two seasons, to visit bogs from which archaeological objects had recently come to the museum and take a series of samples through the top to the bottom of the bog. Then, by studying the succession of pollen grains trapped in these samples, he worked out the history of forest development in Ireland and so placed the discovered object at an appropriate point in history.

Louis Bouvier Smith had succeeded Professor Joly as Professor of Geology and he encouraged me to give up zoology – in which I was specialising for my degree – and turn to geology. I did that and – in due course – became the assistant in the department of geology. He heard about the proposed visit from Jessen and how guides were needed to accompany Jessen – both to show him around the country and to pick his brains. He suggested that I should apply for one of these posts as a guide, which I did and was fortunate enough to be appointed.

Jessen was a most attractive personality – one of the most engaging people I have ever met. I rapidly realised what a privilege it was to be working with him. His assistant was also an interesting man, so we had a tremendous time touring the country. The tour, which would last perhaps two months, would result in enough specimens being taken for more than two years' subsequent study in the laboratory. The counting of pollen grains embedded in the deposits was a laborious and time-consuming process, but it gradually revealed how the proportions of the trees had changed with time – how some had expanded and others had contracted. In those happy days we were not aware of the profound effect that prehistoric farming had had on the woodlands so – to a certain extent – our early work was superseded very rapidly when it was realised that we were not just dealing with nature's effect on the woodlands but also with man's effect. This in turn made it possible to make more precise archaeological correlations, because we were now matching forest change with agricultural activity rather than just seeing a general drift of forest change over time.

Our studies were of the crudest nature compared with what would be done now. We started off by just counting the tree pollen only. Then it was realised that the pollens of a great many herbs and grasses could also be identified, so that was another whole range of material that had to be studied with the new techniques. Pollen grains themselves are composed of a most remarkable substance which practically defies chemical attack, so that if you have a bog composed partly of pollen grains and partly of decayed plant material, you can oxidise and acidify it and do all sorts of things to it to get rid of all the other debris and leave only the pollen grains. We just looked at the crude surface of the pollen grains, but nowadays with the electron microscope you can make identifications with infinitely more precision.

THE MAKING OF A FEMINIST

Writer MARILYN FRENCH *tells how she gradually grew into feminism.*

I CERTAINLY HAD feminist notions when I wrote my first book – the book on Joyce – although it is not considered a feminist book. My feminism has just grown over the years. The novels came out of life, out of direct experience. After the first two, I was doing a lot of thinking and I was giving a lot of talks. Everywhere I went, women would ask me, 'How did the world get this way?' I felt that I knew and I thought I could write.

At that time I had planned to write a thirty-five page essay on how the world had gotten this way, and I would include a number of my speeches and have it all published. My publisher was very happy with this idea and so I sat down to write the essay and it ended up being eighty-five pages long. He handed it back to me and said, 'I don't understand what you're talking about', so I had to do it the hard way. I wrote *Beyond Power*, which took five years of my life, during which I did almost nothing else. It was just constant research and constant thought.

The whole notion of patriarchy became more palpable to me, and what it does to all of us – not just to women but to men. The Book of John says – 'In the beginning was the Word'. In the beginning was *not* the word; in the beginning was the mother. The word began patriarchy, where the word becomes the truth. You say the father is the main parent and you say we will name the children after their father. But the mother is the main parent, the mother is the only parent you are sure of, and children should be named for their mothers. The most basic, vital, essential task we perform on this earth is giving birth. The whole world should be arranged so that having, raising and educating children should be safe, felicitous – a joyful experience. It is the least valued thing that you can do on this earth. It is unpaid, it has no status. This is a perverse world.

Look at what's going on across the world. Greater and greater areas are being brought under the hegemony of one power. They are going to be controlled by global economy, the international monetary fund and television, most of which are emanating out of my country. The rich are getting richer and smaller in number and the poor are getting poorer and larger in number and I see us headed for a really awful stratified world.

The thing about feminism that is so wonderful is that it frees your mind. When I wrote *The Women's Room* I was really setting out to describe the process of liberating the mind from a whole lot of superstitions and fake images. Feminism frees the mind beautifully and it empowers you as a result, so that it's more pleasant to be alive. I always say that it is the first revolution that asks people not to die for it but to live for it. You don't have to win. You don't have to reach the end, the feminine utopia, the egalitarian world, to be enriched and empowered by it.

This is lucky, because we can't figure out how to accomplish the egalitarian world. If you have a lot of feminists in your world, that world is quite a nice place to be. What I am really concerned about – and wish someone else would do – is to come up with a design, a blueprint, for a different way of organising the world, so that it is not arranged into hierarchies as a means of domination; a different kind of political and economic structure that would be more egalitarian, more mutual, that would permit true participatory democracy, which we don't have.

I am so grateful to feminism, feminist thinkers and other thinkers, for allowing me to feel this tremendous joy of thinking, of being. The intellectual ferment and what I feel to be the fertility of the last ten or fifteen years of my life has been tremendous. It's just wonderful.

EDUCATING THE OPPRESSED

MARCOS ARRUDA *tells how he has implemented the ideas of Paulo Freire in Nicaragua and in his native Brazil.*

I ALWAYS FELT that Freire put into words much of what I had envisioned – a process of liberation in which not only the masses are important, but also each individual human being. His thought helped me make the connection between the individual and the collective, between the daily life dimension of our existence and the historic dimension. Every social reformer that came before him was thinking of empowerment on the political level and the economic level. He brought this challenge to the personal level and to the knowledge level – saying that each person has to become a conscious agent of his own education and development. Only when this happens can a collective make sense. Freire gave an answer to a yearning that was already pulsating among human beings.

There are two major difficulties in implementing a Freire-type education. The first is an external obstacle. The powers-that-be resent this kind of approach because it threatens them with democratisation, with decentralisation of power, wealth and knowledge. The second is an internal obstacle. Inside all who are oppressed there is an inertia towards transformation – a weight that pulls people down. For example, in southern Brazil in 1988 the Workers' Party won important elections in a major city. There were three days of celebrations and then the people summoned the elected ones and said, 'Now you go to the palace to govern and we go home'. The elected ones explained that this was a different type of government. It was about participation and they needed the interaction of the people. But they refused and told the elected ones to go and govern while they got on with their lives. Until people are transformed and educated towards taking responsibility for decisions, there will always be that internal obstacle. The attitudes and mindset have to change.

In my work with youth and adult education, we try to see literacy not only as a problem of reading and writing but also a problem of becoming conscious of every aspect of one's individual and collective life. We talk about economic literacy, agricultural literacy, political literacy. Education does not have an end in itself. It exists to serve a development project. So we design curricula and programmes in response to the actual needs of that project.

In Nicaragua I developed a programme for rural workers. They were primarily workers and secondarily students. We started with what they worked on and built the disciplines from what they do, so that everything they learned made them feel better workers and more capable of improving their lives. We began with images and social drama in different areas of agriculture and gradually moved to manuals and books. They learned to read and write by needing to express things related to their work. Then they had sessions in the classroom where they discussed theory and reflected on what they were doing in the field. They had both spaces – the world of their work, social life and family life – and the world of the classroom where they acquired new elements to live beyond what they had already experienced. It is a very localised type of work, but where there is political will this can become a national process – as happened in Nicaragua under the minister Fernando Cardenal.

It is so rewarding to see people transform themselves to become responsible subjects of what they are doing, taking me less and less as an authority superior to them, and more and more as a partner in a common search for knowledge and improvement of their lives. We are seeking ways of rehumanising the world beyond simply directing our lives and energies to always producing more material goods. Paulo Friere died last year but he lives in all of us still. It was only his cocoon that died – the butterfly is still flying around.

FUN WITH PUNS

ROGER McGOUGH *talks about his emergence as a poet during his youth in Liverpool.*

I'M A CHRISTIAN Brothers boy – Star of the Sea primary school and St Mary's secondary school in Liverpool. I enjoyed school. Never enjoyed poetry much at school. I used to mumble a lot – still do! – and went to elocution lessons, where I learned to mumble louder! In doing so, I recited a lot of poetry aloud and did choral verse, which probably gave me my first interest in poetry. I failed English Literature at O level and dropped it from there on. One of the reasons I failed was that for a whole year the Brother did Irish with us instead of English Lit.! The influences that came later did so through the *spoken* word – Dylan Thomas on radio, Robert Frost on television, hearing Christopher Logue and Adrian Mitchell reading at college. A lot of children only see poetry on the page and never hear it spoken – which is a very important process.

> To amuse emus
> On warm summer nights
> Kiwis do wee-wees
> From spectacular heights.

It was also a great shock to me to discover that you didn't have to be dead to be a poet. Philip Larkin was working in Hull University when I went there – what a thrill! I began writing when I was about eighteen. My first poems were published in the university newspaper – not the poetry magazine, which had poems written to please the English department, rather than speak to anybody. I liked Wilfred Owen and the war poets – they influenced me a lot.

> At the going down of the sun
> and in the morning
> i try to remember them
> but their names are ordinary names

and their causes are thighbones
tugged excitedly from the soil
by frenchchildren
on picnics.

Writing for children came later. There is a myth about writers making up stories for their children. It wasn't like that for me – more 'if you don't behave yourself, Dad will read you one of his stories ...' At the same time, a lot of my adult poetry appeals to children – teenagers I suppose – so maybe subconsciously I was always writing for children.

You couldn't smell a rat
If you didn't have a nose
You couldn't tell a duchess
From a herd of buffaloes
And oh! that gorgonzola
As it starts to decompose
Oh wouldn't it be funny
If you didn't have a nose!

A lot of the poems for children is about playing with words, as in 'Pillow Talk' ...

Last night I heard
My pillow talk

Teenage poems are about being angst-ridden and unsure of oneself – as we all are. I always admired my extrovert friends when I was young. They would do wild things like have a few drinks, strip naked and run into the sea. I was the one who stayed behind to mind the clothes ...

Here I am
forty-seven years of age
and never having gone to work in ladies' underwear

never run naked at night in the rain
made love to a girl I'd just met on a plane
at that awkward age now between birth and death ...

I love playing with words. I make notes of little things I see. Saw a sign
yesterday for Demolition Ireland Ltd. I think that's very funny. The other
day I passed a signboard outside a deli. It was headed 'Today's Special'.
I just wanted to write underneath – 'So is every day'.

Over the years my work has been labelled 'pop poetry' and it has been
described as trite. It annoys me at times but the best answer to critics is
to outlive them and keep on writing. The more serious poems come
from somewhere else – from relationships – like 'Aunty Marge' ...

Aunty Marge,
Spinster of the parish, never had a boyfriend,
Never courted, never kissed.
A jerrybuilt dentist and a smashed jaw
Saw to that.

She loved playing cards and she babysat us as children, keeping us up
for hours ...

Falling
Asleep over pontoon, my sister and I,
Red-eyed, would beg to be taken to bed.
'Just one more game of snap', she'd plead,
And magic two toffees from behind an ear.

We grew up and moved away. Aunty Marge lived alone in a council flat
with no phone.

Her death
Was quick as it was clumsy. Neighbours
Found the body, not us. Sitting there for days

Stiff in Sunday best. Coat half-buttoned, hat askew.
On her way to Mass. Late as usual.

Her rosary
Had snapped with the pain, the decades spilling,
Black beads trailing. The crucifix still
Clenched in her fist. Middle finger broken.
Branded into dead flesh, the sign of the cross.

From the missal
In her lap, holy pictures, like playing cards,
Lay scattered. Five were face-up:
A Full House of Sacred Hearts and Little Flowers.
Aunty Marge, lucky in cards.

WE'RE ALL IN THIS TOGETHER

Robert Putnam, *author of* Bowling Alone: The Collapse and Revival
of American Community, *discusses the notion of Social Capital and its
importance.*

Everyone knows what Physical Capital is – a tool, like the humble
screwdriver, that makes us more productive. A quarter of a century ago,
economists were talking of the importance of Human Capital – the
training and education that also makes us more productive. Today we
speak of Social Capital – social networks where people know and care
about each other and through which people are involved in community
life. Such connectedness has measurable benefits for us all – crime rates
are lower, schools work better, people live longer.

Both the USA and Ireland have had high levels of Social Capital in the
past but – certainly in the USA – research has shown that over the last
thirty years there has been considerable decline in the levels of Social
Capital. Membership of voluntary organisations – Boy Scouts, Rotary

Clubs, Parent-Teacher Associations – has declined severely. The same trend is evident in attendance at church and in political involvement and also in many informal ways – people spend less time on family outings, going to bars or dinner parties. We are 'bowling alone'. I was shocked to find in our research a decline of 40 per cent in the frequency of family dinners. Dining on a microwaved meal in front of the television is now so much the norm. I do it myself at times – life is busy – but such a lifestyle is bound to have a powerful negative effect on the family.

In the United States we were in this position before – over a century ago. Towards the end of the nineteenth century the great move towards urbanisation left Social Capital somewhat behind. People were wealthier but not as connected as heretofore. Then between 1890 and 1910 most of the social organisations we know today were founded as a way of creating new forms of connectedness. I understand similar things happened in Ireland with the founding of the Gaelic League, the GAA etc. Those organisations served us well for a century.

World War II created a generation which drew a lesson of obligation to one another and saw the need for community involvement. That generation remained more connected all through their lives, reaching a high noon of Social Capital in the early 1960s, but they did not pass those traits on to their children – the 'baby-boomers' – or their grandchildren – the 'X Generation'. The passing of that generation has coincided with the slump in Social Capital. Of course we don't need another world war but it is true that crisis has a value in reminding people of the importance of social connection. Nor do we need to revisit the 1950s in a fit of nostalgia. We need to reinvent sources of Social Capital in ways that fit the way we have come to live today.

Why have we become so disconnected today? I don't know the answer but it's somewhat like *Murder on the Orient Express* – there are multiple suspects! These are some of them:

URBAN SPRAWL AND COMMUTING TIME: In the USA every twenty minutes more commuting time cuts all forms of social connection by 20 per cent.

ENTERTAINMENT: Television is lethal for civic engagement. Americans tend to watch *Friends* rather than have friends.

GEOGRAPHICAL MOBILITY: Not good for social connection, but still not guilty, I would say.

DECLINE IN RESPECT FOR AUTHORITY: I am sceptical here because places that have most Social Capital are those that are most tolerant and egalitarian.

WOMEN MOVING INTO THE PAID LABOUR FORCE: This is part of the story but far less than most people think.

THE AFFLUENT SOCIETY: This would seem a natural suspect in Ireland but in the USA affluence per se was not a factor. From 1900 to 1960 we were becoming more affluent, but we were also becoming more connected.

GROWTH OF CONSUMERISM AND INDIVIDUALISM: A possible factor but hard to pin down. Having a second car does not lead to life satisfaction as much as good relations with family and neighbours.

Our task now is to find new ways of connecting that fit the way we live. Use our affluence not to buy that second car but to provide public and private institutions that will help us spend more time with each other. The most striking evidence in relation to Social Capital is in regard to health – we live longer, our health is better, we heal better if we are connected. Social isolation is probably as big a risk factor for death as smoking.

There are exciting opportunities out there. The arts can play a major role here. There are two kinds of Social Capital – connections with people who are *like* us (bonding) and connections with people who are *unlike* us (bridging). It is important to have a balance between both. A society that is without that balance is deeply at risk. The arts – choral work, dance etc. – are terrific for bridging. Technology can create new ties but it can also isolate. The trick is not to create fictitious cyber-connections but to use those as ties to real people. A lot of people have membership cards but rarely show up. Woody Allen had it right when he said, 'Showing up is 80 per cent of life'.

THE CURIOUS MIND

There is no contradiction between Social Capital and Social Justice. The former is a prerequisite for the latter. Helping the less well-off is not a matter of do-goodism – it is a matter of *us*. We have to create a more capacious sense of WE. I am optimistic about the future because in our bones we know we need to connect and because – in the past – periods of social fracture were followed by periods when people re-wove the fabric. This problem is not going to be solved by guys from Harvard like me but by ordinary people from Middle America and Middle Ireland.

We are all in this together. We can do this.

A TALE OF TWO CHRISTIES

PATRICIA SHEEHAN *was a doctor who specialised in communication and speech disorders in children. In that capacity she met some remarkable children. Here she remembers two of them.*

I COMPLETED MY internship, married in Southampton and came back and set up house in Clonskeagh. For the first month after I was married I would start getting dinner ready at half past three for Robbie coming home at seven! I soon realised I needed something to do. In Southampton, they had been setting up the speech department and I used to assess the children to make sure they didn't have a medical complaint as well as a stammer or whatever. I went to what was then the Dublin Health Authority and spent a day with Dr Brid Lyons-Thornton. We had a stimulating conversation, but then she told me that the corporation did not employ married women. She suggested that I go round to the spastic clinic that had just opened in Bull Alley street, and that is where I met Christy Brown. It was a pivotal day in my life because, when I found somebody so intelligent, so humorous, so witty and with such difficulty in expressing himself, I made it my *raison d'etre* to help those with cerebral palsy to talk. I stayed on working with them for over twelve years.

Children were brought in by voluntary drivers and St John ambulances to have physiotherapy. I started going in three mornings a week and taking the children for speech therapy. The only constant things I had to refer to were the children themselves, their anatomy, the clothes they were wearing and what was in my handbag. I became renowned for my 'bag of junk'. The children would name what I took out and they would categorise what things went together. We also did rhymes and blowing – trying to teach them to suck and blow was quite a problem. Once they had some breath control, they could start to control the sounds they were making.

When Christy Brown began to learn to write he would flick off his shoe, pick up a pencil and write with the pencil held between his toes. Then he would go home and dictate to his brothers and sisters and they would write down in copybooks what he had dictated. When you think of the battles he had to fight to get himself accepted, he really was a tremendous character.

I learned a lot from the kids I was teaching and what I learned from one I could apply to another. I had some wonderful characters there, some who just communicated with yes and no. I got quite good at asking 'twenty questions' until I hit the right question, when there would be joy and relief! Twenty-five years later, I came across another Christy who gained repute – Christy Nolan. I used to encourage his mum when they came up from Mullingar to the Central Remedial Clinic by regaling her with tales of Christy Brown and telling her that I knew her Christy was going to make it too. There was always something about the look in a child's eyes – you didn't have to do psychological tests to know they were sparking. I realised that somebody who has one channel blocked can be very much more alert in others. We don't always realise how important all the channels of learning are.

A NEW WORLDVIEW

Excerpts from James Robertson's *1990 'Open Mind' Guest Lecture.*

THE MODERN WORLDVIEW has remained hierarchical – it continues to see the world in terms of ladders. But it is mobile, not static. It sees human progress in terms of climbing a ladder of knowledge and power. It sees human life as a competition to climb higher than other people up ladders of career and status and wealth and power. And, when it can, it judges progress in terms of numerical measurements.

But most importantly, the modern worldview has excluded religion and morality. It has offered no meaning to human life, no goal at the top of the ladders, no purpose in climbing the ladders other than climbing for its own sake. 'Ladders to Nowhere' – that is the name of the game the modern worldview asks us to play.

Even the most advanced scientists still suspect the very idea of purpose, and assume that what they call 'objectivity' excludes it. In his recent book *The Ages of Gaia*, James Lovelock endorses the view that:

> The cornerstone of scientific method is the postulate that Nature is objective. True knowledge can never be gained by attributing 'purpose' to phenomena.

That's what Lovelock says, and many people have hailed his Gaia theory as a new milestone in science. But can you really understand people without attributing purposes to them? Or cats? Or earthworms? Or plants? Or the component parts of any organism? And who is to say – how could anyone know? – that true knowledge can be gained of the universe itself by assuming in advance that it has no purpose?

These are difficult questions. But one thing is absolutely clear. The theoretical notion that scientific knowledge and economic behaviour are value-free has left a vacuum. And in practice this vacuum has been filled by values of power and greed and competition.

In short, our European worldview has led us – and now the rest of the world – to err and stray from the ways of wisdom. There is now no health in us, in the old senses of wholeness and holiness. And the kind of wealth we strive for is often not wealth in the old sense of well-being – whether the well-being of other people, or of the earth, or even of ourselves. The world's crisis today is a crisis of values.

REVIVAL OF ETHICAL VALUES

We have seen that the breakdown of the medieval worldview meant the decline of an existing moral order and the rise of a new scientific order. By contrast, I see the breakdown of the modern worldview as the decline of the existing scientific order and the rise of a new moral order. This will be clearer to future historians than it is to us now, but the signs are already there.

Take economics. The existing science of economics has told us that the chief aim of economic life is to make money values grow. So a national economy's chief aim has been money-measured economic growth, a business chief's aim has been financial profit, and the main aim of consumers and investors has been to get best value for money from their purchases and the best financial return from their investments.

But in the 1980s these assumptions have begun to be questioned – even in the most respectable quarters.

For example, the World Bank and the International Monetary Fund are now beginning to recognise the devastating consequences of conventional economic orthodoxy for many Third World countries, and are beginning to face up to the need to resolve the long-running Third World debt crisis. Meanwhile, many people all round the world are not just feeling that the systematic transfer of wealth from poorer and less powerful peoples to richer and more powerful ones is wrong – which it clearly is. They are also recognising it as an inevitable outcome of a competitive, amoral economic system, driven by the aim of making money values grow, and regulated by the impersonal mechanics of supply and demand.

Another example is from the Brundtland Commission's report, 'Our Common Future'. Brundtland pointed out that environmental policy and economic policy must be integrated. It is no longer good enough for environmental policy just to clear up the messes left by economic development, and to deal with what Brundtland called:

> ... after-the-fact repair of damage, reforestation, reclaiming desert lands, rebuilding urban environments, restoring natural habitats, and rehabilitating wild lands.

And it is no longer good enough for economic policy just to 'create wealth' in the narrow and abstract conventional sense, regardless of the environment.

In almost exactly the same way, the World Health Organisation (WHO) – with its strategy on Health for All by the year 2000 – has begun to shift the emphasis away from remedial sickness services to the positive creation of healthier conditions of life. WHO's conclusion on health, like Brundtland's on the environment, is that health goals must be brought into economic policy. Again, 'creating wealth' in the conventional sense is seen as too abstract and too narrow. Economic policy must pursue real purposes, like maintaining a good environment and enabling people to be healthy, and not just money-measured growth.

It is not just the conventional goals of economic policy that are beginning to be rethought, but also the conventional ways of measuring economic progress. A lot of work is getting under way – in the United Nations and national governments, as well as in activist groups like the New Economics Foundation – to develop and introduce new economic indicators and targets. This involves trying to improve existing money-measured indicators like Gross National Product (GNP). But, more importantly, it also involves supplementing these money-measured abstractions – perhaps eventually replacing them – by bringing into economic decision-making indicators of the state of the real world – which will show, for example, whether people's health, the cleanliness of air and water, and so on, are getting better or worse.

There is a parallel at the personal level to this bringing of real goals and purposes, and not just conventional money-measured criteria, into economic policy-making. I am talking about the increasing numbers of consumers and investors who are trying to be 'green' or 'ethical' or 'socially responsible'. They are deciding to bring their values into their economic lives, and to use their purchasing power and their investing power to support the kinds of projects and causes which they themselves favour. They are rejecting the conventional idea that their only economic goal should be to get best money value for themselves.

Even in science itself the idea of value-free objectivity is increasingly under fire. It is becoming more widely understood that, in many fields, objective knowledge is not even a theoretical possibility because the observer cannot observe the subject matter without affecting its behaviour in one way or another. In that respect, the particle physicist is in the same boat as the anthropologist studying a tribal society.

There is also growing awareness that the idea of value-free objectivity in science, just as in economics, has been used as a smokescreen by powerful groups – governments, business, finance, the military and the professions, including the scientific establishment itself – to use science in their own interests. In recent years, more and more people have become concerned with the purposes for which science is used.

EVOLVING A NEW WORLDVIEW

Those few examples of ethical purposes and moral choices being brought back into areas of practice and thought which the modern worldview has seen as value-free are pointers to the new worldview of the future. But what are they pointing us to? I can only give you my own personal thoughts.

Not back to the Middle Ages. Even if we could go back, the medieval picture of a static world is at odds with our knowledge of evolution today. The medieval assumption that the Christian God is superior to the divinities of other faiths does not fit the emerging multicultural one-world community of today. The medieval beliefs that God is masculine, that men are superior to women, and that humans are superior to Nature – special creatures with special kinds of souls to whom God has given dominion over the rest of creation – clash with the feminist and ecological understandings of today.

Perhaps then, in this coming post-European era of world history, we should turn to non-European faiths like Buddhism or Hinduism, or to the cultures of peoples like the Northern American Indians? They all offer wisdom about human life, and the place of human beings in the world, that has been lost in modern European culture. But like Christianity, they have been quite unable to halt the worldwide juggernaut of conventional secular, consumerist development, although it runs contrary to their teachings. I am sure their insights will be reflected in the new worldview that eventually emerges. But – stemming as they did from small agricultural and pastoral and hunter-gatherer societies of long ago – we cannot realistically expect them to offer us a new post-modern worldview more or less ready-made, off the peg.

No. We should draw on the wisdom and insights of the past. But the peoples of the world today and tomorrow will have to create the new worldview afresh out of our own lives and predicaments, out of our own contemporary experience and understanding. I think the new worldview will be a developmental worldview, in which purpose is combined with evolution in a new vision of progress. I think it will comprehend person and society, planet and universe, as aspects of the evolutionary process – a process which includes the evolution of consciousness and purpose – and perhaps of divinity too.

I think that what gives value and meaning to our lives will be the part we play in this process – developing our own potential, enabling other people to do the same, contributing to the development of our society and the emerging one-world human community, maintaining and perhaps even enhancing the natural riches of our planet, and consciously participating in the evolution of the cosmos.

That is the wider context in which the idea of a new, enabling and conserving economics makes sense to me. It is in that context, I foresee, that people in the next century and the next millennium will seek health, wealth and wisdom. It is in that context that we should interpret current issues – such as closer cooperation in western Europe, or the collapse of Communism in eastern Europe, or the crisis in the Middle East. And it is in that context, I believe, that we should now be preparing to chart our common future in 1992, when the European Single Market will come into being.

LEARNING GOOD BEHAVIOUR

MOLLY KEANE *found little to enjoy in her early education.*

FROM THE AGE of about six I was in the care of a governess. We had a succession of these, some of whom I liked more than others. One or two naughty ones used to laugh at everything, including my mother, which was rather disloyal, but I suppose children like a rebellious person. I think that the governesses came through some agency in Dublin. Many of them would have been the daughters of badly-financed secondary Anglo-Irish families and one or two were English, but we weren't really in their 'care' at all. We saw them for lessons and at meal times but apart from that we were absolutely free. They were in charge of our education, in theory, but we learned nothing from them and as a result I'm probably the worst educated woman in the world! When I started lessons I spent about an hour a day trying to learn to read some positively awful 'cat on the mat' book. Later there were books like Mrs Martin's *History of England*, Gill's *Geography*, some terrible French grammar book whose title escapes me and books of little rhymes and poems – some French and some English – but I learned very little from any of them.

We rose each day at about 7.30 (this was at the age of about nine or ten). We had breakfast in the schoolroom with the governess – usually it was something awful like porridge or fried bread (which was particularly nasty) and milk (which was supposed to be good for you). Mother came in just before 'dining-room breakfast' and read family prayers to us. After that we fed the dogs and from ten o'clock 'til twelve we had 'lessons'. We were comparatively free for the rest of the day thereafter – except for something awful called 'Preparation' in the evening. Lunch was at about one o'clock. That was the only meal we had in the dining-room but the food wasn't very good and we were at the mercy of the cook. I imagine that the best food was kept for dinner at night, when the cook would also take more trouble with its preparation, but as children we never saw any of that.

The afternoons were long. Mostly you had your pony and you possibly fiddled around your garden, because above all else you were supposed to be out of doors a great deal (when I was much younger I was out of doors for awfully long periods of time). There were long hours of wandering about with nothing to do, particularly when my elder brother went to school and the others were much younger than me. I do remember spending hours by myself and being easily frightened by things. At the end of the kitchen garden there was a beautiful place called the Great Nut Walk – a long path among all sorts of nut trees. It was a great place for playing – building houses and things like that – but I remember being terrified there by 'Old Nettle'. He was a dotty old fellow who wandered the countryside and he would often walk up and down the field outside our house. I remember being in the Great Nut Walk and hearing Old Nettle 'booing' like a cow outside. I was terrified and dreaded going to the Nut Walk for a long time after that.

Tea was in the schoolroom – horrid bread, butter and jam – before a very small fire. I don't know why the governess couldn't build up a good fire because, God knows, there was enough wood around the place. But I remember a very large fender and a very small fire – and chilblains always, always awful chilblains right through my childhood. We would go down to the drawing-room after tea (though not as regularly as when we were little) but I don't think we were read aloud to or anything. We just talked. Sometimes we took lanterns and went out into the dark – we rather enjoyed doing that – and then we went to bed between seven and eight. I shared a bedroom with my sister and we hated each other. We also shared the room with cages full of budgies and other birds. We didn't have supper – just biscuits in bed. The place was absolutely running with mice – I suppose between the birdseed and the biscuits they had a royal time!

There was a weekly dancing class which I attended when I was about seven. Some might think that a privilege, but I thought it was absolute torture. It was held every Wednesday in a big house in Co. Kildare (Wexford was really much more savage – there was nothing like a dancing class there!). About twenty-five children arrived each week to take lessons from Mr Leggatt-Byrne (how appropriate the name was!) who came down from Dublin. I remember that he had kid gloves with which he would slap you – and if he wasn't slapping you he was slapping himself in time to the music. I never learned anything at dancing class. I had no ear for music, so it was no wonder! I must have had some sense of rhythm because I got on all right with the dancing later, but then it was all gothic to me. There was the barn dance and all sorts of awful exercises you had to do to music; there was the polka that was fairly easy – one could generally jump around to the polka – but the waltz, I could never master.

Overall, I suppose, education had no practical end in my case. It would never have been considered that I should get a job. Girls stayed at home. Many of them grew very sour over that; others adored their fathers and did everything for them.

I suppose that my childhood is pretty well mirrored in the childhood section of *Good Behaviour*. There was the alienation between the grown-ups and the children and the consequent loneliness for the children. There was a complete division within the house – the old upstairs-downstairs thing. There were stairs for children and servants to go up and down and separate stairs for grown-ups. I was more at ease and more friendly with the maids and the farmworkers than I was with my parents.

From an early age it was instilled into one that it was important to be of 'good behaviour' at all times. Modesty was the big thing. I imagine the grown-ups feared that we would grow up rather savage otherwise. I remember having the most appalling row with my mother over what seemed to me an innocuous incident. I was lying on the grass, kicking my legs in the air and exposing navy-blue knickers with elastic around the knees, when my mother saw me from a window and summoned me inside. We had a most awful row. I was very embarrassed by all this. Neither could I understand my mother's reaction to my childish abandon. I queried my sister on this much later in life and she simply said, 'Well you know, Mother's generation just felt that modesty could not be instilled at an early enough age'. It's hard to picture that happening today, but it was a true feeling on the part of my mother – not quite Puritanism, but something that had to be absorbed by a child.

There were other traits instilled also – politeness, good manners, eating properly, table etiquette and, of course, religion was instilled from an early age too. Yet for all the table etiquette we only dined with our parents at lunchtime. We also had two rather tricky aunts who lived with us and they were forever correcting us. One was always being corrected for being greedy. If you dared ask for a second helping you really were frowned on – being greedy was considered a major unattractive quality in a young lady.

A NEW ARK

I had always admired JEAN VANIER, *the founder of L'Arche, an organisation which enabled disabled people to live in a community. Jean had been in the navy and later became a teacher but his life changed completely when he met a Dominican priest, Père Thomas. Imagine my delight when I learned that Jean Vanier was visiting the Kilcornan community in Co. Galway – just three miles from my home! I was over there with my tape-recorder in a flash! Here is part of the story Jean Vanier told me.*

IN 1963, I went to visit Père Thomas, who had become chaplain of a small institute for thirty men with mental disabilities. He had suggested that I come and meet his 'new friends'. I went to visit them with much fear and some misgivings, because I didn't know how to communicate with people who had a mental handicap. How do you speak with people who can't speak? And even if they did speak, what would we talk about? I was very touched by these men with all that was broken in them, their handicaps, their incapacities. Each one was thirsting for a relationship.

Each was asking 'Do you love me? Will you be my friend?' My students in philosophy wanted my head but not my heart. They were interested in the courses I could give them so that they could pass their exams and move on. They were not saying 'Do you love me?', they were saying 'What can you give me to pass my exams?'

I loved teaching, but it was not really my purpose in life. I was seeking my life's work, not just a job. In the navy, and then in the world of studies, I had been in the world of the strong, the 'winners'. Here, I was opened up to the whole world of the poor, the broken, the 'losers' of humanity. I was touched by their cry and by their terrible situations. Many had been living for a long time in institutions or psychiatric hospitals, where you would find a hundred men roaming around in one room, with no work, nothing to do.

Père Thomas encouraged me to take two men from an asylum and live with them. Raphael had meningitis when he was young and would fall over easily. Philippe had encephalitis when he was young and had one paralysed leg and one paralysed arm. He also had a mental handicap, though he could speak well. We started living together – and so began the adventure of L'Arche.

I think L'Arche is a discovery that people with handicaps are beautiful people. They may be slow and more fragile but, if they are loved and appreciated, they are incredibly beautiful. They have great wisdom, but most of the time they are pushed aside. People don't listen to them, so they are unable to give out their beauty, their wisdom and their kindness.

L'Arche is the French word for 'the ark' of Noah in the Bible. It carries with it a beautiful image, because Noah's ark saved people from the deluge. Many people today, particularly those with mental disabilities, are caught up in the deluge of our civilisation of technology, efficiency, rapidity, faxes, unemployment and so on. L'Arche is a community where they can find refuge. Our communities welcome people from different Christian traditions. In India, we welcome Hindus and Muslims as well. The 'passport' to enter L'Arche is not baptism but pain, suffering, rejection. In L'Arche, we are discovering the blessing of eating at the same table as the poor, the lame, the disabled and the blind! To eat together in biblical language means to become friends. The ultimate meaning of *L'Arche* is to become friends, to belong to each other.

As I lived with Raphael and Philippe and others, I discovered that I had to change. I had to listen more to them. They were not calling me just to be generous – to *do* good things *for* people – but to enter into a vulnerable, permanent relationship with people who have disabilities. I discovered the communion of hearts, which is different to generosity. It was difficult, a total reversal for me, as I used to be quite serious and austere. Our meals together would take a long time. We would relax, play games, have times of quiet prayer and few words. Little by little, I was learning what it was to be human. I soon learned that Raphael and Philippe weren't terribly keen to live with an ex-naval officer who thought he could tell everybody what to do. So I have had to change and learn to work with other people.

TV OR NOT TV

LELIA DOOLAN's *experience of working with RTÉ in the early days of Irish television led her and others to question the programming model that the new station had adopted ...*

HAVING SPENT A year studying theatre in Berlin, I eventually found my way into the then bright new world of television. I just simply worked at whatever came along. I did bits of drama there in television plays that were directed by people like Shelah Richards, Chloe Gibson and Jim Fitzgerald. I did some interviewing on programmes like *Broadsheet* and little bits of scriptwriting, and then I trained as a producer-director in America of all places. I don't know if you could call it training, but I went there for three months and sat in on television studios – NBC and CBS, and CBC in Canada.

I came back and started directing the News, which was the most scary thing. In those days you had to actually remember what came in what sequence and call it up and make sure it actually happened at the right time, but people like vision-mixers and production assistants saved the bacon of many a producer-director many a time, and I'm sure they saved mine too. Later, I directed *The Riordans* and I produced *Seven Days* and did some drama as well. Then I became head of light entertainment, looking after programmes like the *Late Late Show*.

I got involved in debates about the meaning of television and the kinds of things we could be doing. The influences at this time, apart from Gunnar Rugheimer – who was a very feisty, very argumentative, lively and humorous controller of programmes – were people like Jack Dowling – who was a titanic figure in the intellectual sphere within the station – and two directors who were working with me, Dick Hill and Eoghan Harris. Together with quite a few others, we began to question and raise issues to do with what were perhaps not the safe things, not the expected things. We felt in some instances that it would be possible to push things to the limit and then found that it wasn't quite possible to push them right to the very edge.

Bob Quinn – who at that stage had been away for a year – came back and found that the station had turned into something of a factory for the production of Anglo-American programmes. He left and we began a debate – based upon his letter of farewell – which more or less escalated into a long series of talk-ins in the canteen. Jack Dowling and I resigned and subsequently wrote a book about what we thought our experiences had been, what we felt television could be in a small country like Ireland which had different cultural traditions, a language of its own, values of its own, and a way of life that in fact the television had been set up to protect and enrich and which we felt had been somewhat diluted and emaciated instead. We suggested that, if we looked at the model of television that we had and if we examined it more closely and interrogated more or less what we were doing, we could do it better. In any event, that didn't happen. The book was called *Sit Down and Be Counted*.

To be around the people who were in television at that time was to be around people who were your teachers. I was learning from everybody there. The unfortunate division of labour which dictated that the intellectual was a higher animal than the manual was something that I had never really been able to assent to. I felt television was a place where the intelligence of the engineer or of the camera-person was of equal value to the intelligence of the director, but in our hierarchical system the director inevitably managed to get the kudos. I think a large number of producer-directors would be on skid-row had it not been for a tremendous bunch of women production assistants and other technical grades who kept the boat afloat. Frankly, I would have perished many a time.

The quality of a man like Jack Dowling was endlessly stimulating, and indeed he wasn't the only one. Jim Plunkett Kelly, Muiris Mac Conghail, Donal Farmer, Michael Garvey, Deirdre Friel – all of these were people who were thinking on the job and presenting questions about politics: what was the government at, what were we supposed to be doing. What should be the stance of a semi-state organisation charged with the good of the commonalty but set up under legislation and also unfortunately set up in order to make a profit?

Nobody for a moment was saying that you could run programmes for nothing. Never. But the question was whether we should try and think of another means, another method, another model for television than the one we had. We felt that the local area was important as the focus and the locus from which the work should come, rather than that it should all come from one centre and then be diffused throughout the countryside. Why does television have to be show business? Could it not also be a two-way event in part?

SECOND CHANCE

Three older people recall their experience of learning in the later years.

EILEEN: I come from Co. Roscommon. I had a wonderful career in
           nursing. I always had the urge to express my creativity.
           Even in my patient reports as a nurse, I was not content

with the facts. I would weave stories around the patients' conditions, much to the annoyance of my colleagues. I always felt there were other areas I needed to explore – especially literature, which I felt remote from. So I recently did a Certificate Course in Literature in St Angela's College, Sligo. It was exhilarating – the discussions, the interaction with other students. The lecturer was enthralled with the creative approach we older people took with our essays. I'm hungry for more learning now. There's a longing deep in my heart that just will not go away ...

KATHLEEN: I live in Dublin city. Like most people of my generation I left school after my Primary Certificate and went to work. I always had a great love of reading, thanks to our local librarian. She engineered our reading, guiding and advising us what to read next. I retired from work in 1986. Suddenly there was a void in my life and I wondered what I could do. I tried the Access to Education course in the National College of Ireland and then went on to do a BA in St Patrick's College. I studied Human Development, English and History. I enjoyed mixing with the younger students. The world wasn't made for young people, you know! It's like a garden – there's room for all sorts. I like to think we older people added to the young students' education. We certainly spoke up more in tutorials!

I got my BA in English and History. Graduation Day was the happiest day of my life. I did it for my forbears. I thought of my grandmother. There's a studio photograph of her at home, seated with an open book on her lap. She would never have been able to read that book. It was just a studio pose. I did my BA for her.

LEO: I'm a Dubliner who left school at fourteen. My mother was a widow, so I had no option but to find work. For forty years

I dreamed of going to university. For a number of years I was a 365-books-a-year man! I read a book a day, thanks to the library. It was free. Everything else cost money. I became redundant in 1994. That was my opportunity to pursue my dream! I was fortunate to be allowed to sit in on Leaving Certificate classes in Ballymun Comprehensive School. I studied English, History and Geography, sat the exam and sailed through it, with an A1 in English. I found it terribly easy. I said to my kids who had done the Leaving Cert – 'What were ye complaining about, all those years?'

I'm now doing the Access course in the National College of Ireland. The whole thing is so stimulating. When I went into the lecture hall I said to myself, 'This is it! This is what I was born for! I'm just forty years late ...'

SISTER OF WISDOM

MARGARET MACCURTAIN *assesses the life and work of Hildegarde of Bingen, disregarded for centuries by historians but now recognised as a formidable composer, poet, mystic and theologian.*
From the radio series 'Millennium Minds'.

HILDEGARDE WAS BORN in 1098, the tenth and last child of Hildebert and Mechtilde Van Bermersheim's family who lived in the Rhineland region between the towns of Trier and Mainz. Hildegarde was an exceptional child, though delicate and subject to severe illnesses. From an early age she saw things invisible to others and – as a small child – told no one of those visionary moments.

Born on the threshold of the twelfth century, Hildegarde experienced and reflected the profound movements in religious and philosophical thought expressed in the art and culture of that great century. She lived for eighty-one years, dying in 1179. Thus she was a contemporary of Bernard of Clairvaux – persuasive preacher of the Second Crusade – and of Abbot Suger who transformed the pokey church of St Denis into a place of dazzling, soaring space – giving the world the first gothic cathedral.

Closer to home, Hildegarde witnessed the strife between successive popes and German kings as to who should invest bishops and abbots in Germany with ring and crozier – the symbols of their spiritual authority. Thirteen popes and ten anti-popes laid claim to the Chair of Peter during her lifetime. The Holy Roman Emperor, Frederick Barbarossa, argued and fought incessantly with the papacy over issues in which jurisdiction between church and state seemed unclear. At one point Frederick even ordered the destruction of monasteries which supported the Pope, but so great was his respect for Hildegarde that he issued a decree of protection to her abbey in perpetuity.

Despite her regard for Bernard of Clairvaux, Hildegarde was not happy with his support for the Crusades – what she called the 'Holy Jerusalem War'. 'Surely,' she wrote, 'it is inappropriate for a cleric to be a soldier and a soldier a cleric?' Hildegarde didn't care for Bernard's unquestioning assumption that those whose lives were dedicated to God should go to fight on crusade for the holy places as if they were secular knights.

Wherever the biographer tests her, Hildegarde's moral courage stands out. She supported the notion of balance and interdependence in the sharing of power between church and state, and also between humanity and nature. With the Crusades pushing east and south, new ideas came pouring into Europe. Towns and cities sprang up and beautified the landscape with great cathedrals and schools. Ten years before Hildegarde's birth, the University of Bologna with its great law faculty had been founded. In Paris the theological centre of Europe opened up to students as she entered old age. Though Paris University never invited her to place her writings and musical scores in its fine library, Hildegarde was in touch with the minds that shaped her century. She herself transcended that century, influencing thought and musical composition down the centuries.

What was she like – what kind of person was Hildegarde of Bingen? No likeness of her is known to exist. We possess several hundred letters written by her and two monks after repeated efforts persuaded her – in her late seventies – to write a memoir which they incorporated into a Life or *Vita*, which gives us details of how she developed into the astounding person she became.

Hildegarde's parents dedicated her to God as an offering when she was still an infant. The promising of children to God's service was not unusual at that period. In 1106 the eight-year-old girl was put in the care of a young noblewoman, Jutta of Sponheim, who was an anchoress in the large Benedictine monastery of the monks of Saint Disibod. In practice this meant that Jutta and Hildegarde – with a couple of servants – were sealed off from the monastery in a tiny apartment adjacent to the abbey church. From Jutta, the child Hildegarde – already a visionary – quickly learned the Psalter or the Psalms of King David and became skilled in writing Latin. From those early years Hildegarde grew accustomed to the liturgical emphases of the Benedictine Abbey – the daily cycle of prayer and of chanting the Divine Office, with music on great feastdays. Her further studies were entrusted to the monk Volmar who became her lifelong friend, secretary and scribe, dying just six years before her.

Sometime in her teens Hildegarde made her profession, receiving the veil and habit of a Benedictine nun. In the ensuing years Jutta's hermitage had expanded as other young women joined Hildegarde and their lifestyles gradually changed from that of anchoresses to being members of a Benedictine monastery according to the Rule of St Benedict. When Jutta died in 1136, the nuns elected Hildegarde as her successor. She was thirty-eight years of age. Five years later Hildegarde tells us she was summoned in a vision to 'tell and write' what she 'saw and heard' in her visions. Amidst bouts of persistent illness she recorded her first books or visions, eventually entitled *Scivias*, short for *Scito Vias Domini* (Know the Ways of the Lord). They were set down and recorded by the faithful Volmar in the presence of her much-loved monastic companion – later abbess – Rikkarda Von Strade.

Though abbess, Hildegarde did not disclose her visions. Jutta had known of them, as did Volmar. She wrote a troubled letter seeking reassurance to Bernard of Clairvaux. Bernard cautiously affirmed Hildegarde's prophetic gift. Then Pope Eugenius III – on a visit to the Synod of Trier – reviewed a section of her writings (on the recommendation of Bernard at the Synod), sending her a letter of apostolic blessing and protection.

With her new celebrity, her convent at Disibod attracted many postulants and overcrowding set in. Hildegarde decided to make a new foundation at Rupertsberg, opposite Bingen, despite fierce opposition. The move released Hildegarde's creativity. Quickly she composed seventy-seven liturgical songs, a musically-complex sung morality play – *Ordo Virtutum* (Order of the Virtues). Her musical compositions were collected into a cycle entitled *Symphony of the Harmony of Celestial Revelation*. She described her compositions thus:

> My new song must float like a feather on the Breath of God ...
> When the words come, they are merely empty shells without the
> music. They live as they are sung, for the words are the body and
> the music the spirit.

With the economic stability and autonomy of her monastery at Rupertsberg secured, Hildegarde turned her vast energies in a new direction. Around 1158 – she was then sixty – a prolonged bout of illness (always a herald of a new initiative for her) was followed by a decision to go on a preaching journey, calling on all the faithful to reform their lives. This woman who had been walled up as an anchoress at the age of eight – who had been cloistered for over fifty years – set out on four journeys to preach the Word of God up and down the banks of the Rhine, into Lorraine and as far as Swabia.

Nor was she free from being regarded as a controversial nun. She scolded the Emperor Frederick Barbarossa in a famous letter when he appointed yet a third anti-pope. Despite her biting invective, he never withdrew his protection from her monastery, nor impeded her in any way.

Her greatest trial was reserved for her last years. Hildegarde buried in her cemetery a young excommunicated noble revolutionary, thus breaking ecclesiastical law in burying him in hallowed ground. The bishops commanded her to dig up the corpse. She refused, saying the youth had confessed and had been reconciled to the Church. Her monastery was interdicted and she and her sisters were deprived of Mass, the sacraments and the music that inspired and sustained them.

In one of her best letters Hildegarde wrote to the Prelates of Mainz about the function of music as humanity's bridge to the heavenly harmonies and how the Devil obstructed the adoration of God by silencing music singing his praise. She places the Prelates of Mainz squarely on the side of the Devil.

She won! The Interdict was lifted in March. Hildegarde died the following September – on the seventeenth day – aged eighty-one.

Hildegarde of Bingen has emerged at this time from a shadowy world of ignorance about her extraordinary giftedness and from a conspiracy of silence about the position of pre-eminence she is entitled to occupy. The reasons are clear – envy of her rich talents in the increasingly controlled world of the cathedral schools of music. It was unthinkable that a woman could make a significant impact on sacred liturgy. It was impossible to think of her as a theologian of her time. Then – shame on her – she left her cloister and *preached* – an office reserved for bishops.

For over seven hundred years Hildegarde's astounding achievements remained buried in obscurity. Her writings were available in Latin only, her liturgical songs disregarded. Honoured as a saint and visionary in her own part of Germany, two attempts at official canonisation have failed.

There is a kind of authority which is a combination of great learning, great holiness, intelligence and modesty, which can terrify and infuriate the arrogant. Hildegarde drew people – she healed them, she was attentive to their needs. She gave a spiritual meaning to their drab lives. She enchanted them with her music and the singing of sacred music. Above all, she had the moral courage – which most of us lack – to speak out against abuses.

In this lovely piece, *O Noblissima Viriditas – O noblest greenness, who have your roots in the sun* ... Hildegarde addresses our age, reminding us of the relationship between the care of the Earth and the Creator of the Universe:

> ... You glow red like the dawn,
> And you burn like the sun's fire.
> You are held all around by the embraces of the divine mysteries.

A SENSE OF THE PAST

SEAMUS HEANEY *reminds us that we all need a sensitivity to the past.*

IN THE STUDY at home I have a table that is as old as this century – maybe older. It is of no great value as an antique and would fetch very little at an auction. It is uneven and the top of it is gapped. The tongues have deserted the grooves in places. The whole thing seems on the verge of caving in. All the same, its value for me will never be determined by its auction value.

Though I write at it now – instead of eating at it – some essential part of me is fed just by having it in the house. It represents continuity, memory, a guarantee of relationship, a communion with the dead. When I was a youngster, it belonged in the house where my aunt and great-uncle lived – a house with an open hearth, a sod roof, a big beam running across the kitchen and a horse's collar hanging on the wall. A house that spoke in every flagstone and rafter of a previous age – bog oak in the roofspace, whitewash and this table, tight against the window, scrubbed twice or three times a day, ingrained with the life and times of a family of which I am a part. So its value to me is as shadowy and incalculable as the past itself.

Generally speaking, I believe that a sensitivity to the past contributes to our lives in a necessary and salutary way. A sense of the past constitutes what Wordsworth would have called 'a primary law of our nature'. Our place, our house, our furniture are present not just as backdrops, but they become influential and nurturing. Our imagination breathes their atmosphere as rewardingly as the oxygen of the air. Yet we grow away from the primary relish of the phenomena – the rooms where we come to consciousness, the cupboards we open as toddlers, the shelves we climb up to, the boxes and albums we explore in reserved places in the house, the secret spots we come upon out of doors in our first solitude – those haunts of our first explorations in outbuildings and fields at the very verge of our security. It is in all such places and at such moments that the reality of the world first awakens in us.

It is also at such moments that we have our first inkling of pastness and find our physical surroundings invested with a wider and deeper dimension than we can just then account for. In my own case, the top of the dresser – in the kitchen of the house where I lived for my first twelve years – was like a time machine. This was where the old nails and screwdrivers, putty, lamp-wicks and broken sharpening-stones would end up. Its mystery had to do with its inaccessibility for me. When I managed to climb up there, the dusty newspaper on the putty, the worn-down grains on the sharpening stones, the bent nails, the singed ends of the wicks, the dust and stillness and rust – all suggested that these objects were living a kind of afterlife. They were not inert rubbish, but dormant energies. Naturally I did not think this to myself at the time. It was all sensation – but that sensation was subtly and indelibly linked with the word 'old'. Old was an atmosphere that brought you out of yourself and close to yourself at once. We read ourselves into our personal past by reading the significant images in our personal world.

The desire to keep a charged object is universal. We all pick up stones from the beach, acorns and chestnuts from long grass under trees. We keep old bottles and nail up old horseshoes – all in the hope that those objects will help us to hold on to the experiences and memories that they stand for. It is an urge that is both primitive and healthy. It reminds me of a story Carl Jung tells in his autobiography. He recalls how at school he carved the top of his ruler into a little Humpty Dumpty figure, ripped it off the ruler and hid it in his pencil-case. Later he stored the pencil-case in his attic and forgot about it. Decades later, when Jung was doing research into the consciousness of primitive tribes, he found among

Australian aborigines the practice of making ritual objects called soul-stones. These too were Humpty-Dumpty-type objects and they were hoarded at a sacred site. Each soul-stone was a storehouse for some individual's life-force, a sort of spiritual battery operating by remote control on its owner's life. Jung was driven to muse upon the deep human impulse that drove the sophisticated suburban western child to carve an image which repeated in its shape and functions those of the aborigine's soul-stones.

To come to the table in my attic. There I have assembled the makings of a small personal museum – keepsakes and memorial bits and pieces that link to moments and places I want to remember. One of these 'soul-stones' is an iron spike I found in New Hampshire when I visited the poet Donald Hall. He lives in an old homestead that still feels as if his grandparents had walked out of the back kitchen, across the yard and into the haybarn. A railway – long closed – had once run across the field in front of the house. The old rails and sleepers had been removed, but I found an iron spike in the grass and brought it home to Dublin – partly because it stood for that nostalgic New England scene, but mainly because that scene had revived my own memories of railwaymen in buggies speeding along the railway line that ran through our farm in Co. Derry in the 1940s. When I wrote a poem about the iron spike, the ghost-life of the old place came flowing back, helped I am sure by the fact that I was sitting at that well-scrubbed, ancestrally-ingrained table as I wrote ...

> IRON SPIKE
> So like a harrow pin
> I hear the harness creaks and the click
> of stones in a ploughed-up field.
> But it was the age of steam
>
> at Eagle Pond, New Hampshire,
> when this rusted spike I found there
> was aimed and driven in
> to fix a cog on the line.

THE CURIOUS MIND

What guarantees things keeping
if a railway can be lifted
like a long briar out of ditch growth?
I felt I had come on myself

in the silent grassy path
where I drew the iron like a thorn
or a word I had thought my own
out of a stranger's mouth.

And the sledge-head that sank it
with a last opaque report
deep into the creosoted
sleeper, where is that?
And the sweat-cured haft?
Ask those ones on the buggy
inaudible and upright
and sped along without shadows.

THE MIRACLE TREE

This was the title I gave to a programme on language development in the young child. It was part of a series for parents entitled 'Learning to Read'. The programme on language development drew heavily on the work of KORNEI CHUKOVSKY *in that field.*

'WAS IT NOT then that I acquired all that now sustains me? And I gained so much and so quickly that during the rest of my life I did not acquire a hundredth part of it. From myself as a five-year-old to myself as I now am, there is only one step. The distance between myself as an infant and myself at five years is tremendous.'

Thus did Leo Tolstoy reflect on the importance of the early years of childhood. His fellow countryman Kornei Chukovsky would agree.

Chukovsky was a much-loved author of children's books and a keen observer of pre-school children's acquisition and use of language. He documented this observation in his book, *From Two to Five*, first published in 1925 and reprinted many times. For Chukovsky the young child is a 'linguistic genius' who through imitation and creativity makes that giant leap in communication.

'It is frightening to think what an enormous number of grammatical forms are poured over the poor head of the young child ... If an adult had to master so many grammatical rules within so short a time, his head would surely burst – a mass of rules mastered so lightly and so freely by the two-year-old "linguist". The labour he thus performs at this age is astonishing enough, but even more amazing and unparalleled is the ease with which he does it ...'

This 'tireless explorer' uses fantasy and curiosity as a means of learning. Chukovsky recorded the following in his diary about his own three-year-old daughter:

> Mura took off her slipper
> Planted it in the garden –
> 'Grow, grow my little slipper
> Grow little one!
> I'll water you every day
> And a tree will grow
> A miracle tree!'

The programme 'The Miracle Tree' won a major international award in Japan, but that is not important. What was important was its message – that the greatest contribution that parents can make to the child's linguistic development is to engage in real conversation with the child and respond to what Chukovsky called 'one hundred thousand whys'. 'Adults who irritably avoid answering the 'boring' childish questions commit an irrevocable and cruel act – they forcibly retard the child's mental growth and thwart his spiritual development ...'

SCHUMACHER ON SCHUMACHER

It is a balmy October evening in 1999. I am sitting in a roof garden in Castle St, Dublin, talking with DIANA SCHUMACHER. *It seems an appropriate setting to talk about Diana's father-in-law, the economist E.F. Schumacher, best known for his book* Small is Beautiful.

MY FATHER-IN-LAW died in 1977. He was a distinguished economist who was considered a maverick because of his dissatisfaction with the way western economics were going. For him, economics had become obsessed with growth and centralisation. In the process it had become dehumanising and disempowering and this would ultimately lead to chaos. His ideas were not popular in his lifetime – apart from in the developing world – but over time there has been an increased awareness of his work and the Schumacher Society endeavours to deepen that awareness.

Contrary to popular belief, Schumacher did *not* say 'small is beautiful'. His publisher coined that phrase. Schumacher *did* say that there is an appropriate size for everything. Small *can* be beautiful, but it must take humans into account. They must feel they are part of the enterprise. The subtitle of his book was 'Economics as if People Matter ...' He believed economics must serve people – and not the other way around. In a finite planet with limited resources, you cannot have exponential growth forever, yet western industrial society is still heedless in pursuit of growth and is running headlong towards a precipice.

According to Schumacher, it is the first-class passengers on Spaceship Earth (i.e. the rich and powerful) who cause problems. Our task in the Schumacher Society is to get the spaceship back on course. We do this through education and consciousness-raising – for example, through the Small Schools Movement, the Schumacher College, the journal *Resurgence*, Green Books publishing, promoting intermediate technology, organic agriculture and so on.

Schumacher was a deeply religious person. He believed in the integrity of the human being. He wrote a famous essay in *Resurgence* on 'Buddhist Economics', which attempted to marry the science of economics with the spiritual, human and ecological values of Buddhism. He argued that if you have a large problem, the answer will come from thousands of small solutions. This is the Mosquito Principle. If you are confronted by a giant with a big gun, the answer is not to look for a bigger gun but to confront him with a swarm of mosquitoes who will attack him from all angles and drive him mad!

One phrase Schumacher *did* coin was 'sustainable development'. He used it at a conference in Stockholm in 1972. For him development was an integrated concept. In assessing any development project, four questions had to be asked:

1. Is it good for the individual?
2. Is it good for the community?
3. Does it create jobs?
4. Is it good for the environment?

You need a 'yes' to at least two of these questions, ideally to all four.

Schumacher was both an idealist and a realist. Practice without theory is misguided, he said. Theory without practice is sterile. He parted company with many of his fellow-economists when, at a conference in Switzerland, he told them: 'You are teaching the seven deadly sins ...' When you look at the ruthless pursuit of growth and centralisation today, it is not too difficult to recognise Pride, Covetousness, Lust, Anger, Gluttony, Envy, Sloth ... .

A DOUBLE ACT

Ireland's great comedienne, MAUREEN POTTER, *pays homage to her stage mentor, Jimmy O'Dea.*

ON FRIDAY 1 September 1939, all the theatres in London went dark. Jack Hylton sent myself and my friend down to Blackpool to his mother and father's place, just to be out of the way of trouble for the time being. The following Sunday morning, 3 September, Chamberlain made his announcement, and it was very odd to see Blackpool empty. An empty strand with those rolls of barbed wire that they thought would keep Hitler from invading. My mother got the wind up completely and sent for me to come home immediately, so I came home and joined Jimmy O'Dea.

He was doing a pantomime that year called *Jimmy and the Leprechaun* and I was the leprechaun, which was very exciting. I had worked with him before I went to Jack Hylton – including in pantomime in 1935 and 1936. I graduated into being his regular feed. I remember my first review was – 'Maureen Potter, surprisingly good in a sketch'. From then on we became a sort of double act, Jimmy and I – Dolores and Rosie, the Totties and so on. I stayed with him until he died.

Jimmy was very meticulous and very neat. He had all his clothes hand-made. He wasn't a comic off-stage – he could be very cross – but he taught me my business and I'll always be grateful to him for that. He was the best in the business at timing a gag and it was from him I learned my own sense of timing, even though I worked with Arthur Askey and all the great comics in England. Tommy Trinder was another beautiful, kind man, who I played with at the Palladium. He used to play hide and seek with me. And then I loved Frankie Howerd. Not long before he died, he came here one night to see me and we had the time of our lives chatting. Bud Flanagan, too, was a lovely man.

They loved the Irish over there. Jimmy and I used to laugh. We were so small that when we went over there during the war, we could beat our way to the bar quicker than anyone else. They used to think we were Canadians – they couldn't believe that Irish people were articulate and could be understood. There were wonderful comics in England, but Jimmy was the one from whom I learned the most. I always felt that Jimmy O'Dea should have been made a Freeman of the city of Dublin. If anyone in this country were to be chosen, it should have been him.

The first time I did a sketch with him, he said, 'A little less characterisation and a little more clarity'. I was acting my guts out but nobody could hear me. He taught me that it is important to be audible on stage if you want to be funny.

In the 1940s and 1950s we toured Ireland a fair bit. Jimmy O'Dea loved touring. The train would break down and Jimmy would take the station master and the train driver over to the local pub while everybody else looked for wood to fuel the engine. Jimmy loved meeting the local doctor, the local bank manager and all the local sergeants while we were doing the work in the theatre.

We always used to bring a rope with a hook to hang our clothes on, because there were no dressing rooms – and the bucket, of course, for the loo, with a curtain between the men and the women. We were an actual 'fit-up'. We fitted up our own stage and made our own footlights out of little cooking dishes and put our boards up on the baskets that we brought our clothes in. It could be pretty ropey sometimes getting on and off the stage. We did sketches and song and dance. Jimmy had sketches like 'Mine's a Pint' and 'Marrying Mary' and I would sing and dance and then we would have acts with accordions and fiddles and maybe jugglers too.

We often used to bump into Anew McMaster, who was a joy. I remember meeting him when he was touring with Harold Pinter. Mac used to leave little notes for us if he was in the hotel in town before us – like, 'Whatever you do, dear, don't touch the beef' and 'Jimmy dear, whatever you do, test the beds'. He was a great man and it was an education for me.

THOMAS JEFFERSON – A MILLENNIUM MIND

Walter Nugent *assesses the life and career of a US president.*

The story goes that John F. Kennedy – not long after he became president – invited all the American Nobel prize winners to the White House for dinner. About fifty of them came. When they were seated, Kennedy said: 'This is probably the greatest aggregation of brains to sit at this table since Thomas Jefferson dined alone.'

Jefferson was, of course, the third President of the United States, holding office from 1801 to 1809. For the forty-one people who have held the job, it is normally regarded as the supreme achievement of their lives. Jefferson, however, did not even include the presidency among the three things he most wished to be remembered for. Before he died, he asked that the obelisk marking his grave in the small cemetery below Monticello, his Virginian plantation, state – 'and not a word more' – that *Here was buried Thomas Jefferson, author of the Declaration of American Independence, of the Statute of Virginia for religious freedom, and Father of the University of Virginia.* He omitted not only the presidency but his terms as the first secretary of state under George Washington, and then the vice-presidency under John Adams's term. He did not mention buying Louisiana from Napoleon Bonaparte and thus doubling the size of the young United States; nor his founding of what became the Democratic party; nor his writings, inventions, architecture or agronomy.

Jefferson was born in the spring of 1743 to a self-made planter, Peter Jefferson, and his wife Jane Randolph – of a renowned early Virginia family. Peter died fourteen years later, leaving Thomas, his older son, nearly three thousand acres of land, a good name among the gentry, and the start of a classical education. The boy learned Greek and Latin and read secular and scriptural texts in them for the rest of his life. In 1760 he entered the College of William and Mary in the provincial capital, Williamsburg, and graduated two years later. He then read law under the eminent George Wythe for the next five years, and practised law until politics fully absorbed his time in the mid–1770s. As a member of the best social and political circles in Virginia, as a student of classics and law, he was preparing himself ideally well for the drafting of the Declaration and a host of statutes – tasks that he would very soon be charged with. Elected to Virginia's House of Burgesses in 1769, he wrote a bill permitting planters to manumit their slaves. It did not pass. In 1772 – then twenty-nine – he married the twenty-four-year-old widow Martha Skelton. Together they had six children, but only two – daughters Martha and Maria – lived to adulthood. Mrs Jefferson herself died in 1782, to her husband's profound sorrow. He never remarried.

Jefferson's role in the Virginia assembly grew increasingly prominent, and his position increasingly anti-British. Biographer Dumas Malone remarked that though 'never an effective public speaker, Jefferson did greatest service in legislative bodies on committees, where his marked talents as a literary draftsman were employed'. Always his *modus operandi* was through pen and personal persuasion, rather than by intimidating or imposing presence. He was anything but confrontational and indeed was hypersensitive. There is reasonable doubt that he could have become a governor or president in our television age. Typically, his first truly major political manifesto – the Summary View of the Rights of British America of August 1774 – was sent to the assembly in his absence. In it Jefferson stressed the natural rights of colonists, denied any authority of parliament over them, and maintained that Virginia was tied to Britain only through the King – a position also held at that tricky moment by the more forthright leaders in New England.

The assembly shrank from adopting Jefferson's views but more than ever admired his 'happy talent for composition', as John Adams then called it. The next summer – 1775 – found Jefferson at the Continental Congress at Philadelphia, and in 1776 the Congress – led by Adams, Benjamin Franklin and others of the American Pantheon – gave him the duty of drafting a declaration of independence. At age thirty-three he produced this most important document, and the Congress accepted his draft with little revision.

The Declaration has three parts: a statement of general principles, a series of indictments of George III, and a brief conclusion. It opens with familiar words:

> When, in the course of human events, it becomes necessary for one people to dissolve the political bands which have connected them with another, and to assume among the powers of the earth the separate and equal station to which the laws of nature and of nature's God entitle them, a decent respect to the opinions of mankind require that they should declare the causes which impel them to the separation.

And then the general principles:

> We hold these truths to be self-evident: that all men are created equal; that they are endowed by their Creator with certain unalienable rights; that among these are life, liberty and the pursuit of happiness; that to secure these rights, governments are instituted among men, deriving their just powers from the consent of the governed; that whenever any form of government becomes destructive of these ends, it is the right of the people to alter or to abolish it and to institute new government, laying its foundation on such principles and organising its powers in such form as to them shall seem most likely to effect their safety and happiness.

But, Jefferson continues, the King has committed 'repeated injuries and usurpations' which require just such a change. The second part is a long list of these injuries and usurpations – among other things:

> He has plundered our seas, ravaged our coasts, burnt our towns and destroyed the lives of our people ... He has excited domestic insurrection among us, and has endeavoured to bring on the inhabitants of our frontiers, the merciless Indian savages, whose known rule of warfare is an undistinguished destruction of all ages, sexes and conditions.

The document concludes: 'We appeal to the supreme judge of the world for the rectitude of our intentions and declare these united colonies are – and of right ought to be – free and independent states', and in this cause, 'with a firm reliance on the protection of divine providence, we mutually pledge to each other our lives, our fortunes and our sacred honor.'

On 4 July 1776, fifty-seven men from all thirteen colonies signed the Declaration, and the United States regards that date as its birthday.

During his congressional term – 1783/84 – Jefferson drafted nearly three dozen reports and statutes, among them the one establishing a decimal currency for the United States. But even more important was his report on what to do with the western lands of the United States. Here he revealed a vision of the American future that he would take much further years later as president – a vision of an 'empire of liberty'. This was a new and peculiarly American form of imperialism that would – before 1850 – extend the boundaries of the United States to the Pacific and triple its land mass beyond its original boundaries in the peace treaty of 1783.

Jefferson – and the United States – inherited a problem by the terms of peace that has been called 'the problem of the West'. The 1783 treaty was exceedingly generous to the new nation in that its boundaries were set hundreds of miles west of its effective settlement at that time. The boundary on the west was declared to be the Mississippi River – although the newly independent Americans had hardly begun to cross the Appalachian chain of mountains. The intervening country – which was even larger than the settled area between the Atlantic and the mountains – was peopled almost entirely by Indians and a sprinkling of whites. Britain had taken over this area (in European terms – Indians would scarcely have agreed) in 1763 from France, and in the next twenty years – until the Anglo-American peace treaty of 1783 – Britain had a disastrous time trying to govern it. Treating it as a subject colony yet filled with suspicious Indians, Britain attempted to placate the French majority in Quebec by recognising its Catholic culture. This only infuriated Protestant New England. Colonial anger soared when the Crown proclaimed that settlers could not proceed beyond the mountains. Few were in a position to, but the prohibition became 'the principle of the thing' and grist – as we have seen – for Jefferson's mill when he indicted King George in the Declaration. Would the United States make mistakes about the West too? What was to be done?

Jefferson was not alone in proposing a solution, but he saw it the most clearly. He was aided greatly by a happy accident. Of the thirteen newly independent states, some had legitimate claims to lands west of the mountains: call them the 'haves'. Some states (the 'have-nots') lacked claims. The largest of the 'haves' was Virginia, whose charter of 1606 (if literally construed) gave it an enormous region – much of what is now the United States and Canada. On the north side of the Potomac river from Virginia was much smaller Maryland – a 'have-not'. As the Revolutionary War drew to a close, the thirteen new states – hitherto independent of each other – desperately needed some kind of central government.

A document called the Articles of Confederation proposed one. But Maryland – and other have-nots – refused to sign it until Virginia relinquished its western claims in favour of the new central government. After three years of politicking, Maryland remained stubborn, and Virginia gave in. The western lands became the United States' public domain – the property of the entire nation – to be administered by the new central government. Now, what to do with it? How to govern it, and how to distribute it to settlers?

Jefferson proposed to Congress in 1784 a plan to accomplish both objectives. The key feature provided that a new state could be carved out of these western lands when it gained a population equal to the least populous of the existing states. Then the new state 'shall be admitted ... into the Congress of the United States on an equal footing with the said original states'. The west would not become colonies or provinces, but states equal to venerable Massachusetts or Virginia. The plan also provided for purchase of land by '*bona fide* settlers'. Jefferson's 1784 plan also provided that 'after 1800 there shall be neither slavery nor involuntary servitude in any' of the new states. Such a clause appeared in the 1787 Ordinance, and slavery never took root north of the Ohio river.

The public domain would be sold in small units at reasonable prices to actual settlers, who would create farms and families, forming a sound and stable small-holding yeomanry – Jefferson's 'Agrarian Dream'. As he wrote to John Jay from Paris in 1785:

> Cultivators of the earth are the most valuable citizens. They are
> the most vigorous, the most independent, the most virtuous, and

they are tied to their country and wedded to its liberty and interests by the most lasting bonds.

By the 1780s, therefore, his idea of an 'empire of liberty' – indefinite expansion driven not by force but (in Julian Boyd's words) 'the sheer majesty of ideas and ideals' – was taking tangible shape.

Jefferson's embassy to France from 1784 to 1789 won acclaim there and at home. He spent the 1790s as secretary of state and then as vice-president. In 1800 he won election as the third president of the United States, and the following spring moved into the new executive mansion in the midst of the decidedly uncompleted city whose mall he had planned. His greatest achievement as president reflected the triumph of the practical over the theoretical in his mind, and a unique combination of intellectual curiosity with great foresight as to the country's long-range welfare.

Thomas Jefferson died at eighty-three – on 4 July 1826 – fifty years to the day from the signing of the Declaration of Independence that he had drafted. He did a great many things. I will always maintain that the Declaration was a great achievement. But so too were his efforts to make possible the 'Empire of Liberty', by which the United States expanded westward. The third legacy I have selected from Jefferson's life is far more ambiguous – the ability to announce the principle that all men are created equal, and then somehow to shrink from acting fully on it. This too is a legacy – paradoxically both bright and dark – that Jefferson gave his people.

AFTERNOON TEA WITH SHIRLEY

Notting Hill, London, 2007. A meeting with the much-loved author and illustrator of children's books, SHIRLEY HUGHES.

ALTHOUGH SHE HAS lived in Notting Hill for over fifty years, Shirley Hughes is a Liverpool lass by birth – growing up in The Wirral just outside the Mersey city, where her father owned a major department store. 'I think the enormous difference between my childhood and the childhood of today is that we had so much time to mooch and wander about ...' And read, of course. From early days Shirley was a voracious reader. The opening line of her wonderful autobiography *A Life Drawing* goes: 'I have to begin with comics ...' At first they were simple, undemanding comics like 'Tiger Tim' and 'Bubbles', whose 'graphic excitement' hooked the young reader. There were lots of books at home (her parents first met 'between the stacks of Ramsgate public library') and Shirley was fascinated by the line drawings in those books which were initially read to her by the maid.

'I always saw pictures and stories as strongly interwoven. Thomas Henry's wonderful line drawings for Richmal Crompton's *William* books made me want to be an illustrator. My whole career has been influenced by people like Ernest Shepherd whose masterful illustrations for *The Wind in the Willows* made the characters and the background come to life. I always wanted to be like him. Then there was Edward Ardizzone, whom I knew. When you looked at a page of his work, the magic of the line opened you to a third dimension. I really loved Will Heath Robinson. He belonged to the golden era of the illustrated classics. He had the good fortune and the bad luck to be famous for those wild inventions, but as an illustrator he had a macabre side. His illustration of *A Midsummer Night's Dream* was absolutely brilliant.'

Shirley's father died when she was only five, leaving her to grow up in a house of women (she had two sisters). She enjoyed trips into Liverpoool with her mother and sisters for shopping, afternoon tea and theatre. 'I loved theatre. I think all illustrators have a theatrical troupe within them. It's as if you are the actor, director, designer and set-builder all in one.' There was also the attraction of the Walker Art Gallery in Liverpool. 'It was full of Edwardian and Victorian narrative paintings. Works like *When Did You Last See Your Father?* thrilled me.'

The young Shirley's mind was set. Illustration would be her career. She went to West Kirby High School where art was '... OK – We did nice pictures once a week under the tutelage of the highly-strung, skeletal

Miss Griffiths ... but most of the artwork I did was done at home'. She moved on to Liverpool Art School for a Fashion Drawing course, where she learned how to cut material and design costumes – experience which would stand to her later as an illustrator. That course lasted only a year and – anxious to move away from The Wirral – Shirley persuaded her mother to let her go to Oxford. She duly enrolled at Ruskin College where she turned up in 'a cashmere jumper and pearls when everyone else was in paint-bespattered overalls – so I had to change very quickly!'

One of the great highlights of Oxford was Kenneth Clark's lectures on the History of Art. 'I knew nothing about Art history but he opened doors for me. From the very first lecture when he showed a slide of the Rembrandt etching "Christ Shown to the People", the hairs stood up on the back of my neck. Door after door opened for me. The following year I went to Florence to see the real thing and I've never stopped looking at paintings since.'

After Oxford, getting started on a career was difficult. Line-drawing for children's fiction was a wonderful apprenticeship but very badly paid and it was only when the author Noel Streatfeild saw Shirley's work and asked her to illustrate her fiction that the major breakthrough came. In the meantime she took on everything including school texts ('"See Tom run. Run, Tom, run!" doesn't give one much scope!') but eventually things improved – particularly when Shirley worked with Dorothy Edwards (of *My Naughty Little Sister* fame). They became friends and soulmates and would go on publicity tours. 'Dorothy was a brilliant storyteller. She would have her audience enthralled, while I stood at the back and did drawings! We were the Laurel and Hardy of the book circuit.'

Romance entered Shirley's life in the most unlikely circumstances. She was visiting a friend who had a small baby. The drain outside her basement flat was blocked and all sorts of muck was swirling about. The baby was crying. She couldn't unblock the drain and was in despair. Along came John – the tenant in the upper flat – who rolled up the sleeve of his immaculate white shirt and plunged his arm into the drain. 'The muck all went away. The baby stopped crying. The sun came out and I thought, *this man knows what he's doing.*' John asked Shirley out and they had a long and happy marriage until, sadly, he died in 2007.

John was an architect so they had an empathy for each other's work. They would go regularly to Florence and he became a very good painter and etcher in later life. John was a great support in the early days when Shirley was juggling a freelance career with motherhood – they eventually had three children. They moved into Notting Hill in 1954 – a very different Notting Hill. 'It was a very run-down, tough area, houses with multiple occupancy, race riots and so on, but gradually it changed. I'm very glad we moved here, and I'm still here, over fifty years later.' Notting Hill became the backdrop for Shirley's first picture-book, *Lucy and Tom's Day,* and for many of her subsequent books. 'It was a very unassuming little book about getting through the day. I was always drawn to realism, portraying the child's real world. I observed children very carefully. I always kept sketchbooks (her autobiography – *A Life Drawing* – teems with sketches from her long career) and once you draw something you never forget it. I'm always being asked are the children in my books my own children or actual Notting Hill children. They're not anybody's children! It's that experience of observation that enables me to draw children – the way they stand and move, their whole body language. The pictures and the words unfold in my head, and once I've got the words right I make a "rough" and the essence of the book is in that "rough". I work with energy and freedom when I'm doing that and the great test of professionalism is to get that same freedom into the finished drawing.'

Her four score years have not dimmed Shirley Hughes's passion for her work and for the world of children one whit. She is concerned that today's children are over-stimulated visually by a succession of electronic images coming at them relentlessly. 'There is a need to slow the pace down. Young children need the opportunity to explore at their own pace – and still images are very important here. Pause, turn the page, turn back, animate the story for themselves.' And she remains convinced that – as she told me twenty-five years ago – 'there will always be story and there will always be the need for story'. She recalls visiting Belfast at the height of the Troubles, watching a 'wonderful librarian' telling the story of *The Three Billygoats Gruff* to a group of little ones in the courtyard of a block of flats. 'They were spellbound until a posse of military came through. The older children threw missiles at the soldiers and the little ones followed the older children. When it was all over and the older ones disappeared into the flats, the little ones came back to the librarian and implored her to go on with the story. I was astonished. It just illustrated the power of story ...'

As a writer Shirley is as fecund with ideas as ever. For her, there is nothing more exciting than a blank sheet of paper before her. 'Mostly I write in silence but sometimes, to liven myself up, I put on a musical soundtrack to my work – Sidney Bechet maybe, or Benny Goodman.' Her latest book is a fairy story set in nearby Holland Park about a stuffed toy who can fly ... Her next big challenge will be 'a strip cartoon with no words. It will be called *Bye Bye Birdie*. That will be my Everest ...'

We conclude the interview with Shirley reading the closing lines of *A Life Drawing*:

> However well you manage to realise your inner vision, at the end of the day you just have to hope that you can take Ernest Hemingway's advice and leave it when you're going good. And, even though I know I haven't a hope of creating the images that were there in my head, attempting to do so is still the nearest thing I know to flying into the sun.

AN IRISH EDUCATIONIST

Adapted from JOHN COOLAHAN *'s series 'Profiles in Education'.*

I REMEMBER THEM vividly – the Vere Foster headline copybooks. How we laboured with tremulous hands, modelling our childish penstrokes on the given headlines which were in turn gems of proverbial wisdom:

Time and tide wait for no man ...
Friendship multiplies joys and divides grief ...

Make flowing rounded strokes, keep between the red and blue lines and above all – above all – have no blot on your copybook!

Generations of students from Ireland and across the English-speaking world owe their penmanship skills to the copybooks devised by one of the great Irish educationists and philanthropists of the nineteenth century.

Vere Foster was born into wealth in 1819 and enjoyed the privilege of education at both Eton and Oxford before taking up a diplomatic career. A visit to the family estate in Co. Louth in 1847, at the height of the Great Famine, changed the direction of his life completely. He now devoted his energies to the relief of the poor who lived in appalling conditions and were schooled in equally appalling conditions. Improving penmanship was but a small part of his concern, which was captured in the motto on the cover of his copybooks:

A nation's greatness depends on the education of its people.

Vere Foster was very much a 'hands-on' philanthropist. He travelled across the country, experiencing first-hand the primitive conditions of ramshackle school-houses in the most remote areas. He was described at the time as 'simply attired in Irish homespun grey, with knapsack strapped on his back and a stout black-thorn in his hand, walking by easy stages through some remote countryside ...'

His agitation brought widespread improvement to school buildings and requisites. A group of teachers from Co. Longford paid tribute to him thus:

You sought us in our dwellings and were not discouraged by the contact; you stood by us in our schools and showed your appreciation of our labours by those generous gifts of educational apparatus ... startled by the suffering of the poor half-clad children, you substituted for the damp, unwholesome clay the dry boarded floor ... and exerted yourself for the promotion of decency, cleanliness and order in our schools ...

Vere Foster further devoted himself to improving the employment conditions of teachers and providing them with an organised voice. When the Irish National Teachers' Organisation was established in 1868 he was chosen as its first president. By the time he died in 1900, Vere Foster had literally given his all for the betterment of the Irish poor. He left an estate of a mere £178.

RESPECTING DIFFERENCES

Excerpts from Nobel Peace Prize winner JOHN HUME's *1994 'Open Mind' Guest Lecture.*

CAST YOUR MIND back fifty years to the end of World War II. Thirty-five million people lay dead across this continent, for the second time in this century. For centuries, the peoples of Europe saw difference as a threat and slaughtered one another. Their answer to difference was to conquer those from whom they differed. Who could have forecast, fifty years ago, that representatives of the peoples of all those countries would be sitting in a European parliament, as part of a united Europe? And the Germans are still German, and the French are still French. Who could have forecast fifty years ago that we would have a united Europe today? It is the best example in the history of the world of conflict resolution.

When you consider the awful bitterness between the European peoples, and the slaughter that it led to, and that now we're all together – how did they do it? That's a question that everybody in every area of conflict should ask. The answer – like all profundities in life – is simple. They decided that difference is not a threat; that difference is of the essence of humanity; that it's an accident of birth what you're born and where you're born, and whether that accident of birth is colour, creed or nationality, it is not the choice of the person being born – it is the way we were born. So why should it ever be the source of hatred or conflict? There are not two human beings in the entire human race who are the same.

Difference is of the essence of humanity. Difference enriches humanity, and diversity enriches humanity. The peoples of Europe decided to respect their differences and to recognise that the divisions of centuries couldn't be healed in a week or a fortnight. They built institutions which respected their differences, which permitted them to work their common ground together, which is economics – bread on your table and a roof over your head, the right to existence, which is the most fundamental right, plus the right to a decent life. By spilling their sweat and not their blood, in building together, they broke down the barriers of centuries. The new Europe is gradually evolving, and it will continue to evolve.

I believe that that is what we have to do on this small island – respect our differences, build institutions which respect those differences, but which create the framework within which our healing process can take place, and within which we too can then work our very substantial common ground, which is economic. The first step on the road has been taken – a total cessation of violence – and it wasn't easy to get there. The decisions of the paramilitary organisations – who themselves are a product of our history – to lay down their arms will, I hope, prove to be historic decisions. The fact that we meet for the first time in a long time in a peaceful atmosphere should help us face up to that major challenge, because you do not heal the divisions of centuries, or the distrusts and prejudices of centuries, in a week or a fortnight. It is no longer the 1920s. When those military checkpoints leave our border, there will in effect be no border on this island. We are all part of a single market of Europe, with its free movement of goods, people and services. Once we start interacting together on the island for the first time in economic terms, some independent people have already forecasted that developing the trade among our island people could create up to 75,000 jobs. But the real border remains.

The real border is in the hearts and minds of our people. There are those who would tell us that partition is the problem of this country – it is not. What partition did was to institutionalise the real problem which was already there, and had been there for centuries. If Wolfe Tone wanted to unite the Irish people in 1798, they must have been divided. That division has been there for centuries. Partition simply institutionalised it and made it worse. The removal of the economic border leaves the real border in the hearts and minds of our people, and that's the challenge that we have to face up to in this new European world. We are living today in a post-nationalist world. There are those around Europe who still think that the nation-state is something that is eternal. The nation-state is only an era in history. Once upon a time there were city-states. Once upon a time we had high kings and we had kings, and then we had clan chieftains. The nation-state has only been an evolutionary period in history and when the history of the world is written it will have proved to be one of the worst periods, because it caused not only imperialism, but two world wars.

Today's world is a much smaller world than in the 1920s, when the parents and grandparents of many would hardly have left their own district in their lives. Today, you can sit in your own room and watch what's happening right across the world as it happens. There's no such thing as an independent country left in this world. We are interdependent. We cannot live apart. We are living in a post-nationalist world. The old traditional attitudes shouldn't harden *our* attitudes when we come to a table. We should recognise that the legacy of our past is still there – the divided people. But let us also work our common ground together, which is non-controversial – and again I'm talking about economics.

We in this small island are the biggest wandering people in the world. In the last census in the United States of America, forty-two million people indicated that they were of Irish extraction, from both our traditions. Most of their ancestry were driven from this island by famine, by injustice, by intolerance. Yet in today's world, they have come to the top – in politics, in government, in economics, in all fields. We have had presidents of the United States of Irish extraction, prime ministers of Canada, Australia and New Zealand of Irish extraction, and likewise leaders of the business communities in all those countries. The time has come to harness that, and to define Irishness today – not just simply those who live on the island, but let us harness the Irish diaspora as we tackle our economic problems, to use their influence across the world to market the products of our small industries on this island, and to seek the inward investment that will provide the basic right of existence to all our people. And doing that together, in both our traditions – using our links with both our traditions across the world, spilling our sweat and not our blood – will make a major contribution to the healing process and to the breaking down of barriers between our people.

In my own part of the world, we have already begun that process. The city of Derry was where the trouble started, and it was one of the worst examples of injustice in the old Northern Ireland. Today, we've put into practice the philosophy of respect for diversity. We alternate the mayor each year, from each section of the community, and chairmanships of committees of council go to all parties. Our differences are obvious, but the city is our common ground. And the community groups do the same on the ground. We have also been harnessing the Irish diaspora, taking small companies from right across the north of Ireland to America. We have got $45 million worth of orders from them in the last few years, and £120 million of inward investment.

We can do that on a national basis, right across the country, north and south, playing both the green and orange cards positively for a change – for the positive benefit of this offshore island of the united states of Europe and of the United States of America. We are not asking them for charity, because we are offering them a foothold in the biggest single market in the world today – the European market – and we are offering them a quality of life which is going to be one of the major features in the new technological world that people will be seeking. If we harness ourselves in doing that, then we'll make a major contribution to the healing process in the main challenge – which is reaching agreement among our divided people. That agreement must, at least initially, create institutions following the European model, which respect the diversity of our people but allow us to work our common ground together.

Let us hope that this generation can face up to that challenge and leave our past behind us. And as we go into the next century, let us hope that it will be the first century in our island's history when there will have been no killing of human beings on our streets, and no guns and bombs, and no emigration of our young. Let us hope that it will be an island in which Catholic, Protestant and Dissenter will truly live together in harmony and peace.

NATURAL WISDOM

Wisdom comes to us in many ways. It is often confused with schooling or academic distinction. One of the wisest men I met in my professional career never went beyond primary school.

HIS NAME WAS Johnny Kelly. He was a bogman – a term often used with derision by slick city people. But Johnny was literally a bogman. He lived all his fourscore-plus years in the same tin-roofed house – a house without electricity or running water – in the heart of the bog in the Irish midlands. In fact the road petered out at Johnny's house. To my childhood eye, Johnny's house seemed to be at the end of the world.

I featured Johnny in a couple of radio documentaries, drawing on his great love for and understanding of his native place. His knowledge of the history, lore and legend of that place was phenomenal. He was well-versed in the craft of turf-cutting by hand and could tell the story of the bog as the turf-cutters mined it layer by layer. He could discern the quality of the turf as it was cut and could even identify the maker of the *sleán* (turf-cutting implement) from a quick inspection. Johnny had a fund of stories, a wonderful memory and an impish sense of humour. He was a truly happy man who acquired his wisdom simply by *being*, living simply in his place and being of his place, absorbing all it had to give him. His language was rich in idiom and imagery. He would recall that his ancestors were 'put out on the soft side of the road' (evicted for non-payment of rent) or complain that he was so hungry that he could 'eat the sock of a plough!'

To me, Johnny Kelly was a truly wise man. And a truly happy man. A bogman, for whom living in the bog was 'the real ass's milk ...' He was the epitome of the poet's words:

> Happy the man whose wish and care
> A few paternal acres bound,
> Content to breathe his native air
> In his own ground.

THE DEATH OF WORDS

DENIS DONOGHUE *muses on the marginalisation of literature in the modern world.*

LITERATURE IS NO longer a central activity in life. It is a diversion. Ultimately it belongs to the history of entertainment. Of course, books are still being written and sold and read. Books are however traded like any other commodity. They are packaged and marketed like any other product on a shelf. They have a shelf life. The preoccupation and almost obsession with – say – the latest *Harry Potter* book, has very little to do with the history of literature, but a lot to do with the history of lore, of gossip, of social life. It is something to be talked about almost more than something to be read – in the same way that names of football or movie stars are given currency.

I am not sure that any work of literature known to me since the publication of Eliot's *The Waste Land* in 1922 could claim the same kind of comprehensiveness – its bearing on a whole way of life and way of feeling. There are works of great splendour like Yeats' 'Among Schoolchildren' – a very powerful poem – but literature since Eliot has been pressed to the margins. It has become a marginal interest. If you are interested in literature now, it is for your own reasons, which may be not at all different from the reasons you are interested in the latest film or CD. They are not the large common reasons such as the first readers of *The Waste Land* would have had.

I would be astonished if we were ever to see another Shakespeare or Eliot. Since the generation of Eliot and Joyce and Yeats, there haven't been the conditions that could produce writers like them. There are good poets – Heaney, Plath, Lowell, Larkin – but they are good within a much narrower concept of literature and its bearing. People will continue to read and have their enthusiasms but – in a certain sense – their enthusiasms will not matter. It is of no great significance whether you consider Janet Winterson a good novelist or not. It is a matter of minor adjectival interest. It may say something about one's life and it is available then to be talked about but that is it. If however you were arguing about Eliot or Pound or Joyce in the 1920s or 1930s, the argument would have had some bearing, some major implications.

Likewise the notion of great committed literary criticism has probably ended with F.R. Leavis. If you read Leavis's hundred-page essay on Eliot's Four Quartets in the book *The Living Principle*, you find a sense of social and cultural urgency that is almost now an anachronism. For the past twenty or thirty years, literary criticism in any recognised sense has been defunct. A great critic like Frank Kermode – now in his eightieth year – represents a phase in scholarly criticism which is probably finished.

So, what are the implications of all this for reading? I have recently written a book called *The Practice of Reading*. Such a book would not have been necessary twenty or thirty years ago. But now the whole notion of what constitutes reading needs to be teased out. Is it possible to teach literature today? It is very difficult to make today's students take terms like 'form', 'structure', even 'meaning' seriously or to concentrate their minds on them. Again this is down to the sheer marginality of the whole exercise. We seem to be moving into a kind of society in which words as such are increasingly unnecessary. In one of his early poems, Yeats said, 'Words alone are certain good'. No writer would say that today. The notion in poetry of regarding each word as having an existence, a value, a density of its own, is very difficult to maintain any more. Our students are not persuaded of that. They think of words as currency to be passed along.

The philosopher Hannah Arendt once said that one of the reasons why we should not trust scientists in relation to political judgement is that they operate in a world where words are not necessary. It has become very fashionable in the last twenty years to say that there is no such thing as literature – there is no way of certifying the differentiations in literature. I don't accept that myself, but it is very difficult to establish the notion that there is such a thing as literature. A famous critic once said that 'literature is the only form of language which is free from the fallacy of unmediated expression', i.e. most uses of language presuppose that language is a transparent medium, but in fact language is a distorting mirror – what the poet Christopher Hill calls 'enemy country'. Language is not concessive but recalcitrant, difficult and opaque. How do you convey that to students? Part of the marginalisation of literature is that it is something that must be studied rather than apprehended as part of one's life. The main home of literature today is the colleges and universities.

I am currently trying to write a book on teaching literature and that book will have to go much closer to square one than I have gone before, because it will have to start out with fundamentals that I and my colleagues have long taken for granted. What is a language? What does it entail in relation to words, meaning, usage, convention? What do we mean by forms of language? etc. The book will be almost an ABC of literary understanding – the basic co-ordinates upon which we might proceed. If this means that I don't write as much as I should about Seamus Heaney or Christopher Hill, for example, then that's too bad.

IN THE FOOTSTEPS OF THE HERMIT

GEORGE CUNNINGHAM *visits the hermitage of St Colman in the heart of the Burren.*

ONE OF THE aspects of this site that I like is that it's there – and nobody has put in a car-park or a road to it. There isn't even a sign to tell you that St Colman's Bed is here. You search it out for yourself. We are walking across a carpet of alpine flowers and it takes a good fifteen minutes to reach the site since we left the Carron-Kinvara road.

And here it is in the shade of Sliabh Carron – St Colman's Dysart or Hermitage. Here – the Annals tell us – St Colman had 'his bed in a cave ... crystal fountains supplied him with drink ... the wild herbs of the forest were his only food and the skins of the wild deer formed his coarse and scanty raiment, either in summer heats or wintry snows'. We have an oratory here – probably thirteenth–fourteenth century. Colman's original oratory would probably have been made of timber. The 'crystal fountains' came from Tobar Macduagh – one of many wells ascribed to Colman in these parts. These wells were often said to have cures – this one reputedly cured sore eyes. Here it is today almost magically bubbling out between the moss-covered stones under the hazel trees. Hazel was so important in the Burren – providing food and shelter. This is a hermitage just as much as Sceilig Mhichíl was or any of the midland dysarts in the bog.

Colman came here with his faithful servant to fast and pray. After a particularly harsh Lenten fast, the servant was dying with hunger, but Colman told him not to worry – that God would provide. At the time the local king – Guaire – was holding a lavish feast in his castle near Kinvara. Suddenly the dishes rose from the table and raced away. The scared king and his retinue followed all the way to this place. The king and his followers were rooted to the limestone. The path they took is traditionally known as Bóthar na Mias – the Road of the Dishes.

The other lovely story about Colman is about the creatures that kept him company and were of practical use to him – the cock whose crowing woke him every morning, the mouse who nibbled at his ear when he dozed off and the fly that walked under the words as he read and thus helped him concentrate. These and other stories have come down to us through oral history – although Colman's life is also well described in medieval documents. When King Guaire saw the remote area where his kinsman was living, he persuaded him to move to a more fertile spot and Colman thus founded a monastery at Kilmacduagh – to which many people subsequently came. But as for this place – St Colman's Retreat – it is a place to savour for its peace and tranquillity – a landscape that has hardly changed since Colman's time. As we look up at St Colman's Bed – the little cave were he slept, forty feet above us in the rock-face – we are reminded of the lines written by an anonymous eighth-century monk:

Alone in my small cell
Peace for company
Before meeting with death.

A very cold bed
Fearful, like the sleep
of a doomed man.

Sleep, short and restless,
Invocations
Frequent and early.

Let this place shelter me
These holy walls,
A spot beautiful and sacred
And I there alone.

MULTIPLE INTELLIGENCES

Howard Gardner *proposes his theory that there are seven kinds of intelligence, not one.*

My research over the past twenty-five years has convinced me that each of the claims of the standard view of intelligence is wrong. It isn't a single thing ... it's not something you are born with ... it's not something you can't change ... and it certainly isn't something you can assess adequately with a paper and pencil. I became convinced of this through my study of child development, of different cultures, and of the brain and nervous system. My definition of intelligence takes intelligence partly out of the head and puts it in the interaction between the mind-brain and the opportunities and the needs of society.

I came up with the concept of multiple intelligences. My theory is that the brain has evolved so that people can analyse at least seven different kinds of information and any theory of intelligence has to encompass at least those seven frames of mind. I define an intelligence as the ability to solve a problem or to make something – to fashion a product – that is valued in at least one culture. By 'make something' I mean write a symphony, make a painting, organise a meeting, conduct a successful class, choreograph a dance, hunt an animal and so on. 'Intelligence tests' tell nothing about whether you can ever do anything. People who do well in intelligence tests belong to Mensa, where they congratulate each other about being in Mensa! They may well be able to do other things but that has nothing to do with the 'intelligence' that was measured in tests ... The other important criterion is being valued in at least one culture. You could be very good at doing something but if it is not valued in a culture, it is not intelligent. If you have a wonderful verbal memory and there's no printing around, you are extremely valuable. Once printing is invented, you become a curiosity, because you can look it up. There is no need to memorise any more.

In my book *Frames of Mind*, I propose seven different human intelligences. Any intelligence can be used for lots of different things. All of us have each of these intelligences, but no two people have exactly the same profile of intelligences. Strength in one area does not predict a strength or a weakness in other areas.

– Poets exude *Linguistic Intelligence*. They think in language. I don't believe that any race or ethnic group has a monopoly on any one intelligence but many would say that the Irish have a wide distribution of linguistic intelligence. I wouldn't say it – other people might!

– Logicians, mathematicians, computer experts, scientists have high degrees of *Logical-mathematical Intelligence*. In school these first two types of intelligence are very important and even more important in test-taking. As long as you stay in school, you won't find any discrepant information!

– Many people think in music and have strong *Musical Intelligence*.

– Next is *Spatial Intelligence* – the ability to imagine a large spatial world as a pilot would, or a more circumscribed spatial world as a chess-player or an artist would.

– Then there is a *Bodily-kinaesthetic Intelligence* – the capacity to use your whole body or part of it to make something or solve a problem. Dancers, actors, craftspeople, surgeons, all need high degrees of this intelligence.

– *Inter-personal Intelligence* concerns the capacity to understand the intentions, motivations and desires of other people.

– And *Intra-personal Intelligence* denotes knowledge of self, having a good sense of who you are, what your strengths and desires are, how to navigate your way through the world. For me, this intelligence is becoming more and more important today. In the old days we did what our ancestors did, but today we make our own decisions and choices.

These are the seven major intelligences. There may be more and there are sub-components of these seven. All of this has profound implications for education. In our uniform education everyone is taught the same things and examined in the same way. This is patently unfair and discriminatory in the light of my theory. I favour individual eccentric schooling. We should take our differences very seriously and fashion schooling so that we can reach as many children as possible. The job of the 'assessment specialist' is to figure out the intelligences of the children in a school. If you give them a paper and pencil test, you are passing all the intelligences through a language-logic lens. Information from assessment specialists needs to be shared with 'student curriculum brokers', whose job is to match students with curricula – a mix of required and elective subjects, taught in a plurality of ways. There is also a need for a 'school community broker', who will work with children who don't connect well with school and who will help them find opportunities in their environment which make the best use of their blend of intelligences.

School doesn't have to be the way we remember it! Alas, part of the unschooled mind is to remember school as a big person up front who knows a lot while we all feel very little and unimportant. If we sit in our desks with worksheets we're doing good and if we are talking to other people, we're doing bad. If we know the answer, raise your hands, otherwise duck! This too will pass! It doesn't have to be that way. Multiple Intelligences theory is not a cure, but it does suggest a lot of things we can do with youngsters and there are very few youngsters who cannot connect with something. The most important moment in a child's education is when he connects to something that engages curiosity and stimulates further exploration. For me it is a tragedy that the richest country in the world has so many children – rich and poor – who are bored, alienated and never connect to anything.

EVERYONE IS GOOD AT SOMETHING

A personal claim to ownership of the Theory of Multiple Intelligences!

THE HARVARD EDUCATIONIST, Howard Gardner, has revolutionised much of our thinking on teaching and learning with his Theory of Multiple Intelligences. Whereas we once saw intelligence as a singular concept, Gardner argues that there are many dimensions to it. One may be endowed with musical intelligence or linguistic intelligence or spatial intelligence. The list goes on. At a very basic level this theory argues that everyone is good at something.

I did not realise it at the time but I proposed this theory some twenty-five years ago in one of the first scripts I wrote for radio. It was a story for tiny tots in a programme called *Knock at the Door*. It dealt with the Frog Family's exploits at the Woodland Sports.

Being good sports, the frogs gave every event a try. They entered the Beauty Competition but – as you know – frogs are not the most beautiful of creatures so ... They entered the Singing Competition but – as you know – frogs are not the greatest singers so ... They entered the Jumping Competition and ... well! Fred Frog made such a leap he sailed right over the judges' heads! 'First prize in the Jumping Competition goes to Fred Frog,' proclaimed the startled judges. All the woodland creatures cheered.

The Frog Family went home happy (or – as we would say long ago in our clichéd compositions – 'tired but happy'). 'Well,' Fred Frog croaked, 'we may not be much to look at and we cannot sing very well ... But toddling tadpoles! We surely can jump – can't we?'

Eat your heart out, Howard Gardner!

FROM BRAY TO CALCUTTA

Sr Cyril Mooney – *a Loreto nun from Bray, Co. Wicklow – talks about her pioneering work in education in Calcutta.*

I was born and raised in Wolfe Tone Square in Bray and from an early age I was aware of poverty and injustice. My parents were thrifty and provided well for me, but during the war years I went to school with children who were barefoot and often hungry. At the age of thirteen I felt the Lord calling me to do his work. I joined the Loreto order and have been working in India since 1956. I am principal of a 1,400-pupil girls' school in Calcutta. Our policy is an open-door policy. Entrance is totally random and our children are of many faiths and come from backgrounds that range from reasonably well-off to the homeless children of the streets.

Some years ago I became concerned about the plight of rural schools outside Calcutta, where villagers would erect a mud shanty and employ a master. If they could keep the master alive for five years, the government would then give him a salary. These schools might have up to four hundred pupils with two masters. I arranged a meeting between the teachers in my school and about forty of those masters and discussed how we might improve the education of the rural children. We arranged that our city children would go out and teach the rural children. Initially this was done at weekends in nineteen schools, with the masters monitoring what was going on. We were not trying to impose our ways or pontificate. We were offering a service from which we hoped the masters would develop their own ideas.

The reaction was positive. They wanted to see us more regularly, so now our children go out every Thursday (our school holiday) to teach 2,500 rural children. We send out 150 of our secondary girls (aged ten upwards) each week. There are about 600 girls in the secondary school, so each girl goes out once every four weeks. Every girl goes out. The ten-year-olds teach four-year-olds, the eleven-year-olds teach five-year-olds and so on up through primary school. This means that in a school where there might be 120 pupils to one master, those pupils get individual

THE CURIOUS MIND

attention once a week. I constantly remind our girls that they are receiving more than they are giving. There is no sense of 'we're the grand ladies from the city going out to help the poor'.

Our own well-trained teachers do a mini-teaching course with our children before they go out – how to teach a lesson, how to prepare a lesson plan. The topics for teaching are put up on a big notice board at the beginning of term. The rural children are divided into groups of ten and they will work with the same four children from the city. Each Friday the four 'teacher-children' meet, discuss what has been taught and plan the next week's lesson – this provides continuity. The curriculum would embrace the environment, health, nutrition, science and mathematics – expanding the work the masters are doing. The ten-year-olds are the best teachers – totally enthusiastic and dedicated. It does wonders for their dignity and self-confidence. It is marvellous to see a child who has come in to us from the slums walking tall when she goes out to the village and sharing what she has learned with other children. Often I notice that the children who are struggling with their own lessons are the better teachers. They are more patient, more understanding.

We explained this project to the parents also – how it would develop qualities of responsibility, service, patriotism in their children – and won them over in this way. India is the fifth most technologically advanced country in the world and yet has the greatest number of people living below the poverty line. When you draw people's attention to that, they rise to the challenge. The teachers are equally supportive. They go out with the children to supervise. It means giving up one or two Thursdays per term. They aren't paid for this. You don't pay people for patriotism. The parents can see the tremendous return their children are getting – in self-confidence, responsibility and character-formation. Interestingly, our children's academic performance has improved enormously at the same time. A local charity gave us a bus and every Thursday we pack 150 children into that bus like sardines! This couldn't happen in Ireland but it is very much the Indian way.

We have also opened up our school to the street children. They literally live on the pavement under a tarpaulin or cardboard shelter. They have drifted into the city from outlying areas in search of a living. Some of them have their parents with them and may have to work to help out, so school attendance is irregular. There are other street children with no parents – no adult influence – and they are at the mercy of total exploitation. Our school is available to the street children whenever they are available.

During the school day there will always be one period devoted to work education where craftwork is taught, so at any one time we have a reservoir of about fifty regular students at one end of the terrace. The Rainbow children from the streets come in at the other end. (We call them Rainbow children because they unite all of us and because they come and go like the rainbow.) We might get fifty or seventy or twenty rainbow children. The regular children meet them and teach them on a one-to-one basis. They teach them their letters and work their way up to books. The rainbow children learn the letters in a little pot of sand, tracing the letters in sand, before moving on to paper. For homework they search for the letter of the day on buses, hoardings etc. If they are reasonably regular, the rainbow children can be literate in three months. They value reading greatly and become very eager students.

For me this work is simply living out my religious ethics. I am not evangelising or trying to spread Christian ethics. I myself want to live that Christian ethic (do unto others as you would have others do to you). If others, seeing that, receive a witness of Christ's love for other people, that is fine but it is not my objective. Within the hearts of our children we plant the seed of compassion, the capacity to put yourself into another person's skin and feel what that person feels. The projects we run in our school are my way of responding to what Christ asks of me.

FLYING KITES WITH MR YEATS

Sean McBride *recalls a colourful childhood in France and Ireland.*

I was born in Paris in 1904 and, on and off, I would have spent five or six years of my childhood in Paris. I was actually christened in Terenure,

Dublin, despite the objection of the parish priest to my godfather, the Fenian John O'Leary. I learned later that there was a police file on the whole event – I suppose because my father was on the run after the Boer War. My very earliest memory is of travelling around Donegal and Mayo with my mother in a long cart and seeing a priest in a tall hat.

I went initially to a Jesuit school in Paris and did very well academically. Our house in Paris was very much an open house. John O'Leary and Roger Casement came there, as did some Indian revolutionary leaders. My favourite visitor was the writer James Stephens. He was a great storyteller. He told me about his namesake, the Fenian leader. 'He wasn't small like me. He was a big, burly man. Once when police tried to arrest him, he lifted four of them in the air at once, and escaped!' He would take me out to indulge in my passion for stamp-collecting. He gave me a certain amount of money to spend and then sat in the corner of the shop reading while I made my choices. Then we went to Rumplemeyers for ice-cream and cake – and lots of stories from James Stephens. I idolised him. Yeats was a regular visitor too. We had a house by the sea in Normandy. Yeats bought me a kite and taught me to fly it. He was really good at it and probably enjoyed it more than me. I was maybe too young at the time.

In 1914 I was brought to St Enda's School in Rathfarnham to be interviewed by Pádraig Pearse. It was really to find out how advanced I was in the various subjects, but most of the time was taken up with mother and Pearse discussing political issues. They were particularly concerned with Roger Casement's idea of developing new shipping lines with the USA and Europe so as not to be dependent on British lines in the event of war. When war did break out we were in the Pyrenees Mountains. Mother rushed back to Ireland and that was an anxious time for me until she returned. On her return to France she was asked to set up a hospital for war casualties. I remember being involved with her in that, even though I was only ten. We stayed on in Paris. I recall having to do an hour's daily compulsory reading of Irish history during the school holidays – to make up for what I was missing in the French school.

When my father was executed after the 1916 Rising, the Jesuits were very kind to me. There was a Commemoration Day each week for parents who had been killed in the war. The Director made a most moving speech, explaining that France was at war to protect the freedom of small nations and my father had been fighting for the freedom of his small nation. They had, therefore, tremendous sympathy for what the Irish were trying to do. In the middle of my personal trauma, his speech was a great comfort to me. It smoothed things out with the other boys.

We eventually returned to Ireland in 1917. Mother was under police surveillance and was ultimately arrested and detained in London. I travelled over and stayed in Yeats' house, so that I could visit her. Later I stayed with Yeats near Coole in Galway and then I moved to Tulira Castle to stay with Edward Martyn. I cycled in to Gort to a teacher for lessons in English and Irish. I was very fond of Martyn and I loved Tulira. Martyn would not appear until the evening time. We had dinner in the huge dining hall, after which he would smoke a big clay pipe which invariably broke when he let it fall. The morning papers arrived in Tulira in the evening and I would have to read the headlines to Martyn. He retired early to his bedroom on the ground floor. My room was upstairs. I had to climb the winding stair by candlelight and make my way down corridors. I was terrified. If ever there was a place for ghosts, Tulira was it. However, I never met any.

Martyn was quite a character. He was expelled from the Kildare Street Club in Dublin when it was discovered he was a Catholic. He took legal action and won his case. Subsequently he would sit in an armchair in the big window overlooking Nassau Street with a huge wooden rosary beads. This daily performance would enrage the other club members. It was one of the sights of Dublin at the time. A crowd of forty or fifty people would gather in the street to watch the performance.

Later I spent about eighteen months in Mount St Benedict school near Gorey in Co. Wexford under another marvellous character, Fr Sweetman. Because I was more advanced than my peers in Latin and Mathematics, I had a lot of time off – which I spent delivering telegrams for the local postmistress, or catching rabbits which I then sold to the school. My early ambition had been to be a farmer-cum-lawyer. I would live off my farm and chose the legal cases I would take on. Sadly, due to my subsequent political involvement, it didn't quite turn out like that.

SUNLIGHT

Her name is PATRICIA SUN. *And yes, she comes from California. And yes, now that you ask, she is a psychologist. Here comes the West Coast psychobabble, you say. No. Here comes a lot of common sense, lively, positive thinking on how we learn.*

WHEN I MET Patricia Sun in the mid-1990s, she began with the Indian parable of the six blind men who were asked to describe an elephant.

> 'It's like a rope,' said the one who felt the tail.
> 'Not at all, more like a tree-trunk,' said the one who felt the elephant's leg.
> 'A wall, I should say,' said the one who stood under its belly.
> 'Ridiculous,' said the fourth man, holding its trunk. 'It's a serpent.'
> The fifth man caught hold of the elephant's tusk. 'It's a spear.'
> 'You're all wrong,' the last man pronounced, fondling the animal's ear. 'It's a fan.'

The problem is, Patricia explains, they were all right but they were also all wrong. Just as every experience you have ever had is correct, except that it's wrong!

Excuse me, Patricia! Elaborate please!
Well, it's simply this. There is a whole lot more to reality than we can ever know. The problem has to do with the two hemispheres in our brain. The left brain controls the right side of our body. For a long time left-brain thinking has dominated our approach to learning and teaching.

The left brain produces logical, linear, cause-and-effect thinking. Did it happen or didn't it? Is it right or is it wrong? Is there a book on it? What's the answer? I need to know *now*, before I start! The linear-mind approach to learning was the old approach of *I tell you – you hear it – now you know it*. It was Mr Gradgrind's way. Give them the facts! Not any more. If you had never seen an elephant before and I presented you with a rope, a tree, a wall, a serpent, a spear and a fan – would you know what an elephant was? I doubt it. But if I brought an elephant into this room and you could see it, feel it, smell it, hear it – I guarantee you, you would know what an elephant is and you would never forget it!

So what are you saying to me, Patricia?
I'm saying to you that you have only heard half the story. There is also the right hemisphere of the brain. And for too long it has been ignored.

Did you know, Patricia Sun asks, that the medical profession often refers to the right brain as the 'minor hemisphere'? (*She gives a little sigh and continues*). We are a relatively young species. We are growing up. We are still learning about the right brain. The right brain is not logical. It thinks in pictures, feelings. It is very involved in art, genius, music. The ancients spoke of the Muses who would take them over. Call it inspiration, if you will, but the ancients produced art, music, poetry and didn't know how they had got it.

This is the intuitive mind. It is open, receptive, innocent. It is the child, open-mouthed in wonder, asking 'how did that happen?' Everybody has that innocence. It takes a conscious will to call it up, but once called, it has endless possibilities. The intuitive mind functions by being asked. It is 'supposing ...' It is 'what if ... ?' It is how great discoveries are made in science, in art. The scientist, the artist cannot quite explain the discovery. They began by just wondering ... They gave expression to their feelings. Depression on the other hand is simply de-pressed energy. There is talent, ability, the desire to move, but every door is closed. The linear mind locks us into a kind of paralysis, but the trick is to invent a new door ...

To live, to be alive, you must engage with *risk* – not necessarily big risk but 'one step at a time' risk. If you try very, very hard not to be wrong, you are close to death ... It's like the child learning how to tie her shoelaces. If the parent repeatedly says, 'No! No! No! You don't do it that way ...' the child will give up and say 'You do it for me, then ...' We learn from mistakes. Wasn't it Edison who invented the light-bulb? He is said to have failed a hundred times before getting it right but he saw nothing 'wrong' in that. 'On the contrary,' he said, 'I learned a hundred things that don't work!'

So Patricia, are we all to become intuitive thinkers and ditch the linear mind?
Of course not. The linear mind is logical and I am pro-logic! The linear mind is a great computer that discerns and sorts reality. That is wonderful, but reality is larger than logic can hold. So I am pro-intuition too. We must accept both minds and find new ways of approaching learning. There are thousands of questions that have not been asked before and thousands of solutions. The intent to know – the curiosity – should lock into both hemispheres.

That's learning. What about teaching, Patricia?
Teaching is making room for that to happen. The great teacher will orchestrate this 'wholebrain' approach ... be willing to digress, to follow the interesting, the curiosity, the joy of discovery. The great teacher will be innocent, open, in search of a new way. And when that teacher gets stuck, 'doesn't know', admit it and ask the students. And be prepared to be surprised ...

A HIDDEN, WASTED IRELAND

SEAN O'CONNOR, *an extremely influential civil servant with the Department of Education, recalls a boyhood friend and a book, both of which motivated him.*

IN MY EARLY days in school in Dingle, Co. Kerry, I had a very close friend from my own street, who was in my class. Every morning when I arrived at school he borrowed my home exercise book and copied about two-thirds of what I had done in Maths. Four out of six answers got him above the danger line for a whack from the teacher.

I was always unhappy about this – not because he cogged: others did it too, but because he didn't have to. He was bright, sharp, the leader of our street group and a natural musician. Any instrument that came his way – flute, fife, melodeon, mouth-organ, Jew's harp – he could play it. But he had no interest in schooling. He could read, write and add – that was all he needed from school because he was leaving as soon as ever he could. His parents, apparently, had no interest in education; the older members of the family had left school early and emigrated to the USA. He also would leave in a year or two, so why waste time now on algebra or Latin verbs or Irish verse? Because I admired him, and indeed envied his musical aptitude, I felt in a rather incoherent fashion that he hadn't got a fair deal – that here was waste.

I went to another school and later entered the civil service in the early 1930s. I got myself involved in the language movement and, in the course of my reading, read Daniel Corkery's *The Hidden Ireland*. Corkery's book is mainly about the Munster poets, in particular Eoin Rua O Súilleabháin, most of whose poetry I don't greatly admire. But it did not bring me any closer to the poets themselves. Rather did it bring into focus for me the enormous disadvantages suffered by the ordinary Irish people since the Battle of Kinsale, particularly the lack of educational opportunity. This I knew about already, but had never made much of it until Corkery's book forced me to think seriously about it. The disdain of my boyhood friend in Dingle exemplified for me not so much the lack of opportunity but the fact that continued denial of opportunity breeds indifference so that, when opportunity presents itself again, there is no hurry to take it up. This matter of educational opportunity became my first and lasting priority in education.

Many years later, in 1968 to be exact, as head of the Development Branch of the Department of Education, I was involved in meetings throughout the country in pursuit of the development and expansion of educational opportunity. On a particular day in March I undertook to speak at an education meeting under VEC auspices in Tallaght, Dublin, at eight o'clock in the evening. On the same day I had to attend a meeting in Enniscorthy. Because I was extremely busy I did not have a script for the Tallaght meeting, but I had prepared some notes.

I should say here that some three or four days previously I found in a bookshop a paperback copy of Corkery's book *The Hidden Ireland* (the copy I had in the 1930s had long disappeared). I had started to leaf through it again and had found that it still affected me as before. Now however I was trying to do something to remedy the disadvantage where it existed. On the way back to Tallaght from Enniscorthy, instead of giving thought to my notes for the meeting, four lines quoted in the book from a poem by Eoin Rua dominated my thoughts.

I was the last speaker that night and when my time came I found I couldn't speak from my notes. Instead I told the audience about my re-reading of Corkery's book and about the four lines that had been disturbing me all day. I recited the four lines and gave an off-the-cuff translation. The lines were:

> *Iar gcaitheamh an lae má's tréith nó tuirseach mo chnámha,*
> *Is go n-abrann an maor nach éachtach m'acfuinn ar ráinn,*
> *Labharfad féin go séimh ar eachtra an bháis,*
> *Nó ar chathaibh na nGréig 'san Trae d'fhúig flatha go tláith.*

> At the day's end should my bones be sore and weary,
> And the ganger say I am no great shakes with a spade,
> I will speak evenly of the exploits of death
> Or of Greek wars in Troy where the blood of princes flowed.

I centred my address on parents, spoke about the total lack of formal education in the poet's time, and besought them, first, not to let the opportunities in education then available go unused by their children, and second, to look for further improvement in the provision of educational facilities.

ON DISCIPLINE

ALFIE KOHN *argues against the use of rewards and punishment as ways of maintaining discipline in the classroom.*

EARLIER IN MY career I taught in a secondary school. I felt I had to maintain control over the classroom. I used grades to motivate students and the more I tried the worse things got. In 1986 I wrote a book entitled *No Contest: The Case Against Competition* – in which I argued that competition is the very opposite of excellence. When we set children or adults up against each other in a race to win, they end up losing interest in what they are doing, not doing it as well, starting to doubt themselves and feeling alienated from just about everyone.

I haven't found a shred of evidence to support the notion that competition is part of human nature. All the research I did led me back to the classroom – to think about how we can create classrooms in which children learn with each other rather than against each other, where we can promote caring and responsibility and tap into the potential goodness in humans, where we can engage in learning for its own sake instead of being based on rewards and punishment. This – I acknowledge – may seem to run counter to the culture of competition that besets our society generally, but the fact that competition is a pervasive part of society is not an argument on its behalf. There is research that shows that when workers try to best each other, they tend not to be as innovative or creative as when they didn't have to compete. W. Edwards Demming – the great management guru – argued very strongly that competition kills quality.

Most of us experienced the 'doing to' approach of our schooldays.

'Doing to' is about manipulating students into acting the way we unilaterally demand – by coercion, by punishment or by rewards. The child either asks, 'What do they want me to do and what happens to me if I don't do it?' or 'What do they want me to do and what do I get for doing it?' In both cases it's about conformity to what others want and it's about myself, not others. When children are punished, they learn about power, aggression, making others do what you want. Equally when they are rewarded they tend to be less generous with others. Punishment and rewards can only buy temporary compliance. They cannot help develop commitment to an action when the punisher or rewarder is no longer around. I'm not arguing against love and acknowledgement and encouragement, but *praise* is often a way of manipulating children to do what we want. It is more a method of control than support.

The alternative to keeping control over children is not to let them run wild, but to take a more democratic approach. We would do well as teachers and parents to talk less and ask more. When we ask children about their experience, we help them to become thoughtful and reflective people who are compassionate and responsible. A lot of children and young adults who do horrible things are children who experienced too much discipline, too much control, whose opinions were never valued. Every human being needs to be autonomous, to be self-determining, to have some say over the things that happen to them. If you're told what to do all the time, you grow up trying to reclaim your autonomy, and you may well do that in unproductive and anti-social ways.

I recognise this can cause major psychological turmoil for parents today, because at a very deep level we desperately want to believe that our parents had the right idea and punished us – often with physical force – out of love. If someone like me comes along and says the old ways were not the best ways, a lot of people will become very defensive about their parents. It's much easier to dismiss critics by saying that's utopian or that's liberal nonsense. There are many impediments to implementing a 'working with' approach in the classroom instead of a 'doing to' approach. Large class size would be at the top of this list. That militates against creating a community in the classroom. Covering the curriculum can be another impediment. The most effective teaching is not about covering a curriculum but about discovering ideas, where the teacher is a guide in exploring issues that matter to children.

Despite those and other impediments, I have seen many classrooms where teachers work magic – discipline problems are virtually nil and children are excited to come to school and to learn. I love the kind of classroom where I walk in and it takes me a minute to find the teacher. He's not up in front of them, lecturing them, pouring facts into empty vessels. He's on the side, as a guide, facilitating the process by which kids come to answer their questions and solve their problems and learn to be responsible.

People will say to me, 'I came up through a punishment and reward system. It never did me any harm ...' I have two questions for them. One is rather pointed. 'Did you *really* come through unscathed? Are you *really* as healthy as you like to believe?' I look around at US society and see people who are unsure of themselves, or too full of themselves, whose relationships are unstable, who are indifferent to others' suffering ... precisely what we would expect from a pattern of punishment, reward and control. The second question is more gentle. I ask, 'Did you come through unscathed because of or in spite of that system?' I think it is the latter.

'Working with' children is very demanding. Creating a warm, caring relationship with children, giving children choice about what they are doing but helping to guide those choices takes care and time and talent and skill and courage. There's a range of talent and skill within teaching as within any profession, but I see a lot of teachers who are not able to live up to their own potential because they are placed in a system which limits their capacity to develop a relationship with children. 'Working with children' also demands a lot of principals. A good principal has to create opportunities for teachers to come together to form a community of adults who care about each other. A principal must not be a dictator, must not run most faculty meetings. That job should rotate among interested staff members. And of course we must open dialogue with parents as to their long-term goals for their children and how those goals might best be attained. It's all about curriculum, community – and choices.

THIS PLACE SPEAKS TO ME
(Three Further Scenes)

SCENE FOUR: *On the side of the holy mountain of Maiméan,*
JOHN O'DONOHUE *contemplates a Connemara landscape.*

LANDSCAPE IS THE first-born of creation. It has a huge pre-human memory. It was here for hundreds of millions of years before plants, animals or humans came along. It must have seemed very strange to the eye of landscape when we humans arrived here. That of course depends on whether you think of landscape as dead matter or as a living presence. For me there is life and memory here. The more you live among mountains, the more you become aware of the cadences of the place and the subtlety of its presence and personality.

As we look across this landscape on this June morning, we see a whole narrative unfolding through mist and fog. How lunar it looks! Of course it is mainly bog – which is the afterlife of a forest. Looking down now on the major emptiness and the bare granite, it is hard to believe that there was a time when all of this was covered in forest. I wrote a poem that tries to capture that concept.

THE ANGEL OF THE BOG

The angel of the bog mourns in the wind
That loiters all over these black meadows.
Remembers how it chose branches to strum
From the orchestra of trees that stood here;
How at twilight a chorus of birds came
To silence in nests of darkening air.

Raindrops filter through leaves, silver the air,
Wash off the film of dust to release nets
Of fragrance on which the wind can sweeten
Before expiring among the debris
That brightens each year with fallen colour
Before the weight of winter seals the ground.

The dark eyes of the angel of the bog
Never open now when dawn comes to dress
The famished grass with splendid veils of red,
Amber, white, as if its soul were urgent
And young with possibility and dreams
That a vanished life might become visible.

If the human eye could have looked out here, ten thousand years ago, what a sight it would have beheld – everything covered in grey, dead ice. It must have been incredibly frightening for the landscape to have been suffocated under hundreds of feet of pack ice and to have lived that way for thousands of years. Imagine then the first trickles of water as the ice retreated and the sun touched the landscape again and seeds hidden for so long began to waken. Landscape has a memory of that time of ice that humans know nothing about.

It's lovely to see how animals are at home in the landscape. Look at the sheep – the undercover mystics of the Connemara landscape – in their Zen mode of stillness, lying in the middle of the road ruminating on something totally different from us! And then there is a huge population of birds here. They know this landscape better than any human foot or eye. Who knows – maybe the next breakthrough in the evolution of human consciousness might be the subtle complexity of that hidden inner world that animals carry around with them.

Animals carry huge witness to the silence of time and the depth of nature. Of course, silence tends to frighten us as humans. Meister Eckhart said that nothing in the universe resembles God so much as silence. To come into silence is to come into the presence of the divine – that silence of intimacy where no word is needed, where a word might even be a fracture. One of the great healing functions of landscape is that it is the custodian of a great unclaimed silence that urbanised post-modern society has not raided yet. This landscape, living in a mode of silence, is wrapped in seamless prayer.

My gran used to bring me down here. No day was complete without a visit to the Coalquay. The morning was the best time. The dealers would come at about eleven o'clock and take up their stands. The clothes-dealers would throw down bundles of old clothes and start selling. The vegetable-sellers came in from the market gardens out in Ballyphehane. 'Balls of temptation, Mam,' the potato-seller would cry out. The pubs opened at seven a.m. to catch the early trade and there were 'eating-houses' for the farmers where they could have big mugs of tea and rough 'boats' of bread. Nothing very dainty, but wasn't it grand for them to have their breakfast before going back to the country. The most famous house in Coalquay was Kattie Barry's shebeen, which only opened after the pubs had closed. It wasn't a very posh place but patrons sat around and talked and drank while Kattie might be out the back boiling up a big pot of crubeens!

After the war, bananas came in and we went stone mad for them. We didn't want 'poppies' or cabbage. We would have bananas for breakfast, dinner and tea if we could and we plagued our poor mother for them and she would buy a shilling's worth every day. The dealers knew she was a widow with seven children, so they kept the biggest bunch of bananas for her. She was a dressmaker, so she might buy an old woman's coat for twopence from a dealer, take it home, turn it inside out, rip it and make it into a coat for one of us. Put a bit of velvet on the collar and you would be handsome on a Sunday for threepence ... The greatest bargain of all was the card of sample buttons. There was a gross of buttons on each card, all different colours. The dealer had a tea-chest full of cards, so my mother would root through it until she found six identical cards, which cost her a shilling. These lasted forever – she could have six identical buttons to sew on a coat or dress. When we lost the markers for our Ludo game, we replaced them with buttons.

The foodstalls were not the most hygienic. The fish stall was an old block of wood and a chopper to cut the heads off the mackerel or herring.

Sprats were very popular in Cork. Small little fellows. You cut the head off with a scissors and the little gut came away. Boil them up lovely and the little bones all melted. My grandfather always said that sprats were the cleanest fish in the sea. Over there were the randy butchers – not that they were randy themselves, mind! Quick as they would look at you, they would pass off a bit of goat for mutton or lamb – and of course the goat is known for being randy, hence the name!

Other stalls had books and gramophone records – stacks of them a few feet high at threepence each. My mother loved John McCormack but we loved Jimmy O'Dea's sketches – *Casey at the Dentist, Casey at the Pawnshop* etc. Our gramophone took thirteen windings – any more and you broke the spring. Then you had to load it into the pram and take it down to a man in a little room on Bachelor's Quay to have it fixed. On Saturday mornings little stages were set up for entertainers. One fellow – a contortionist – could turn himself into a monkey. Another would lie on a bed of nails or glass. And there was the fellow who claimed he could remove all stains out of clothes. He took a boy from the audience, threw ink on his shirt and then made it disappear by rubbing 'magic' blue stuff on the stain. My mother was very impressed, bought the stuff and tried the same trick with my brother's Communion shirt. She destroyed the shirt. 'The divil hoist that fellow,' she cried. 'If I ever see him again, I'll reef him!' Of course, she never did see him again. There was Banjo Annie who sang songs like *Two Little Girls in Blue*. There would be fights too but it was all an act. On Saturday night, a fellow in a candlelit booth used to do Shakespeare speeches. He'd get them all wrong, but it was brilliant altogether. Where else would you get such entertainment for nothing?

This was the real heart of Cork in those days. All life was here, but now it's all cars and progress.

Patrick Pearse called Cave Hill 'Ireland's Holy Mountain'. He was obviously referring to Wolfe Tone's visit here in 1795 with Thomas Russell, Henry Joy McCracken and others. Tone recorded in his diary that they undertook a solemn obligation 'never to desist in our efforts until we had subverted the authority of England over our own country and had asserted our independence'. So Cave Hill has political associations but in my time here – I spent twenty years of my life in Belfast – it was a playground for the people of North Belfast. There was a dancehall, cafes, concert parties around the bandstand.

As a young lad I loved to climb up to McArt's Fort – a basalt cliff jutting out over Belfast. You were eleven hundred feet above the lough and it was great on a summer evening to watch the tiny boats below sail out to Heysham, Liverpool, Glasgow and Ardrossan. From the city you could hear the clangour of the shipyards and the hooting of the factory sirens. With my friend I would make a fire and we would boil up a billy-can for tea and maybe fry eggs and bacon. Heaven, with wild bilberries to follow! I got the fright of my life one evening when standing at the edge of the cliff. A big white face appeared in front of me. We stood looking at each other until it dropped away. It was my first time to encounter a barn owl.

Alice Milligan wrote about this place in her poem 'Ben Madigan':

> Look up from the streets of the city,
> Look high beyond tower and mast;
> What hand of what Titan sculptor
> Smote the crags on the mountain vast?
> Made when the world was fashioned,
> Meant with the world to last,
> The glorious face of the sleeper
> Slumbers above Belfast.

Not far from here stood a famous house – now demolished. It was 'Ardree', the home of Francis Joseph Biggar. It wasn't just his home. It was a cultural centre. Frank Biggar encouraged and subsidised various writers, musicians and artists. He was a remarkably open-minded, generous man. No one who had a project that would advance Irish consciousness would be turned down by him. He had an insatiable desire to see his country improved and its heritage maintained. He had a big stone placed outside the church in Downpatrick to mark the alleged grave of St Patrick. He had Jordan's Castle in Ardglass restored. He even restored a number of public houses, although he was a non-drinker. He was known as the Franciscan Presbyterian. Although he was a Presbyterian, he had great devotion to St Francis and indeed to Mary.

Ardree was an open house for all. No one was turned away from Biggar's door. He poured out money for a variety of causes and projects. Eoin McNeill, Roger Casement, Bulmer Hobson would be regular visitors. Joseph Campbell described Biggar as 'the lordliest type of Irishman it has ever been my luck to meet'. A most remarkable man was Francis Joseph Biggar. He is buried at Mallusk in Co. Antrim.

CULTIVATING GOOD HABITS

A meeting with one of the world's great gurus of leadership and effectiveness,
STEPHEN COVEY.

A JUNE EVENING in 1998. I am in the Europa Hotel, Belfast, to meet with Stephen Covey of the Covey Leadership Centre and author of the ten-million-selling *Seven Habits of Highly Effective People*. Belfast is the last stop in a gruelling world tour for him and he has just spent the evening leading a family renewal meeting in a Belfast church. He is exhausted but still finds time at a late hour to talk about those seven habits.

HABIT ONE: Be Proactive
We are each responsible for our own lives. Proactive people don't blame circumstances, conditions or their conditioning for their behaviour. Their behaviour is a product of their own conscious choice, based on values.

HABIT TWO: Begin with the End in Mind
Have a clear understanding of your destination. You can be very, very busy climbing the ladder of success only to discover it is leaning against the wrong wall! Imagine yourself as an observer at your own funeral. What would you like family, colleagues, friends to remember about you?

HABIT THREE: Put First Things First
Learn how to say No, how to delegate. The way you spend your time is a result of the way you see your time and the way you set your priorities. Deal with the things that are not urgent, but important.

HABIT FOUR: Think Win/Win
Win/Win means agreements or solutions that are mutually beneficial, mutually satisfying. It is a belief in the Third Alternative – not your way, not my way, but a better way. The recent Peace Agreement in Northern Ireland is an example of Win/Win. There are four steps to Win/Win:

1. See the problem from the other point of view.
2. Identify the key issues and concerns.
3. Decide what results would constitute an acceptable solution.
4. Identify possible new options to achieve these results.

HABIT FIVE: Seek First to Understand, Then to be Understood
We need to get outside our own 'rightness', our own story. We need to develop empathic listening. When we really understand each other, we open the door to creative solutions and third alternatives. Habit Five is the essence of professionalism.

HABIT SIX: Synergise

Synergy means the whole is greater than the sum of the parts. In a relationship, there is a part between the two parts and if that part is good, full of high trust, you release tremendous creative energy and new ideas come up, so that you produce a larger pie. A cornucopia of opportunities is opened up to people who are synergistic. I can see this happening in Ireland. If there is true synergy between North and South and if there is commitment to constant development and investment in people, this country could be a tourist haven. Synergy demands risk and spontaneity and often works best on the edge of chaos.

HABIT SEVEN: Sharpen the Saw!

A man is worn out sawing down a tree for hours. Someone says, 'Why don't you sharpen the saw?' He replies, 'I'm too busy sawing'.

We need to renew ourselves regularly – physically, mentally, emotionally, spiritually. This habit helps to develop and cultivate the other six habits. If you sharpen the saw for one hour a day, it affects the quality of every other hour of the day. It affects the quality of our decisions, our relationships, every aspect of our lives. The key thing is to get centred on that which nourishes the deepest part of your life – and do that for an hour each day.

CORNELIUS RABBIT AND OTHER FRIENDS

In the very last 'Open Mind' Guest Lecture (2002), PATRICIA DONLON *celebrated 'a life with books'. Here she tells how books enriched her childhood.*

OURS WAS A house that respected books – although we owned very few. Still Christmas and birthdays always brought a book for me – even when I couldn't read them for myself. I had a big sister, May, who would read to me – to help coax me to eat, to get me to go to sleep, or simply just to amuse me. She'd read from *Bunnikin's Picnic Party*, or *Mabel Lucie Atwell's Annual*, or best of all from the *Cornelius Rabbit of Tang* books.

Mary Flynn, the author of these books, was a primary school teacher who clearly had a great empathy with her young students and understood very well how they would respond to her stories. The other wonderful thing about Tang – the setting for all three Cornelius stories – is the realisation that this is real, this is home and this is Ireland. For 'Tang is a town in the middle of a wide, wide bog'. It has a railway station with a big glass roof so that 'it always seemed to be a fine day no matter how gloomy the weather is'.

The hero of these stories is Cornelius, eldest in a family of rabbits who live in the tallest house in Tang. His best friends are Edward Elephant and Una Lamb. They dress as we do, and live as we do despite appearances to the contrary – and the best bit is that they are almost all the same size, which never struck me then as even remotely odd. They have adventures that are just a tiny bit out of the ordinary, maybe the sort of thing that could happen to you and me, only it never did. They go on the train on holidays, and picnic by the river. They help with the haymaking and go to the bog where Cornelius finds an old gold goblet, which is promptly taken to the local museum, where due credit and a small reward come our hero's way. Cornelius can get ahead of himself sometimes and can't resist showing off or having the odd boast – but never for long, because inevitably life and the wise writer take him back down to earth with a bang.

The illustrations were by Eileen Coghlan, and were produced in a two-colour ink process in those Talbot Press books, which were modestly printed and bound. Yet despite their modest appearance, those books were memorable, and I read and re-read them constantly. Some decades later, before I had actively rekindled my passion for children's books, I was at a dinner party where somehow or other the topic of conversation got around to the books we read when young. To my amazement, three or four of those present not only had read the Cornelius books but also were as big fans as I was. The room rang with questions such as: Do you remember when he slid down the banisters, only to find the cushion was gone? Can you remember the Test? And Old Grey Rabbit's long, long cottage? And Cornelius as Mayor? ... I'm sure it is no coincidence that Phelim – my husband of thirty-seven years – also had Cornelius as part of his childhood reading.

There were other stories too – *The Wind Fairies* by Elizabeth Brennan, who employed a clever device where each of the Winds has its own troupe of fairies, some good, some downright bad. On windy nights, I would disappear underneath the bedcovers, convinced that it was the wicked East Wind Fairies that were rattling the windowpane and making the curtains blow, as they came to seek me out.

My father too would read to me and the memory of the prickly tweed of his jacket, the rough stubble on his chin at the end of his day's work, are forever linked to his reading aloud from *Curly Wee and Gussie Goose*, the annual compilation of the cartoon strip in the daily paper. Once I could read for myself then life was different and by then the whole world had expanded. The effect on me was similar to the effect on Dorothy when she walks through that door in the Land of Oz. Suddenly I had lots and lots of new and exotic friends – Milly-Molly-Mandy and Little Friend Susan – in their quintessentially English setting; Heidi, with her grandfather high up in the Swiss mountains; and William of *Just William* fame and his female counterpart Jane.

I read whenever and wherever I got the opportunity. Because my sister was older than me, and because my mother had notions of me 'making something' of myself, I was not allowed to play with the local children – too rough you understand. So my childhood was a solitary one that would have been a lonely one but for the company of my books and book friends. I lived my life to a certain extent through those books and characters. My clothes were all either hand-me-downs or home-made and how I empathised with Anne Shirley of *Anne of Green Gables* when she proclaimed: 'It's ever so much easier to be good if your clothes are fashionable.'

Our family was small, but I lost myself in the bustle and warmth of the March family of *Little Women*. In truth I was probably much more like silly, priggish Amy but fancied myself as Jo, as she climbed into the

THE CURIOUS MIND

attic to munch apples and cry over some heroine in *her* book. I even took to saying 'Christopher Columbus' – the boldest utterance from Jo's mouth – and I wept bitter tears when she refused Laurie, the boy next door. I read it so often that I'm almost convinced I could recite it by heart.

In between multiple readings of *Little Women*, though, I met Ratty and Mole and fell under the spell of *The Wind in the Willows*; was caught up with Sheila and the little goose Betsy in Patricia Lynch's *Grey Goose of Kilnevin*; and met lots and lots of indistinguishable, hockey-wielding, midnight-feasting, jolly school girls, with wonderful names like Penelope. There was, of course, the odd madcap or orphan, such as Judy in Jean Webster's *Daddy-Long-Legs* whose pronouncement – 'I've determined never to marry; it's a deteriorating process, evidently' – I chose to ignore.

When I was about twelve I had a strange fit of piety. I was going to renounce the world, become a nun and be promoted to Reverend Mother on the ladder to sainthood. I'm glad to say that phase didn't last very long – just long enough for me to decide that a major sacrifice was called for. I decided that I would give away all my old books to the local orphanage (such sacrifices gained you lots of heavenly brownie points). I regret to say that I spent most of the intervening years either begrudging the poor orphans, or else plotting a raid to reclaim that precious hoard. Over the years I've managed to buy back most if not all of them – and each reunion has reclaimed for me the magic of the first reading.

These days I wish I had not been so mean-spirited about my 'gift'. For it is impossible to think about Ireland over the last fifty to sixty years and not be shocked, ashamed and bruised by the appalling treatment, negligence and abuse of those most precious, vulnerable members of our society – our children. We have failed miserably to understand that all children are precious; we have failed to watch over them, to protect them from abuse and neglect. We have – over and over again – contravened the United Nations Convention on the Rights of the Child – a charter for any country that wishes to be considered civilised. I don't know what it was that they read – these children in homes and institutions where abuse took place. I harbour a tiny seed of hope that they had books and stories to escape into, that they too journeyed into 'once upon a time' or to 'over the hills and far away' – to a better, kinder world of happy families, or enchanted forests, or most likely to Neverland and the island of little lost boys.

My life with books has passed its half-century, yet I never cease to marvel at books, at their construction, the paper, the typography, the illustrations, the binding, the beauty, the touch and feel of books. All parents are an embarrassment to their children at some stage or other and I am proud to say that I am no exception. When my children were very much smaller than they are today and were forced – or so they would have it – to come into endless second-hand and antiquarian bookshops, they would inevitably plead as we headed for the door, 'You won't smell the books, will you?' But I did, and I still do. I love the smell of print on paper and continually hunt for a particular smell which brings me right back to my hiding spot for a little bit of secret reading – under the stairs. It is a heady mix of poor quality paper, damp and moist, but I still find it utterly enchanting.

DREAMING THE DREAM

Senator GEORGE MITCHELL *steered the Northern Ireland peace negotiations through two difficult years, culminating in the Good Friday Agreement. In 1998 he honoured me by agreeing to give the 'Open Mind' Guest Lecture for that year. This is the closing part of that lecture.*

THROUGHOUT THE NEARLY two years of the negotiations, there was constant speculation by the media that I would leave, out of frustration and disgust at the lack of progress. Indeed, almost every time I faced the press in Northern Ireland, the very first question was – 'Senator, when are you leaving?' For a while I got the feeling that some of them wanted me to go, but I accepted the legitimacy of the question. I will confess to you that I often thought of leaving, especially in the spring of 1997 when we had a lengthy break in the negotiations for elections held for the

British Parliament, and then District and Local Councils in Northern Ireland. Things looked very difficult, and the prospects were slim. I discussed with my wife and friends of mine the possibility of leaving, and that was much on my mind throughout that summer and early fall.

And then, on 16 October 1997, a transforming event occurred in my life: my wife gave birth to our son. Every parent here knows what that means. In my case, it involved my role in Northern Ireland. On the day that my son was born, I telephoned my staff in Belfast and asked them to find out how many babies had been born in Northern Ireland on that day. There were sixty-one. And I became seized with the thought – what would life be like for my son had he been born in Northern Ireland? What would life be like for those sixty-one babies, had they been born Americans?

The aspirations of parents everywhere are the same – to have children who are healthy and happy, safe and secure, who get a good education and a good start in life, who have the chance to go as high and as far as talent and willingness to work will take them.

A few days after my son's birth – in what was, for me, a very painful parting – I left home to return to Belfast, to resume chairing the negotiations. And on that flight, I resolved that I would not leave, no matter what. I committed myself to the end, and promised to redouble my efforts to bring the negotiations to a successful conclusion.

And when I returned to the negotiations the next day, the delegates were very kind and expressed their congratulations on the birth of my son, and I told them of my thoughts. I told them that I was committed to stay until the end, that I was prepared to redouble my efforts, and I asked them for the same commitment. And I reminded them of the high obligation that they had as the elected representatives of the people of Northern Ireland not to let this opportunity pass.

We were able to bring it to a successful conclusion, thanks to their courage and perseverance. After the agreement was reached, we came together for one last time. It was very emotional. Everyone was exhausted. We had stayed in a negotiating session for nearly forty consecutive hours. For most of the previous two weeks, everyone had gotten little sleep, and so some cried. There were tears of exhaustion, of relief, of joy. I told the delegates, in my parting words, that for me the Good Friday Agreement was the realisation of a dream – a dream that had sustained me through three and a half of the most difficult years of my life.

Now that dream has been realised and I have a new dream. It is this. My dream now is that, in a few years, I will take my young son and return to Northern Ireland. We will tour that beautiful country until, on one rainy afternoon, we'll go to visit the new Northern Ireland Assembly. That won't be difficult, because almost every afternoon is a rainy afternoon! And there we will sit in the visitors' gallery of the Assembly and watch the delegates there debate the ordinary issues of life in a democratic society – healthcare, education, agriculture, fisheries, tourism. There will be no talk of war, for the war will have long been over. There will be no talk of peace, for peace will be taken for granted. On that day – the day on which peace is taken for granted in Northern Ireland – on that day I will be truly fulfilled.

SHEEPMEN AND SITKA SPRUCE

Brian Leyden *gives a writer's perspective on rural Ireland as part of his contribution to the 1992 series 'The Rural Development School'.*

These days the mountain farm fields carry cattle and sheep. The mountain sides are paved with wandering sheep. On Palm Sunday after holy communion the parish priest has a message from the altar for his own people.

'I've had complaints,' Father Egan says. 'The flowers and the fresh wreaths in the graveyard have been eaten. Last week I discovered a number of sheep with purple markings around their necks in the front porch of the chapel, digesting the Bishop's Lenten pastoral letter. I would remind you that when the bishop set down his thoughts on paper he had a different flock in mind.'

The sheepmen kneel on their caps at the back of the chapel, unmoved by his appeal. Back when the talk was about landing men on the moon, a debate arose whether the Americans would find any life up there.

'There's no grass on it, anyway,' said Eddie Brannigan. 'If there was, Pat Shields would have had sheep on it long ago.'

The sheepmen deal in black-faced mountain ewes, all scrag ends and torn woollens, bred in large numbers and then left to wander about the forestry plantations until the inspection for the sheep premium payment. It's the same with the cattle.

'Auld reindeers' is what Mrs Lenehan – who cleans the chapel for Father Egan – calls them. 'With their hungry calves climbing the ditches for ivy. The country is polluted with bad cattle.'

'Too much milk and butter', the bureaucrats had said, chewing the tops of their pencils in Brussels at the sight of the rising dairy produce mountains. 'Switch to beef, that's the thing.'

The dairy cows were dumped on the sides of the roads – not worth the price of their feed – when the money moved to beef production. It's the grants and subsidies that the smallholders have come to depend on for a living – not market prices. Now the same see-saw action can be witnessed again as the intervention beef deep-freezers stand full to the rafters. They know that the market for subsidised lamb is another bubble waiting to burst, but the sheepmen are getting what they can, while they can.

After second Mass the men take up position outside the church porch for a smoke as a blustery rain-shower sweeps down the valley. They cock their ears for the met office weather forecast coming over a car radio. *The meteorological situation at twelve hundred hours. A vigorous depression centred over the Northwest will extend to all parts of the country ...*

Their attention wanders back to the parish newsletter, bought by every household for fifteen pence per photocopy. *For Sale: white veil and first communion dress. Wanted: second-hand school books. GAA news: the parish team wishes one of last week's opposition players a speedy recovery.* There is a notice from the Credit Union giving details of life and loan cover. And another item on the illegal dumping of rubbish on the mountain. 'Our fine scenery, which can compare with the ring of Kerry,' says Father Egan – a Cork man originally – 'is being ruined by this dumping of old cars, gas cookers, fridges and black bags.'

These and other goings-on in the valley are out of the national news now and limited to the parish newsletter. But for a couple of days the newspaper and television reporters came and noted the token protest before the valley was written off as running at a loss to the European Economic Community. There was an item about it on the *Today Tonight* current affairs programme.

'With Olivia O'Leary, all lustre and bluster,' said Eddie Brannigan. A man who summed up his time in the coalmines by telling the reporter that, 'The work was hard and the pay was small, and no matter how little you did, you earned it all'.

Just like the milk, sheep and cattle, the coal too was subsidised to the hilt. When the industrial iron ore furnaces had consumed all the trees for firewood and charcoal, the companies went in search of other fuel. They found coal on the mountain. The coalmines outlived the iron ore workings but the mineral fields were never viable. The coal was there only in small amounts, and for every bucket of coal you burned you seemed to take from the grate two buckets of ash and cinders. But when the second world war started, the United Kingdom paid well for industrial coal and for the fuel needed by the stevedores to stoke their warship boilers.

'That Harry Hitler,' said Martin Reynolds. 'Let no man say but he made up this valley. He should have been canonised.'

Like the Gulf War on the satellite television news channel, the second world war didn't have a whole lot to do with this place. The LDF hid the milestones in the ditches to confound any crack German invasion force that might enter the valley. And you couldn't get hold of proper tea – you had to make do with bottles of Irel coffee.

It was the strategies of peacetime Europe that posed the most real threat to the small Land Commission farms of the Northwest. The region was acknowledged as a disadvantaged area. Twenty-acre farms were only nesting boxes for curlews, with the frogs spawning in the waterlogged fields. Rushy fields where the rain pooled on that blue daub the way it stood on a cement front street, and then the same blue daub cracked open like the desert with the first sign of drying.

'That land,' the experts said. 'You don't measure it by the acre – you measure it by the gallon.' What else could a bureaucrat in an air-conditioned office on the continent do only earmark the region for planting? For every job gone there would be a thousand trees to take its place.

The lifeless pine woods seeping their acids into the water-table appear as the inevitable next phase – the next cycle in that turning wheel called progress. But after every industrial closure the government agency committees, the jobs task forces, come to spend the European relief funding.

'The brandy boys,' said Eddie Brannigan. 'If you could bottle and sell hot air we'd all be made up.'

He was talking about Mr Newgent who 'co-ordinated' – one of Mr Newgent's own words – the first task force. He had a telephone installed in the parish hall and changed its name to the Community Resources and Development Centre. On the first day he opened his briefcase and passed out an armload of glossy folders full of leaflets. After dinner he began to blue-tack more big full-colour glossy posters to the walls around him. Finally, he turned to Eddie Brannigan.

'Have you ever thought about starting a small business?'
'I did have a small business,' said Eddie.
'What happened?'
'It got smaller.'

Father Egan greets the sheepmen as he steps out of the vestry door into the blustering rain with his bundle of first quarter church collection envelopes in his hip pocket. Until the recent let-downs these men had offered up most of their prayers in thanks to the beef barons, but they touch their caps this morning. Father Egan's sermon was a bit on the long side today. In it he said that the people of the parish should all spend more time talking to God. But he may be underestimating the depth of faith of his people.

One hundred years ago the annual gatherings – or patterns – at St Lasair's holy well were memorable events. Crowds of people took the shortcut across the mountain on foot, in carts, traps and jaunting cars. More visitors walked from the Mount Allen station house of the narrow-gauge railway after stepping off the Ballinamore train. Stalls stood in the fields selling biscuits and boiled sweets. There was prayer and there was match-making, there was drinking and there was fighting. Enough for the parish priest to read out from the altar about the 'roaring porter, the courting porter and the fighting porter, and biddy with the stones in her stockings'.

Finally the bishop arrived from Longford and had the altar stone at the well broken in half and the two parts carted off in different directions. But the twelve-hundred-year-old rural tradition of harvest festival pilgrimage to the well continued. The procession with banners and staffs with pictures of the saints from the church to the well was gradually revived, and in time the outside Mass returned.

To this day you will find private offerings – strings of beads, coppers, prayers of appeal in tiny plastic envelopes, tissues, ends of coloured fabric and baby clothes – tied about the branches of the tree sheltering the holy well. For this is, increasingly, a region where prayer – not government – is seen to be the best hope of survival. Divine intervention will be needed to quell the waves of change that are coming every day with increasing speed and fury. There can be no doubt that our elected government ministers would vie for all the credit, but the arrival of an alternative industry now – offering wide employment to this part of the Northwest – would be viewed as the holy well's first documented miracle.

HERMAN THE HERETIC

Economist HERMAN DALY *on the limits of economic growth.*

I HAVE BEEN branded a heretic by the church of *The Economist* because its major dogma is economic growth forever. For me that is impossible. We live in a finite world and we're encroaching on the larger eco-system which provides all the services that sustain our lives and to date the world economy has not counted that as a cost. We have to learn to live within a sustainable scale of that eco-system.

I worked for six years in the environment department of the World Bank but the bank simply sees the solution to every problem as economic growth – whether it be poverty or environmental destruction. But what if growth is costing you more in sacrificed environmental service than it is benefiting you in increased wealth? Of course you can have growth in some areas, but the problem is with aggregate growth – which is what we mean by GDP. We cut down forests, we exhaust mines, we deplete fisheries beyond their sustainable productive capacity and we count that – wrongly – as income. It is not income but capital and that is one of the major corrections that ecological economics is seeking to make – to live off our income and not run down capital.

What I am seeking is qualitative improvement, subject to a quantitative physical limit – like the librarian who has to get rid of one book from the shelves for every new book she adds. How you decide which books go to the shredder is the dilemma. Do you go populist and shred the books that are least often taken out? The latter may include classics of literature and thought, so a careful balance is required. If you try to generalise the current material standard of living of the wealthy part of this planet to the entire world, the result would be an environmental catastrophe – yet this is precisely the goal of the World Bank.

There are three basic things that need to be done in order to tackle extreme poverty:

1. We must face the issue of population control – the world population cannot continue to increase at its present rate.

2. We must address consumption control – per capita consumption cannot continue to increase. We need to find a way to redistribute existing wealth.

3. We must increase the productivity of the resource flow. Whatever resources we can sustainably extract from the natural eco-system, we have to use them ever more efficiently. One way to do that is through ecological tax reform – shifting our taxes away from labour and capital and onto the resource flow.

I am opposed to globalisation in the sense of a single integrated world economy, in which the ideal is the disappearance of the nation-state for economic purposes. We do not have a world community. Community exists at the national and sub-national levels. Ideally, each nation should internalise the costs of depletion and pollution in its prices but globalisation and free trade award the prize to the nation that has the *lowest* standards of cost internalisation. Government needs boundaries but markets do not like them. Transnational corporations seek to buy where things are cheapest and sell where they are dearest, so they try to buy off the politicians. In the USA we say we have the best government that money can buy – to the detriment of our own workforce. I admit that the nation state doesn't have a happy history. Many sins have been committed in its name. On the other hand it is the quality of our community relationships which determines our welfare far more than the amount of goods and services we consume.

We need to distinguish between man-made capital (e.g. fishing boats) and natural capital (the fish in the sea). Fifty years ago man-made capital was seen as the limiting factor to growth, so we invested in more and better boats. Today the limiting factor is natural capital. We have not yet learned to shift our economising behaviour on to natural capital. We need to 'invest' in it by leaving natural systems alone in a sort of fallowing system. As of now, we have gone too far in exploiting natural systems beyond their capacity and this can only lead to increasing poverty. We would do well, before it is too late, to heed the words of John Ruskin:

THE CURIOUS MIND

'That which appears to be wealth, may in verity be the gilded index of far-reaching ruin.'

MY FAVOURITE THINGS

Sir PATRICK MOORE *cherishes some childhood possessions in the study of his West Sussex home.*

MY FIRST ASTRONOMY BOOK

I had a lot of illness as a child and had a very patchy formal education. I remember sitting in that armchair when I was six – in 1929. There was a bookcase behind the chair. My mother had some interest in astronomy and had some books on the subject. I reached up one day and took down one of those books – *The Story of the Solar System*. I sat in the chair and read it from cover to cover. It wasn't actually a boy's book but I could read it and I would not be hooked out of that chair until I finished it. I later bought a companion volume with my sixpence pocket money and both of those books got me started on a lifelong passion for astronomy.

MY FIRST TELESCOPE

I saved up and bought a three-inch refractor telescope for seven pounds ten shillings when I was eleven. Prior to that I had used borrowed binoculars to study the heavens. It was a very nice telescope and I published my first research paper (on the moon) based on the study I did with that little telescope at the age of fourteen. I still have that paper too.

MY CUCKOO-CLOCK

When I reached the age of six, my mother asked me what I would like for my birthday. 'Mummy,' I replied, 'I would so like a cuckoo-clock.' So we drove in our old car from Sussex up to London, parked in Oxford street, bought the cuckoo-clock (I think it cost thirty shillings), drove further down the street, parked again outside a restaurant, had high tea and came home. Wouldn't be possible now.

MY TYPEWRITER

When I was eight, my bible was Pickering's book about the moon, but it was totally unobtainable. I wanted that book so badly. A friend of the family – a fellow of the Royal Astronomical Society – loaned the book to us for three months. I had a brilliant idea. If I typed this book out – all 60,000 words of it – I would learn how to type, I would learn how to spell, and I would have a copy of the book. So I did – starting as a one-finger typist and gradually moving on to touch-typing. The plan worked like a dream. I still have the typescript and the typewriter – which I still use.

MY CHESS SET

My father gave me that for my ninth birthday and I got a lot of enjoyment out of it. I was a serious chess-player at one time.

LEARNING TO LIVE

Fifty years ago SEAMUS DORAN *was principal of the local vocational school in Mooncoin, Co. Kilkenny. He had seen a film about the '4H' clubs in America – clubs that offered teenagers opportunities to be better citizens and to learn by doing. Seamus had a dream ...*

IT IS OCTOBER 2002. I am talking with two men in a furniture store in the village of Mooncoin. It is Rosedale Furniture Superstore – a veritable maze of three-piece suites, cabinets, tables and chairs. I have not come to buy furniture, however. This superstore was once a humble three-roomed vocational school, and its former principal – a tall, lean man now in his eighties – is telling me his story.

'In the 1950s there was great poverty in Ireland. Transport was largely restricted to the bicycle. There was mass emigration to Britain in search of work. There was very little for young people to do. Few of the rural

THE CURIOUS MIND

children went beyond primary school. They were largely confined to their homes. I wanted to change that ...'

A number of vocational schools had 'Home Garden schemes'. Seamus Doran called a meeting of teachers involved in those schemes and proposed the setting up of clubs for young people which would involve them in learning by doing. He managed to get two government ministers down to his little school – Sean Moylan, Minister for Education, and Tom Walsh, Minister for Agriculture. They backed his idea and thus in March 1952 the organisation *Macra na Tuaithe* (Sons of the Countryside) was born.

'The young people reared their own calves, pigs, chickens. They did gardening. They learned homecrafts. This might seem simple now but it was crucial then to get young people *active*. The leader (usually a teacher) attended meetings and advised, but the young people ran the clubs themselves, electing their own officers, making their own decisions. We wanted to get them active and questioning. Being members of *Macra* made them better people. It improved the home environment and got them involved in community affairs. Citizenship was one of our prime aims – it was unheard of in 1952. At a very basic level *Macra* changed the eating habits of people. Prior to 1952, vegetable-growing was confined to potatoes and cabbage. Now they were growing lettuce, tomatoes, radishes ...'

Seamus Doran's dream was realised in a way he could never have imagined. *Macra na Tuaithe* grew and grew. In 1981 it changed its name to *Foróige* (Youth Development), reflecting a changing urbanised Ireland. My other guest is Michael Cleary, current director of *Foróige*. Fifty years on, he tells me, you will find *Foróige* clubs in towns and cities, getting involved in the Special Olympics and Tidy Towns, visiting old people, developing parks, setting up businesses – they hope to set up a Youth Bank soon. 'We did a millennium survey of young people. They told us they wanted to be listened to, to be respected, to contribute to the community. I think that is wonderful ...'

Seamus Doran leans back in his armchair, smiling.

A CIVIL SERVICE EDUCATION

T.K. (KEN)WHITAKER *is one of the great economic architects of modern Ireland. Here he recalls how his days in the Civil Service shaped him.*

FOR BOYS WHO had a Christian Brothers education at the time, there were very few outlets. The civil service and local authorities and a few other jobs of that kind were the only things on offer. In the very early days when I was in the Civil Service Commission, I sat with a man who was the father of Eithne Fitzgerald. Our job was somewhat like that of Laocoön, who was wrestling with all the serpents in that famous sculpture. We were wrestling with great big sheets of sticky paper on which we had to put the marks for various examinations. We then had to put them into numerical order, which meant getting all these narrow perforated sheets and putting them back on a new background – a very sticky and unexciting job! However, we were rescued from that because, once you're in the Civil Service Commission and want to do another competitive examination, you are hounded out to somewhere else for fear you might see the papers in advance. I was sent to the Department of Education at a very early stage and actually became private secretary to Tomás O Deirg, who was the minister at the time.

I wasn't too impressed with Education as a department. My impression of it was that people did not cooperate well. There were a lot of people whose main interest was not to help you but to 'walk you up the garden'. There was a great deal of unnecessary competitiveness. They didn't have enough input from outside – the kind of graduate intake that Finance and some other departments had was not available to them – and that continued for quite some time.

I spent a little while in Revenue as an assistant inspector of taxes, which was another rung of the ladder. For that examination, economics – or commerce – was on the syllabus. I had never heard of economics until then, so I decided I had to do something about it. I started doing first of all a London University arts degree in Mathematics and Celtic Studies, Latin and Law. I got some credit for the mathematics to do an economic/science degree at London by correspondence, as an external student. Later on I completed it by doing a Master of Science/Economics, as they put it.

I went to Finance in 1938. I have always likened it to entering an officer corps. No matter how junior you were, you had access to the officers' mess, you could ask the general something and you wouldn't be frozen out. It was a completely new experience – an exhilarating one – to be in a place where that kind of *esprit de corps* existed. It was very much like an academic institution. There was a good deal of talking amongst ourselves about economic problems. There were people there in my time like Paddy Lynch and Jack Nagle, with whom one could talk over problems one had with one's own study.

In my thirty-one years in Finance, one of my great mentors was Arthur Codling, an Englishman who stayed after the Treaty to help in the new department and who became assistant secretary there. He was quite a disciplinarian; you made sure that you got your file numbers correct on your documents and so on. He was also someone who – by his own example – taught you how to mix intuition and logic to good advantage.

Professor George O'Brien of UCD was also extremely helpful to me. I was somebody outside his own immediate sphere, somebody who had never gone to university, but I was always included by him amongst those he called his 'swans', the people he invited to dinner and pleasant debates in congenial company.

In the post-war period, Seán Lemass was one of my great political heroes. I admired him a lot for being a man of decisiveness. He was a pragmatic patriot, a man who was in the right place at the right time, though perhaps not timely enough. I would agree with those who think that de Valera probably stayed on too long.

It was clear to everyone – and became clear to Lemass in particular – that protectionist policies, the self-sufficiency policies, were outmoded. So, after the war, Lemass began the process of dismantling it all. First of all, he introduced a bill to restrict protection, to force the infant industries to become adult. However, that was never passed, because in 1948 there was a change of government. Once he came back into power and we reassessed policies in the mid-1950s, I think everyone agreed that there was no future for either employment or improved standards in Ireland if we were relying on an impoverished home market. We had to break out – we had to sell in the export markets competitively.

We also learned a lot from civil servants like John Leyden and J.J. McElligott. We observed them when we went on trade talks or negotiations of an economic kind to London or Paris. We were the young people briefing them, doing the groundwork, but also watching how they dealt with cross-table discussion and argument. Leyden in particular was quite a fierce terrier in those situations.

In the late 1950s, we prepared the programme for economic development. It made the change from a self-sufficiency policy to an open export-oriented policy. The significant thing about it was that it was a product of the most unlikely place in the world – the hard-bitten, negative Department of Finance. People were impressed and said there must be something in it, there must really be some potential for development in the country if those people in Finance say there is. I think that helped to create confidence, that psychological factor which I would regard as one of the most important factors of production.

De Valera, who was just in his last months as prime minister, had the magnanimity to say we should publish the book and let it be known that the authorship was a group of civil servants. That was a big step for him, because other people – like Sean McEntee – opposed it. De Valera, Lemass and Dr Jim Ryan said publish and be damned, as it were. Of course, they were very astute politically in doing so, because it would have been much harder for them to embrace a complete reversal of traditional policy on their own account, much easier when it was apparently the advice of objective non-political civil servants.

It was a time of great satisfaction, because most of us who were engaged in that process felt that we were the first privileged generation of the new Ireland. We'd had good jobs, a good education, and here was a chance to apply what we had learned for the benefit of the country, as we saw it. That was a source of great satisfaction. I remember thinking, going back to Wordsworth, how apt it was when he said –

Bliss it was in that dawn to be alive,
but to be young was very heaven.

THE MASTER'S VOICE

SHINICHI SUZUKI *devoted most of his life to a new approach to education
in general and music education in particular. Suzuki modelled his method
on the way children learn their mother-tongue.
'Everything catches,' he argued. That was the title of a documentary I made
on the occasion of Suzuki's visit to Cork in 1985.
These thoughts of the Master are taken from that programme.*

MAMA HAS VERY good heart, and the child – the new-born baby – catches
Mama's feeling and heart – everything. For example the wolf-girl
Kamala. The wolf 'educated' the wild child's heart. Everything catches.
That is education ...

My devotion to art helped me to develop and educate my own ability.
People say 'I have no ability' – what sadness and despair are occasioned
by this nonsensical belief! For years people everywhere have succumbed
to this false way of thinking, which is really only an excuse for avoiding
work. After long studies over a period of time I finally learned that man
is the product of his own environment. Had I known before that ability
can be developed by training, I would have followed the right path much
earlier. Every child can be educated: it is only a matter of method of
education. Anyone can train himself: it is only a question of using the
right kind of effect ...

I consider that seventeen was the age at which my foundations were
laid. In a manner of speaking it was the year I was born, the year I
emerged as a human being ... I went into a bookstore and looked around
among some books on a shelf at random. After some time fate led me
to a copy of Tolstoy. It was the small *Tolstoy's Diary*. I casually took it
down from the shelf and opened it at random. My eyes fell on the
following words: 'To deceive oneself is worse than to deceive others ...'

I had been inflamed by Tolstoy; I had learned to realise how precious children of four or five were, and wanted to become as one of them. They have no thought of self-deception. They trust people and do not doubt at all. They know only how to love, and know not how to hate. They love justice, and scrupulously keep the rules. They seek joy, and live cheerfully and are full of life. They know no fear, and live in security. I played with children so that I could learn from them. I wanted always to have the meekness of a child. A big revolution took place within me. I feel that this is when the seed was sown of the Talent Education movement that was to be my life-work.

Most of these beautiful children would eventually become adults filled with suspicion, treachery, dishonesty, injustice, hatred, misery, gloom. Why? Why couldn't they be brought up to maintain the beauty of their souls? There must be something wrong with education ...

It is in our power to educate all the children of the world to become a little better as people, a little happier. We have to work towards this. I ask no more than the love and happiness of mankind, and I believe that this is what everyone really wants. Love can be had only by loving. Our life is worth living only if we love one another and comfort one another. I searched for that meaning of art in music, and it was through music that I found my work and my purpose in life. Once art to me was something far off, unfathomable and unattainable. But I discovered it was a tangible thing ... The real essence of art turned out to be not something high up and far off. It was right inside my ordinary daily self. The very way one greets people and expresses oneself is art. If a musician wants to become a fine artist, he must first become a finer person. If he does this, his worth will appear. It will appear in everything he does, even in what he writes. Art is not in some far-off place. A work of art is the expression of a man's whole personality, sensibility and ability ...

My prayer is that all children on this globe become fine human beings, happy people of superior ability, and I am devoting all my energies to making this come about, for I am convinced that all children are born with this potential.

LISTENING TO THE PEOPLE

Matthew Coon Come – *Grand Chief of the Assembly of First Nations of Canada – on the struggle of Canadian Indians to assert their rights in their own territories.*

I REPRESENT A very diverse group of some eighty nations, comprising about one million people. My own nation is the Cree nation in Northern Quebec. Many years ago King Charles gave the First Nations' land to the Hudson Bay Company in the name of Prince Rupert. Our people could not understand this. How could a man who had never set foot on our land make a gift of it to someone else in the name of someone we had never heard of? Nobody had asked us.

Our people were and are hunters, fishers, trappers. The land is our life. I was born in a hunting camp, where I lived until I was six. One day a plane landed on the lake. Our parents put all the six-year-olds into canoes, paddled out to the plane and handed us over to government officials. We were flown to a residential school three hundred miles to the south. Our parents had been forced to do this under threat of the loss of welfare services. Under the Canadian Constitution, authority was given to the government to rule over the Indian lands and peoples. This was enshrined in the Indian Act under which we became wards of state. To me, this was a form of discrimination. We never heard of a Greek Act or an Irish Act ...

The government created these residential schools in order to assimilate us into the mainstream of society. They took children out of their homes in order to 'kill the Indian within the child' – as one official put it. There was a loss of language and culture and sex abuse was rife in those schools also. There were five hundred children in my school. We cried for weeks at first, but I spent ten years there. When I graduated, I wanted to come home but my father told me there was a higher school I should go to before I came home. I ended up in Magill University doing political science, economics and law. When I came home I asked my father to show me our land. I had a map with me. He took it and ripped it up.

'You are thinking like a white man,' he said. 'Just walk the land with me the way your forefathers did. We have names for everything. I will show you where I saw my first moose, where the fish spawn, where the caribou calve, where the beavers dam the river.' This was a real learning curve for me, understanding how life depended on our living in harmony with nature.

I came from a community called Big Rock (today the young people call it Rock City!). It was very isolated. There was no road into it until 1978. My grandmother did not see a white man until the 1940s. She once had a vision on the shore of the lake. She saw something eating the trees surrounding the lake. She saw rivers flowing backwards and people having to buy water. In my lifetime, her vision has been realised. The forests have been cleared by logging machines. The rivers have been dammed and diverted for a hydro-electric scheme which involved flooding an area the size of France. The 'Project of the Century' the premier of Quebec called it. We knew it would change our whole way of life and we fought it – and lost. And now we must either boil our own water or buy bottled water.

Eighty per cent of the natural resources of Canada are in traditional Indian territories. The development of these resources brought us into conflict with the government. We were not anti-development – we were concerned about the way it was happening. It was not involving us and our way of life. We eventually negotiated an agreement that gave the Cree people more local autonomy – control of our schools, health boards, policing. In taking on the government, we were forced to look at ourselves and make choices for our future. There was much dialogue and debate. If you want to promote your own culture and way of life, a central government won't do it for you. It will provide services but you must fund and support your own identity.

When subsequent 'development projects' were mooted, we had learned our lesson. We mobilised domestic and international support, used the judicial system and the media. I was accused of using guerilla tactics but I was simply using the white man's system that I had studied so well. Eventually we made the officials in their ivory towers down south listen to the voice of our people and we broke the stranglehold of central government. We decided on our own school curriculum, not theirs. We introduced our own language in junior schools. When the geese fly in springtime, we close the schools for three weeks – because we are hunters after all.

There are great challenges ahead, however. As society consumes more and more of everything, more and more of our resources are taken. Our land is shrinking and can only support a limited number of families. My own children are growing up learning about our land and traditions, but it may be different for my grandchildren. Government will only deal with you when they want your trees, your oil, your water. It's unfortunate but that's the way it is.

ROOTS

HARRY BOHAN recalls how his experience of pastoral work as a young curate in large industrial cities in England led him to organise a practical approach to revitalising a community in his native Co. Clare.

THE DAY I was ordained, Bishop Joseph Rogers told me that he was sending me off to do a postgraduate course in the University of Wales, because it was a time of change and because Shannon was beginning to emerge within our diocese as a new town and one of the centres of industrial development. He wanted someone who would have some understanding of what that change was all about.

I went in October 1963 to Cardiff and my thesis was 'The Growth of Cities in Britain'. I looked at the movement of people out of Ireland, from the Famine days right up through the second half of the last century and the first half of this century, and the kind of conditions they lived in in the cities of Britain. We often hear of people emigrating from this country and dying on the way to far-off places, but what we don't always hear of are the numbers that suffered and died from diseases like typhoid in the cities of Britain. They lived in hugely over-crowded accommodation and they worked in horrific conditions in factories there. The thesis convinced me that the industrial city is wrong and that I should go back and make some contribution to the little villages of this world.

I was asked to go and work with the emigrants in Birmingham and so I left Cardiff with a heavy heart in the late 1960s. I worked for two and a half years with these emigrants and came to love it and to love them. I worked in a parish that had thirteen thousand Catholics and got heavily involved in their lives, in the housing and the pastoral scene there. Again, this was another step in the inevitable direction. The night before I left Birmingham, I was called down to a one-room flat where a man and his wife and six children were living. She had been beaten up by the husband and he said to me, 'I'm sorry for doing what I did to my wife, but if you or anyone else had to live in these conditions you would probably do the same thing'. They and others like them convinced me that something has to be done for families that have to uproot from rural Ireland to go and live in conditions like that. It is very definitely not a recipe for good family life.

I came back in the late 1960s to Shannon. The whole of Ireland then was flying – there was progress everywhere. Whereas people were talking about full employment in a number of 'growth centres', I felt, despite popular opinion, that we were on a disaster course in Ireland. However, to say that – which I did publicly and privately at the time – was almost considered to be a mortal sin. We were over-reliant on transnational money and transnational technology. We were putting all our eggs into one basket and we were only putting the new industries into a few centres. Effectively, that meant that families that I had grown up with would simply be suppliers of labour to those centres. We were totally neglecting our own natural resources and putting millions and millions of pounds into multinational companies. They gave a great service to this country in the 1960s, but it became very clear to me that some of the companies that were coming here then would be in another part of the world – and for the most part in the Third World – ten years on. And that is exactly what happened.

I began to say publicly and privately that if we continued on the course we had embarked on, we would soon face mass unemployment and urban breakdown. Because I was so convinced of this, I borrowed £1,500 in 1972. I went to a bank manager and told him that if we could get young families to come to live in small villages, then maybe we could reverse the trend. Not only did that bank manager, Johnny Mee, say that this was a good idea and give me the loan, but I asked him to come onto a committee with a few other experts to see if we could build twenty houses back in Feakle. I felt that if I couldn't do it in Feakle – my native village in Co. Clare – I couldn't do it anywhere.

We discovered that in 1972 – in spite of all the apparent progress in Ireland – in a village population of 120 there were only three people between the ages of twenty and forty, and that spelt disaster. In other words, the village that I had grown up in and loved had been written off. All the experts told us that people would not go back to live there. I asked the parish priest to announce from the altar that if there were young families who would like to live in Feakle, they should come to the hall the following Friday night. We got representatives of twenty families into the hall that Friday night and eventually – through a lot of scraping and bowing and a lot of backbreaking work – we got twenty young families back into Feakle. That was an enormous input into a small village population, because not only was it an increase of about a hundred people but this was in the age group that was needed.

We formed a company and we moved on from there and since then we have built 2,500 houses in 120 communities and thirteen counties, and the spin-offs became obvious very quickly. For example, in Feakle, Con Smith built a village hotel; the school, instead of losing a teacher, got an extra one; young farmers stayed on the land. People started to look at setting up little enterprises and this happened in many of the other villages as well. All of that effort by a voluntary organisation represents an investment of about two hundred million pounds in rural Ireland.

It was often said to me that I was a romantic, that it couldn't work – and obviously that was a challenge. We had to make it work on the ground and we had to make it work practically. I was convinced then and am more convinced now that the era of the industrial city is over and done with. There is too much crime, too much family breakdown. I believe that family breakdown itself has come about largely because families became consumers and not producers – they were not working together. The father and mother that I grew up with trained me in a whole lot of things. Many sons today don't see their fathers at work, and so are seriously deprived. The togetherness, the praying together, the working together, have been taken away from family life. I am completely convinced that we are entering a new era where we'll return to the family and to the community to solve the unemployment problem and to solve a lot of the other problems we have in society.

DO THEY STILL LIVE IN IGLOOS?

This was the title of a documentary (my first!) about Eskimos. Here EILEEN KANE *describes the houses and clothing of traditional Eskimos.*

ESKIMOS LIVED IN a variety of houses. In warm times most of the Eskimos had tent-like structures. Sometimes these structures were used into the colder parts of the year and were simply covered over with snow. However, you had permanent or semi-permanent kinds of houses as well. In the western areas they tended to have sod houses until you got into coastal areas where they had to build igloos. Most sod houses had a kind of porch arrangement or a long passage leading into the central chamber which was usually circular. They were not very spacious inside. A man, his wife and their complement of children might live in a house that was only six or seven feet in diameter. The main function was protection against the elements so this porch was very useful because it was a long entrance tunnel and it kept the cold air from entering the main room.

The long entrance porch was semi-subterranean and a lot of things were stored in it. For example, in very cold weather, the dogs were kept in this porch. The family clothing was hung to dry in the porch, spare utensils were kept there and – in a little room off the porch – sexual relations were engaged in. Then as you proceeded down the passage you went through a central opening – a kind of flap – and up into the main room. This was usually two or three feet above the ground so you were actually putting your head up through a hole and going into the main room. It was more or less sealed against the elements.

The Alaskan Eskimos wore caribou clothing, which they got from trade relations with inland Eskimos. The women made the garments. They chewed the skin to make it soft, then they tanned it with human urine. In fact outside every Eskimo hut or in the porch passage there was usually a bucket of human urine which was used for tanning and for treating wounds as well. By the time they reached middle age, most Eskimo women had no teeth because of this process of softening the skin by chewing. The process of the saliva acting on the skin and the tanning process made the skins beautifully soft. They were sewn in a kind of stitch which people use today to make waterproof clothing. It is a kind of double stitching system so that moisture can't seep in. It was absolutely essential that no water be able to get into these skins. The boots were a work of art. They had sealskin soles and various kinds of animal skins for the sides but they were often lined with moss or down to ensure that the feet were kept comfortable.

I think the most interesting thing of all of this is how comfortable people were, considering the environment they were living in. The houses had always been described as comfortable – dark perhaps and not as hygienic as we would think would be desirable – but warm in such an environment.

AN UNHAPPY CHILDHOOD

Newspaper magnate CECIL KING *reflects on a childhood in which he experienced little affection.*

I SPENT SOME of my very earliest years in Simla, India, where my father was head of the Salt Revenue for Northern India. We returned to Ireland in 1905 to live in Roebuck Hall in Dublin – a lovely family house with eleven acres, two walled gardens, two cows and a pony. (I won second prize of £15 on the latter at the Dublin Horse Show, but then there were only two competitors!) My father subsequently became Professor of Oriental Languages at Trinity College Dublin.

I was fifth in a family of seven children. My older brother was killed in action in the Great War and my younger brother was one of 500 who died aboard the steamship *Leinster* when it was torpedoed by the Germans in the last month of the war. The loss of her eldest son nearly drove my mother mad. She never got over it. She told me I was her favourite but in truth that meant very little.

We had a schoolroom in Roebuck Hall where a very strict little governess gave us a basic education. She had an iron discipline and what she taught, we learned. At the age of eight I was sent to boarding school in Surrey but I was very unhappy there and was taken out after a year and sent to a day school – Strangways – in St Stephen's Green. I was always a bit of a lone child. I read a tremendous lot. I remember at the age of ten or eleven lying on the floor at home by the fire and reading all I could lay my hands on – Dickens, Austen, Thackeray, and Scott, whom I found very boring. I was always a bit of a scavenger and when I saw a notice outside Henshaw's Ironworks in Clonskeagh offering money for scrap, I would fill up a little donkey cart with bits and pieces of scrap I found in the ditches and duly sell it for a few shillings.

There were some notable characters around in my childhood. One was Endymion – a large man who carried a swordstick and binoculars. He just drifted around the area, occasionally peering through his binoculars. It was said he was looking for his dead fiancée – but he was quite harmless. Another was a very, very old woman who could recall the news of the Battle of Waterloo (1815) being brought to Dundrum.

Two major events stand out in my childhood. In 1911 King George V came to Ireland after his coronation. There was a ceremonial march-past in the Phoenix Park – 14,000 troops, all in full dress uniform. Lancers charging, horse artillery at the gallop with their guns – it was such marvellous pageantry. There was a big fleet in Dún Laoghaire harbour and I was taken to see one of the gunships – the *Dreadnought*. The most exciting event was the 1916 Rising. Even in Roebuck we could hear the rattle of machine-guns. I walked down Foster's Avenue to watch the Sherwood Foresters march into town from Dún Laoghaire. My sister was at school in Mount Anville, so I was invited to watch from the rooftop. We could see the gunboat *Helga* shelling O'Connell street. Later my father took me into the city. It was devastation in O'Connell street – shells of still-smouldering buildings all around.

My uncles were the Harmsworth family who became the great press barons of the age. Alfred – who became Lord Northcliffe – was the family hero. He was born in Chapelizod and, starting with nothing, he made a huge fortune setting up the *Daily Mail* and the *Mirror* newspapers. I remember getting a gold sovereign from him when he got his peerage. He would visit my grandmother regularly and I sat at my uncle's feet as they discussed the need to overthrow Asquith as prime minister and replace him with Lloyd George.

I eventually went to Winchester Public School, which I disliked intensely. I hated being cooped up with my peers. You were never allowed be alone. Another uncle – Harold, Lord Rothermere – paid my way through Oxford. Northcliffe had promised me a job with *The Times* on my graduation but he died shortly afterwards and Rothermere gave me a job on sufferance. We didn't get on very well. He was a most unhappy man. He lost two sons in the war. His marriage was not a success and even though he had amassed £25 million by 1925, it brought him no happiness. He seemed to take to making money like some people take to drink. Northcliffe left £6 million but he was not very happy either.

Overall, mine was not a happy childhood. Maybe the fault was mine but my mother was most unmaternal and selfish. If you don't feel affection and security from your mother at an early age, it doesn't make for happiness. And my father? He was just an old gentleman in his study ...

THE BOOK THAT BECAME MY BIBLE

From the radio series 'Heroes and Heroines', SEAN BOYLAN *recalls the story of a doctor who had a profound influence on his professional life.*

SOME YEARS AGO, in gratitude for my treatment of her condition, a nun from the USA gave me a present of a book. It was entitled *Fearfully and Wonderfully Made* – a collaboration between a writer, Philip Yancey, and an orthopaedic surgeon, Paul Brand, on the miracle that is the human body. The title is taken from Psalm 139, verses 13–14: 'You created my inmost being; you knit me together in my mother's womb. I praise you, because I am fearfully and wonderfully made ... '

Paul Brand spent a lifetime treating leprosy and studying and observing the human body. He wrote:

> I have come to realise that every patient of mine, every newborn baby, in every cell of its body, has a basic knowledge of how to survive and how to heal, that exceeds anything I shall ever know. That knowledge is the gift of God, who has made our bodies more perfectly than we could ever have devised ...

For Brand, studying the human body yielded a bonus – it sheds light on the likeness that exists between the human body and the Church, the spiritual Body of Christ.

Yancey, an eager young journalist, learned about Brand in the 1970s. Brand was then a distinguished surgeon, working in the only leprosy hospital in the United States, where Yancey accompanied him on his rounds and then recorded conversations with him on subjects ranging from leprosy and theology to world hunger and soil conservation. The resultant book – *Fearfully and Wonderfully Made* – had a profound and lasting effect on my professional life.

Paul Brand was born in India in 1914 and educated in England before returning to India in 1946. He intended to stay for a year but stayed for seventeen years with his wife Margaret – an eye specialist – treating leprosy patients. He made an amazing discovery when he shook the hand of a leper whose grip almost crushed the surgeon's hand! This totally confused him until he realised he was experiencing power without sensitivity. He began researching the subject and discovered that all the manifestations of leprosy – missing toes and fingers, blindness, ulcers and facial deformities – all trace back to the single cause of painlessness. Leprosy silences nerves and as a result its victims unwittingly destroy themselves, bit by bit, because they cannot feel the pain. When he left India and continued his research, he then applied his knowledge of painlessness to other diseases such as diabetes, thus helping to prevent tens of thousands of amputations each year.

It was in India, though, that Paul Brand honed his skills as a surgeon and gathered his knowledge as a researcher. While his physician friend treated the leprosy and brought it under control, Paul and Margaret Brand worked surgical miracles – restoring rigid claws into usable hands through innovative tendon transfers, remaking feet, transplanting eyebrows and fashioning new noses. Brand worked tirelessly in the very fine and tender skin tissue until power eventually came back and then sensitivity. He became a sort of cobbler, inventing special shoes with a heel bar that exercised the feet. He himself would surprise everyone in the hospital in the United States by walking around in his bare feet! He is fascinating about feet, as shown in this conversation with Yancey:

> I find bone's design most impressive in the tiny jewel-like chips of ivory in the foot. Twenty-six bones line up in each foot – about the same number as in each hand. Even when a soccer player subjects these small bones to a cumulative force of over one thousand tons per foot over the course of a match, his living bones endure the violent stress, maintaining their elasticity. Not all of us leap and kick, but we do walk some sixty-five thousand miles, or more than two and a half times around the world, in a lifetime. Our body weight is evenly spread out through architecturally perfect arches which serve as springs, and the bending of knees and ankles absorb stress.

Think of the stress those little bones have endured in the footballing career of Brian Stafford, say, or Colm O'Rourke!

Page after page, chapter after chapter of this remarkable book pay tribute to the miracle of the human body – a miracle we forget about in our daily lives. Brand quotes Saint Augustine to make this point:

> Men go abroad to wonder at the height of mountains, at the huge waves of the sea, at the long courses of the rivers, at the vast compass of the ocean, at the circular motion of the stars; and they pass by themselves without wondering ...

Brand draws on his long years of work in India with the poorest of the poor, outcasts and beggars, to provide case studies to make his points about the human body and in painting the bigger picture:

> My body employs a bewildering zoo of cells, none of which individually resembles the larger body. Just so, Christ's Body comprises an unlikely assortment of humans. Unlikely is precisely the right word, for we are decidedly unlike one another and the One we follow ... The basis for our unity within Christ's Body begins not with our similarity but with our diversity.

For someone like myself, dealing with the ailments of the human body, *Fearfully and Wonderfully Made* gives wonderful insights into the working of that body. Here, for example, is Brand on the human eye:

> Inside my human eye ... are 107,000,000 cells. Seven million are cones, each loaded to fire off a message to the brain when a few photons of light cross them. Cones give me the full band of colour awareness and because of them I can distinguish a thousand shades of colour. The other hundred million cells are rods, back-up cells for use in low light. When only rods are operating, I do not see colour ... but I can distinguish a spectrum of light so broad that the brightest light I perceive is a billion times brighter than the dimmest ...

Brand is brilliant on skin. He quotes Richard Selzer:

> What is it then, this seamless body stocking, some two yards square, this our casing, our facade, that flushes, pales, perspires, glistens, glows, furrows, tingles, crawls, itches, pleasures and pains us all our days, at once keeper of the organs within and sensitive probe, adventurer into the world outside!

Skin is a window on which we read the health of the activities within. It is a source of ceaseless information about our environment – touch is one of our most complex senses. Skin's most crucial contribution to the human body is – for Brand – waterproofing. Sixty per cent of our body consists of fluids and these would soon evaporate without the moist, sheltered world provided by skin. Skin is also a frontline defence against the hordes of bacteria that attack the human body:

> It is a rough world out there, and the epidermis provides a continuous rain of sacrificed cells ... People who count such things estimate that we lose ten billion skin cells a day ... Up to 90 per cent of all household dust consists of dead skin ... Just shaking hands or turning a doorknob can produce a shower of several thousand skin cells; one trembles to calculate the effect of a game of racquetball.

Or for that matter, a game of hurling or Gaelic football! And of course, as manager of a football team, I am interested in Brand's treatment of muscles and their role in movement and balance:

> Six hundred muscles, which comprise 40 per cent of our weight (twice as much as bones) burn up much of the energy we ingest as food in order to produce all our movements.

And it was muscles that started Brand on his journey, when his own hand was almost crushed by the grip of a leper's hand:

Somewhere in that severely deformed hand were powerfully good muscles. They were obviously not properly balanced, and he (the leper) could not feel what force he was using. Could they be freed? ... That single incident in 1947 changed my life.

The other aspect of *Fearfully and Wonderfully Made* that resonates with me is Brand's concept of service. When he looks back over his life it is not the greatest meals, thrilling vacations or awards ceremonies that bring him pleasure. Rather it is his work as part of a surgical team in the service of others – often in primitive conditions, working in intense heat with the help of a flashlight:

> Our culture exalts self-fulfilment, self-discovery and autonomy. But according to Christ, it is only in losing my life that I will find it. Only by committing myself as a 'living sacrifice' to the larger Body through loyalty to Him will I find my true reason for being.

This book – a chance gift by a grateful patient, to whom I am eternally grateful – has practically become my bible. At times I might feel I know it all, when of course I know so little. Just a glance through *Fearfully and Wonderfully Made* will always bring something home to me and will especially remind me of the greatest healer of all – Jesus Christ. It has been and is a huge and ongoing influence on my life and work.

AFRICA – MY UNIVERSITY

JOHN SEYMOUR *was an Englishman who settled in Co. Wexford. He was a writer and practitioner in self-sufficiency.*
Largely self-educated, he considered Africa his 'university' ...

IN SOUTH-WEST AFRICA, in a place called Namibia, I got a job managing a farm. It was very remote, as far into the desert as you could possibly get. It took four days to get there in an ox wagon from the railway line.

There I came across an old box of books with which my boss's father –
who was of Scottish descent – had tried to educate himself. There was an
enormous amount of English literature in this box, but the white ants
had eaten bits out of nearly all the books. White ants like books, but they
don't read them, they eat them. So, I would be reading *Henry IV* and I
would come to a gap and have to work out for myself what Shakespeare
would have said there. I recommend that as an educational device. I had
to use my imagination because of the white ants! I read all of the
Shakespeare, all of Shaw and Fielding. It was the first time I really knew
there was such a thing as English literature and I really got a lot of
enjoyment out of it.

I stayed in Namibia for about two and a half years. I was managing a
Carical sheep farm – a breed of sheep which come from central Asia.
Their wool makes fur coats for rich ladies. That was the chief industry
of the place. I had to look after about 4,000 sheep and 200 head of beef
cattle. I was stuck away in the bush with nothing but African people – I
couldn't speak a word of their language and they couldn't speak a word
of mine. I learned to speak Afrikaans, which was the *lingua franca*, but
I never learned any African language because there were four different
language groups on the farm and if I learned one language then I
wouldn't be able to speak to the other three-quarters.

I loved Africa. I moved from the farm and spent a year deep-sea
fishing in the south Atlantic and line-fishing off Capetown. I spent six
months copper mining – every young man in those days had to have his
term down the mine, otherwise he couldn't hold his head up. Then I got
a job inoculating native cattle in northern Rhodesia, which is now called
Zambia. I travelled over a huge area of central Africa. There were no
roads and no cars – you walked and you had porters to carry your gear.
You lived by your rifle, on what you could kill. I learned a great deal there
– how to look after myself and be more or less self-sufficient. I would call
Africa my university.

Later on I learned to speak Swahili fluently. I speak it better than I do
English, but that was because I joined the army in World War II. I was
in the King's African Rifles – which was an East African regiment – for

six years and we spoke Swahili. There are so many languages in Africa that to learn one is pretty pointless, because if you travel twenty miles you are in another language area, whereas Swahili does take you over the whole of East Africa. I spent six years living in the bush – first in Ethiopia chasing the Italians and then in Burma chasing the Japanese. It was like being in Africa, even though it was Asia, because I was surrounded by Africans. I had a platoon of forty men who were all African. I got to know my men and they got to know me, and there was mutual respect between us. To be with forty men in conditions like that taught me a great deal. The Japanese were a very tough enemy and the jungle was not a friendly place, but we learned to rely on each other and that did me a lot of good.

Having been brought up in an agricultural tradition, I was always interested in the soil, because right from the beginning I realised that we human beings are soil organisms. Everything we eat comes from the soil. I saw the soil being destroyed on the big white-owned farms in northern Rhodesia. They ploughed land which should never have been ploughed and they grew nothing but maize. I could see the soil was being destroyed and that gave me what has been an abiding obsession for looking after the soil. We can't treat it as something to make money out of – pouring chemicals into it, getting inferior food out of it and selling it for as much profit as we can get. That is not the way we are meant to live. We have to remember that we are soil organisms, we are creatures of the soil, and therefore we must look after it.

AN UNCONVENTIONAL MOTHER

CLARE BOYLAN *remembers a mother who was different.*

MINE WAS A Dublin childhood – a totally urban middle-class childhood. We were kids who played in the lane and went to the pictures and ate chips.

'We' were my two sisters and myself. We were very, very close. I was the youngest and at various stages my elder sister, who was three years my senior, was a 'twin' to me, while at other times she was a 'twin' to my eldest sister. We circled round each other like little moths in motes of dusty light.

The earliest experience I had of closeness with my sister was of stealing 'snoke'. 'Snoke' was glucose powder. I don't know where we got the name, but we would wake up with this incredible longing for snoke and steal down the stairs in the dead of night to get it. We piled up chairs to get to the high shelf in the pantry where the box of snoke was kept. And it might as well have been coke – such was the high we got from thieving it.

I don't think that either my mother or my father really saw children as children. My father was a shy, reticent man who was unlikely to get into the hurly-burly of parenthood. He wasn't a disciplinarian, but then he grew up among generations of rather vaporous ladies who were inclined to faint away at the first hint of a rough wind! It must have been terrifying for him to have a whole house full of these delicate creatures – he wasn't quite sure what to do with them. He was quite old-fashioned, in the sense that he could not envisage women having careers. We would all be well-educated, and he would see to it that each of us was kept in one piece until we were handed over to a husband. We were even forbidden to ride bicycles or roller-skate in case we knocked our front teeth out. I don't think my father ever saw us as being independent.

My mother saw us as potential people rather than as cuddly babies. I don't imagine that she was all that keen on babies, but she did like older children. She had endless patience with children's questions, because she saw all that as a process of growth. When visitors came, we were always there at the table to hear the conversation. But as I remember, it wasn't a very enlightening experience – the adult conversation of the time was extremely boring!

My mother was a writer for as long as I can remember. She wrote essays and short stories. And she composed a children's book for us, which entertained us greatly. I remember summer evenings when she sat writing in the drawing room while we played in the front garden. At some stage we were sent to the shop for pineapple bars and sailor's chews, which were promptly devoured by all – including Mother – with great gusto. When I was a little older – about seven – I used to type out her articles with two fingers, as a reward for which I would be taken to the movies.

To encourage creativity in her children, my mother took the unusual step of painting one of the kitchen walls black and providing us with a box of coloured chalks. She felt that – because children cannot scale things down – they should not be made to contain their idea of a person or a flower to a page in a notebook; they should draw something as they see it – lifesize or even larger. So we used to spend our days drawing on the black wall. This had a number of advantages. As far as my mother was concerned, it meant that we were very quiet and that she could keep an eye on us. For our part it encouraged self-expression and we were given prizes for the best drawing. We never realised, of course, that my mother gave the prizes exactly in rota.

My mother was in many ways a most unconventional woman. When my father was away on business she would keep us home from school for two or three days at a time, switch off the radio and turn the clocks to the wall. She would write and we children would undertake curious and elaborate – if often useless – pieces of housework, like washing rugs in a tin bath or making toffee at the kitchen table. We had a glorious time. We went to the pictures in the evening and extended the fantasy by always trying to eat whatever the people ate in the pictures.

I realise now that this was my mother's silent protest against the extremely conventional lives that women lived then. She dressed up to go to the shops as other women did – she put on her high heels, pearls and gloves to go down to the shop for a bag of potatoes! She obviously hated all this, so in the privacy of her own house – when there was nobody around to approve or disapprove – she lived as she wished to live. Of course this behaviour wasn't very much approved of in school, but she felt that she could 'educate' us just as well at home on the odd days that we took off school – and indeed she did. But then she would provide us with a very haphazard excuse, like 'Dear Sister Immaculata, I kept Clare at home from school because she ate too much and got sick'.

Of course, appalling retribution followed at school! I was dragged up and made an example of – 'the frightful little glutton who ate so much that she got sick and couldn't do her lessons ...'

Retribution apart, I enjoyed school. It was, in a way, another excursion into fantasy. I loved the company of all the other girls. I thought that was tremendously exciting. I loved the competitive element of school – not the academic end, but any competitions involving learning poetry off by heart or singing a song. It seemed full of possibilities. Lessons were frightfully dull. I thought then – and I still believe – that school textbooks were monstrously dull and that it is an absolute offence to children to teach them lessons in the way they are taught through textbooks. I think that the teachers are doing much more now than they did then, but the textbooks – especially geography and history books – were simply appalling. But as I sat there through this torrent of dullness, I had a fantasy that an enormous American with a cigar in his mouth would burst in the door, point at me and say, 'That's the child, I want her', and that I would be cast in a starring role in *Pollyanna 2* or something. It never happened.

Every year in the convent school, four little girls were chosen as flower girls for the Corpus Christi procession. To be chosen was considered a tremendous honour. You had to dress up in white and scatter a basket of petals – just the sort of thing that little girls love to do. I was thrilled to be chosen as a flower girl and I wrestled into my First Communion dress – which I had long outgrown – and other bits and pieces. As we were going for a rehearsal, I overheard the head nun remark to our teacher, 'Look at the cut of her. We can't have someone like that leading the procession'.

Another child took my place, and of course I was heartbroken and ran home screaming hysterically to my mother. Instead of being sympathetic as I had expected, my mother was quite angry. 'I quite agree,' she said. 'Why can't you dress up decently? There are plenty of clothes.' I was quite puzzled by this, as I knew there were not plenty of clothes. Why should my mother be so angry? Of course it was because my humiliation reflected on her.

That was the first time that I became aware that we were short of money. As I grew older I resented the fact that we had been excluded from this knowledge. I felt that it would have been much better to explain the facts to us and have us all pull together, rather than protect and exclude us. I feel differently now. I realise that my parents were very brave to have hidden their worries from me and I am grateful to them for that because it enabled me to grow up free of financial insecurity. It means that I can do things like leave a very secure job to become a full-time writer – which I did. I always feel that there is more money where the last lot came from and I think that if I had gone through the horror that my parents went through at that time, I certainly wouldn't have that freedom.

SWEET OMAGH TOWN

Writer BENEDICT KIELY *recalls memories of the Co. Tyrone town where he grew up.*

Ah! from proud Dungannon to Ballyshannon
And from Cullyhanna to old Ardboe
I've roused and rambled, caroused and gambled
Where songs did thunder and whiskey flow.
It's light and airy I've tramped through Derry
And to Portaferry in the County Down.
But with all my raking and undertaking
My heart was aching for sweet Omagh town.

That ballad sums up my feelings for Omagh, where I spent my childhood and youth. I was actually born near Dromore but we moved into Omagh when I was small. My earliest memory is of wandering out of the house, down Kelvin road, along John street and up to the Courthouse that dominates the town – until someone found me and brought me home! The rivers of Omagh are also part of my early memories. My elder brother was a great fisherman so we would spend many hours down on the banks of the Drumragh or the Camowen, which come together to form the Strule.

> Thrice happy and blessed were the days of my childhood
> And happy the hours we wandered from school
> By old Mountjoy's forest, our dear native wildwood
> On the green flowery bank of the serpentine Strule.

I grew to love the town and its people and in later years I loved to bring visitors like my good friend Thomas Flanagan around the town. Starting at the Courthouse, we would make our way down High Street and beyond to Market Street, where that abominable explosion happened in 1998. Then down the steep hill of Castle Street, where the church spires rise above you. Past the military barracks, which was an important part of the town. As secondary schoolboys, we did our training in the barracks gym. Over Campsie bridge and on to Killyclogher where we enter a lovely park between the rivers. This is Lover's Retreat – although the soldiers had another name for it ... If the day is fine we might ramble out to Lough Muck, which is the lake of a mythological pig. My brother-in-law Frank McRory – a Shavian and a Wellsian – wrote a comic ballad about Lough Muck in which two local boys went on a drinking skite and imagined they got lost in a storm out on the lake:

> Till a man with a big dog drew near
> He shouted out – Hi! clear away out of that
> Faith, I want no drunk Omey boys here!
> He said we'd been drinkin' and sleepin'
> Since the clock in his parlour four struck
> And that was the end of our ill-fated cruise
> On the treacherous waves of Lough Muck.

The town was full of versifiers. There was a postman who emigrated to America and always wrote home in verse. Andy McLoughlin – a small, crippled man – was the town poet. When a new powerhouse was built, the Town Council advertised for an electrician to take charge of it. There were two applicants – a local man and a Portadown man. The Council gave the job to the Portadown man, so Andy decided to satirise the Council:

> Micky Lynch you did it dirty
> Have you any eyes to see?
> And Alec, what's the matter?
> You're our Nationalist MP.
> McConville and Frank Cassidy,
> You are not the poor man's friend
> Nor our well-famed bookie
> W.F. Townsend.

That's as good as Alexander Pope would write any day!

My father loved ballads, although my mother was the singer in the house. I can still hear her sing 'Carraig Donn'. They met when she was working in a local hotel. He came in 'under the influence' and she gave him a lecture for presenting himself like that. A week passed and he came in again, quite sober. Another week passed and he came in – and proposed to her! She was a Gormley from Drumquin and he was the son of a Limerick RIC sergeant who was posted in Carrigart, Co. Donegal. My father joined the British army and had been involved in the Boer War in South Africa. He used to joke that the only shot he ever fired was at a snake, but he marched around South Africa six times. He always carried a stick and from an early age I did too – long before I needed one.

I was schooled by the Christian Brothers – all gentle and good men. There were two Brothers Burke. One was a charming man from Tipperary, who was into hurling, and the other – known as 'Busty' – was a rugby man. He had a thing against me because of my brother Gerry who was a big GAA man. My friend Joe Gilroy used to say that Gerry changed Omagh from a soccer town to a GAA town. 'We used to play street Gaelic Football in Campsie Crescent,' he recalled, 'and one day you went up for a high ball, got hit from behind, fell and hurt your back.

Then you went mad in the head – as we thought – and went off to be a Jesuit. But the back came at you and you left the novitiate and spent eighteen months in hospital. The point is if Omagh had been left a soccer town, you wouldn't have got that back injury and you would now be a Jesuit!'

Brother Hamill was another interesting man. He had been in China and when we went for walks he was forever talking about Hong Kong. He put me on the stage in the Town Hall at a tender age to recite 'The Man from God Knows Where' ...

Into our townland', on a night of snow,
rode a man from God-knows-where;
None of us bade him stay or go,
nor deemed him friend, nor damned him foe ...

Later I was part of the Omagh Players and played a double role – Annas the High Priest and one of the Magi in *The Coming of the Magi*, but Hollywood never called. We had two cinemas – the Star and Miller's – in the town and a number of bands, so there was no shortage of entertainment. People got on well together. Religion didn't matter – whether Catholic, Protestant, Greek or Jew, we were just neighbours. Davy Young would put up the football results in the window of his tobacconist shop and it became a meeting place. Freddie Armstrong's shoemaker shop was a calling-place for grown-up schoolboys. The smoking was wild there. You couldn't see yourself for smoke.

I grew up in a bookish household. My parents and brother were readers. Frank McRory had a great library and gave me the run of it. He found me reading Chesterton once – of whom Frank was not a fan. I went with him to the Eucharistic Congress in Dublin in 1932. It was a late-night train excursion and I fell asleep waiting for High Mass in the Phoenix Park. I got a kick in the tail-end from Frank to wake me. 'There's your favourite author, carrying the canopy like any respectable Irish publican,' he said. Sure enough, there was the fat man carrying the canopy in the Eucharistic procession. At secondary school I had a great teacher – M.J. Curry – who also loaned books to me. Omagh was a reading town.

> And when life is over and I shall hover
> Above the gates where Saint Peter stands,
> And he shall call me for to instal me
> Among the saints in those golden lands;
> And I shall answer 'I'm sure tis grand sir
> For to wear the harp and to wear the crown,
> But I, being humble, sure I'll never grumble
> If Heaven's as charming as sweet Omagh town'.

THIS SACRED EARTH

MIKE COOLEY *explains why the insights of American Indian Chief Seattle led him to nominate the Chief as a 'Millennium Mind'.*

I FIRST ENCOUNTERED Chief Seattle on my car radio when someone told me of a programme of the chief discussing with a US government representative the future of his people in 1854. His people would have all the advantages of written language and literature, science and religion. This would constitute progress, he was told. Chief Seattle replied:

> Every part of this country is sacred to my people. Every valley, every hillside, every glade is hallowed in the memory and experience of my tribe. Even the soil on which you stand responds more lovingly to our footsteps than to yours, for the soil is rich with the life of my people. Our religion exists in the hearts and minds of our people. Your religion was written on tablets of stone by the iron finger of an angry god ...

Those words were so compelling to me because they encapsulated so many of the things that I held to be important. Seattle pointed out –

knowingly or unknowingly – that our religion is a rule-based religion and that it is only in the Judaeo-Christian tradition that we have the kind of science that is completely about the control of nature and the manipulation of data. I went in pursuit of more knowledge about Chief Seattle.

He belongs of course to an oral tradition, but while there is no written history extant, there is another way of knowing the world – by living the knowledge, which is what Seattle and his people did. We know he was in his sixties when he made that speech. A Dr Smith is said to have taken notes and then wrote it up and published it. Seattle could foresee the awesome future that awaited his people in reservations following the 'opening up of the west'. Subsequently he is supposed to have written a letter to the US President. There is controversy about this letter but the essence of his philosophy is there. He wrote:

> The President in Washington says he wishes to buy our land, but how can he buy or sell the sky or the warmth of the earth? The idea is strange to us. If you do not own the freshness of the air or the sparkle of the water, how can you sell them?

If the Indians could not understand the colonists, the reverse was also true. The white people could not accept that Indians were competent. They had no respect for Indian languages, and with horrific missionary zeal 'they took our tongues' – as one Indian account puts it. Chief Seattle represented many nations with their own languages and culture, which had at its base a love of nature and an understanding that if we damage nature we damage ourselves.

> This we know. The world doesn't belong to man. Man belongs to the world. All things are connected, like the blood that unites us all in one family ... The earth is our mother. Whatever befalls the earth, befalls the sons of the earth. Man did not weave the web of life – he is merely a strand in it. Whatever he does to the web he does to himself.

If we could have that understanding built into our education system today – the way we relate to nature, the kind of agriculture we develop, the way we treat animals – all of these would be entirely different. Part of our problem is in clinging to the notion of a 'one best way'. We need to validate the diversity which Chief Seattle and others understood so deeply. We cannot continue to treat nature in the way we have done. Science has always been a double-edged sword. It has given us the beauty of Venice and the hideousness of Chernobyl, Roentgen's caring x-rays and Hiroshima. We need to look at what we can learn from the likes of Chief Seattle and how that knowledge can advise our science and technology in taking care of the environment. We must *love* the countryside. And yet I have seen a scientific paper recently entitled 'The Optimal Level of Pollution' ... Chief Seattle would have said that the optimal level is none, but that is not what modern science would say.

Today, the majority of the world's population lives in cities. Chief Seattle foresaw the problems that would bring:

> There is no place in the white man's city for quiet – no place to hear the leaves of the spring or the rustle of insects, but perhaps because I am a savage I do not understand ... What is there in life if man cannot hear the cry of the whippoorwill or the arguments of frogs ...

This might sound very simplistic but I think it is very sad that there are city children who have never seen a starry sky because of light pollution or have never heard natural night sounds – only police sirens and heavy traffic. Of course we cannot transplant a particular culture in a much-changed world, but we can be advised and forewarned by it in laying the basis for a sustainable future for our children. Listen to Chief Seattle on one of today's great problems – pollution:

> The whites too shall pass, perhaps sooner than the tribes. Continue to contaminate your bed and you will one night suffocate in your own waste. Your destiny is a mystery to us. What

happens when the buffalo are all slaughtered, when the wild horses are all tamed? What will happen when the secret corners of the forest are heavy with the scent of men? Where will the thicket be? Gone. Where will the eagle be? Gone. And what is it to say goodbye to the swift pony and the hunt? The end of living and the beginning of survival ...

That to me is so insightful. I would suggest we are in the survival stage now. I regret that our educational system and our way of understanding the world cannot find space for a great mind like that.

CROMWELL'S QUARTER AND ROUSERSTOWN

Oisín Kelly *recalls a childhood in the heart of Dublin.*

My father was a teacher in James's Street, Dublin and I was born next door to the school in No. 183 James's Street in 1915. The area was known as Cromwell's Quarter. It was a very poor area. You could have beggars knocking on your door ten times a day. I seem to remember men with skin diseases and soldiers suffering from shell shock. We lived opposite the South Dublin Union – now St James's Hospital. Every Saturday afternoon for quite a while we would visit it as a family. We would sing evangelical hymns (of which my mother had quite a repertoire) for the patients. I found it very depressing. The men had shaven heads and wore clothing made from rough frieze. Some of them were very old and I wasn't used to the sight of old people together.

For all that, ours was a sheltered, happy household. My father had reached a very high standard in a number of crafts – he was a shoemaker, a carpenter, a tailor and a plumber. He was very austere and had strict moral standards. He had a horror of war and was strongly pacifist. I was named Austin (after an uncle who was killed in the Dardanelles) Ernest (after an uncle who was killed in the Boer War). My father saw no humour in violence and objected to my reading comics like *Kinema Kuts*. I wasn't allowed play with toy soldiers, but ironically my father made a bow and arrows for me. The cult of the noble savage impressed him! I was enrolled in the Irish League of Woodcraft Chivalry – a boys' organisation somewhat like the Boy Scouts, minus the overt militaristic element. I was a member for four or five years and I owe it a lot for the company and companionship it provided and the opportunity to face a simple primitive situation. I had no great interest in team sport but I excelled at Marbles! I had a steel taw which could split other marbles. It was a killer! I'm sure I decimated the marble population of James's Street during the season!

My mother was a great devotee of the cinema and we would go to the Inchicore Grand or the Fountain to follow the adventures of Tom Mix and Rin Tin Tin. There was also a film show every Saturday in Swift's Hospital and we got into that with the porter's children. I had violin lessons with Miss Kavanagh, but dancing lessons in Rouserstown (on the way to Kilmainham) were a disaster for me. I was the only boy and while the girls tripped around like angels I felt big-footed and awkward. I refused to go back after the first lesson. As for artistic promise, I did some childhood drawings but they showed no merit or promise whatever. We had a large extended family, so most of my early friends were cousins. We crossed the city a lot to visit relations. The number 21 tram went every three minutes and you could travel from the Union to College Green for three halfpence.

Summer holidays every year were spent in my father's home in Clonmellon, Co. Westmeath. It may have been a quiet backwater but it was the centre of the world to me. I think it is the essence of a child's holiday that it should recur in familiar surroundings. I went to Mountjoy secondary school. I didn't like it much. The boys there seemed rougher than in James's Street. I never liked casual masculine violence. I'm afraid I was not a manly little chap! At the end of secondary school I went to Spiddal to perfect my Irish. That had a profound effect on me. This was a different civilisation. I realised that there was a living language there and that Irish was not the 'con' we had suspected at school.

THE CURIOUS MIND

Overall, mine was a happy, placid childhood. I loved the Dublin of then. I dislike the Dublin of now. I have lived a lot of my life outside of Dublin but I don't feel any pleasure in going into it now. It means nothing to me. I suppose to an extent, the motor car has ruined it.

IVAN ILLICH COMES TO COROFIN
Writer-philosopher IVAN ILLICH *creates a buzz in a Co. Clare village.*

COROFIN, CO. CLARE, is a quiet village. On a May evening in 1989 when I arrived to record an event in the parish hall, it seemed unusually quiet – but it was the eve of Corpus Christi and Mass was in progress ... A banner draped across the front of the parish hall proclaimed that something unusual was about to happen. It said simply –

COROFIN WELCOMES IVAN ILLICH

Yes, the man who would 'deschool' society was coming to Corofin. Ivan Illich, whose book *Deschooling Society* challenged the school as an institution by claiming that it hinders learning and real education. 'In schools,' Illich argues, 'we confuse teaching with learning, a diploma with competence and fluency with the ability to say something new.' He was in Corofin as the guest of Dara Molloy who was leading a campaign for alternatives in education.

By 9.30 p.m., over three hundred people had packed into the parish hall. They had come from as far away as Galway, Cork and Tralee. Illich is a broadcaster's nightmare. He does not give interviews, abhors microphones and quite readily walks away from them. He does not believe in giving lectures but prefers 'dialogue'. So rather than stand up on the stage, he sat in the middle of the hall and invited everyone to sit around him in concentric circles. He agreed that we could do a fly-on-the-wall type of recording – which was fine as long as he sat still. But when the dialogue heated up, Ivan the Terrible was jumping all over the place. I ended up crawling about after him on my hands and knees, causing sound technician Ted Berry all kinds of headaches.

Illich warmed things up with statements like 'People who go to school – believing that they need to be taught if they are to learn something – are crazy ...' But when he got on to the teaching of reading, the temperature went up considerably. 'There is something completely crazy about a society which takes eight months or more to teach children to read ... I have taught adults in Spain to read in three or four hours – not to pass an exam, but in response to their need to read a newspaper or a book ...'

A teacher in the audience reminded Illich that 'most teachers spend four to eight years teaching children to read ...' Illich replied: 'If by *reading* you mean deciphering the written word for silent understanding and if that competence must be acquired by everybody in society, then it will take you ten years to *teach* it! The book was *read* for thousands of years before compulsory education and the majority of people understood what was in books much better before schooling came in, because they *listened*. You couldn't be an employee in a doctor's house without knowing everything the doctor knew, because he read everything aloud ... Maybe we should get rid of teachers today, because the more we teach reading in this modern way, the more the reading of textbooks goes up and *real* reading goes down.'

The teacher was having none of this: 'If Dr Illich is right, then all teachers are stupid and he is a genius!' An equally irate Illich retorted:

'They are not stupid. They are *professionals*. There have always been artisans who have claimed a monopoly on doing what they do. In certain medieval cities, only people who belonged to a guild of shoemakers were allowed to make shoes. They were professionals who would not tolerate people who did not make shoes according to their standards. The modern professional – e.g. a physician – belongs to a completely different kind of association. It defines what constitutes disease and how one identifies it and it monopolises the way that disease will be corrected. This is monstrous.

'Professionals in modern society have the power to legislate, to judge and to monopolise the administration of correction. We live in a democracy which is based on the separation of those three powers, but with the multiplicity of professionals the separation of those powers is more and more taken back and relocated in small groups. These groups collapse into one hand the power to define, to judge and to correct – *to give what is missing*. We live therefore in a professional society. My concern is that the rediscovery or re-enlivening of traditional culture falls into the hands of professionals and their little executors. In this sense, I see schooling as a destructive procedure.'

At this stage – probably fortuitously – somebody suggested a break for tea, biscuits and music. During the break, Ivan Illich moved around, continuing 'dialogue' on a one-to-one basis.

It was after midnight when I left Corofin. It had been quite an evening.

A CLASSICAL EDUCATION

Former Archbishop of Armagh, CAHAL DALY, enjoyed a classics-based secondary education in St Malachy's College, Belfast.

FATHER HENDLEY WAS president of St Malachy's College. He was a man who had a tremendous spiritual influence on his pupils because of his integrity, his utter sincerity and conviction and his lack of all pomp. He was a man of a very compassionate heart but he was anxious not to spoil his students, anxious that nobody would have ideas beyond their station and that we would genuinely give thanks to God for the gifts we had and not pride ourselves upon them. I had done the equivalent to the junior certificate examination and I think I probably had the leading results in Latin and Greek, which were my favourite subjects then and afterwards. I came back rather proud of my results and not unwelcoming to any compliments that might be directed towards me. I met the president on the stairs on the first night and he looked rather sternly at me and said, 'Daly, you didn't do very well in your mathematics. You'll have to pull up your socks in mathematics.' I discovered afterwards that he was in fact quite proud, because he had taught me Latin and also mathematics, but he just wanted to make the point that I mustn't get ideas above myself, and I think that was good for me.

The study of these languages was a great help to me then and afterwards, particularly when I went on to specialise in the ancient classics in my university course. I did honours in Latin and Greek with subsidiary subjects in modern history and philosophy, which was part of the requirement for admission to a major seminary. I liked philosophy and was to specialise in it afterwards, but at that time my horizons were within the world of Greece and Rome. I still remember the classes in translation and in Latin prose conducted by the professor, R.M. Henry, who was a venerable figure, just as old as I am now but I thought he was as old as the hills then. When he had a good student, he took a great personal interest and was very encouraging. He gave compliments sparingly but when he did they were worth receiving.

The appeal of the classics for me was the insight they gave into the structure of a language, into how language works and how you construct a sentence that will concisely and grammatically express your meaning. Thinking yourself *into* a language with a different structure from a modern language, and yet which is at the root of modern linguistic development, was a tremendously mind-stretching experience. There are very few experiences in life that have ever stretched me intellectually to the same extent as Latin prose translation. The philosophy of translation which R.M. Henry taught was that you take an English paragraph and ask yourself, 'What did this writer mean to say?' and then you say it in the language that Cicero might have used in his time. It is not a question of word-for-word literal translation, but a thinking into the meaning of the English sentence and then thinking yourself into the mentality and thought patterns of a Ciceronian. In an examination, for example, when presented with a Latin prose text, one would have been expected by R.M. Henry to spend at least half the time just thinking into the meaning of the passage and then saying it as a contemporary of Cicero might have said it. You didn't take your pen in hand until at least half the time had elapsed and the rest of the time you spent in sheer hard thinking, thinking *into* the mindset of the person who wrote the passage.

Only one other teacher had the same effect on me as R.M. Henry and that was Dr William Moran, the priest who was professor of dogmatic theology in Maynooth. Again, when a written examination was required, his questions were so penetrating that he would ideally have wanted every student to spend more than half the time thinking about the meaning of the question and preparing a clear and succinct answer to it. The sheer thinking involved was quite an exhilarating experience, exhausting but exciting.

WORDS FROM THE WISE

In 1993, to mark International Year of Older People, I convened a senate – a gathering of older and wiser people – in Tinakilly House, Co. Wicklow. This became the Tinakilly Senate. Its theme was 'Renewing the Spirit of Ireland'. This is PATRICK LYNCH'*s address to the Senate, under the title 'Is Economic Growth Enough?'*

IRELAND HAS SEEN vast changes over the past seventy years. Some of these have been for the good, some not. Our historians often judge our performance too harshly, though indeed there have been aspects of that performance of which we have little reason to be proud.

Let me begin with our greatest achievement, something we often overlook. We have preserved democratic government in circumstances that have no parallel – that I am aware of – anywhere else in the world. The victors in a bitter civil war governed with consent from 1922 to 1932. The vanquished in that conflict, after some years, became a peaceful parliamentary party, formed a government in 1932 and survived for sixteen years until 1948. During those years representatives of their opponents in the Civil War formed the main opposition party. From the beginning of the State, the foundations of an efficient and honest administration were laid.

Within the context I have just described, substantial and material progress was made, as most Irish economists would agree. But have we let the economists away with too much? We must, of course, encourage and promote economic growth, but have we been concerned more with the quantity of that growth than with its quality?

The development of any society is, I believe, far too important to be left exclusively to the economists. An increase in economic growth is not the only measure of achievement. As the American economist Herman Daly observed, 'If people die of exposure to pollution, their funerals and burials add to gross national product'. Economics has been drifting away from the other social sciences for the past forty years. Price theory cannot apply to the environment. It is absurd for some economists to claim that everything must have a price. You will recall Oscar Wilde's cynic who knew the price of everything and the value of nothing. Keynes regarded economics as a moral science, as did Marshall and Pigou whose book *The Economics of Welfare* examined the disutilities of the market economy, explaining why firms which profited from their smokey chimneys should compensate those whose clothes lines were victims of the soot.

In the measurement of growth, compromises are essential. Uncertainty is part of the human condition. We must begin by agreeing on the kind of environment we want and measuring the costs of maintaining it. Within that context, let market forces prevail. Economic theory has precise methods for forecasting change when people are motivated by competition for direct monetary or material reward and when outside factors do not intrude on the market. In the real world, however, such conditions cannot exist over any considerable period of time. The great economists, who were also wide-ranging thinkers – such as Adam Smith, Marx, Pigou, Marshall, Keynes and Joan Robinson – all made social and political assumptions.

Change is continuous. The real world is more complicated than the simple, static equilibrium assumed by many economists. Brendan O'Regan accepted the inevitability of continuous change by adapting to a new situation in 1960 when the long-range jet aircraft began to overfly Shannon. He created a new industrial region at Shannon while others were whining about a past which had already become part of history.

THE CURIOUS MIND

Today we need men and women such as Brendan O'Regan in a new situation to help the renewal of the spirit of Ireland.

The classical economists from Adam Smith onwards extended their analysis outside the narrow realm of economic facts because national policy-making must draw from a variety of disciplines – from the sociologist, the economic historian, the administrator and others. In the early years of this state, many aspects of public policy were unduly influenced by able civil servants and economists whose background and training had closed their minds to most ideas outside the British liberal and *laissez-faire* tradition. We were rescued from economic and social stagnation by the Whitaker programme that was published in 1958. In many ways, that survey was a reminder that economic growth, however essential, is by itself not enough. Today the fashionable word is privatisation. Many economists are enthusing about the wild race towards an unfettered, unrestrained free-market economy which worships an unthinking consumerism, inspired not by considerations of social responsibility but by a desire to grab the fast buck and let tomorrow look after itself.

In general, we have been slow to adapt to this concept of continuous change. Arthur Griffith's belief – that political independence implied economic independence – lived on until it no longer made sense and was dispelled by the Anglo-Irish free trade agreement and membership of the European Economic Community. Progressive industrialisation and television are changing Irish institutions so rapidly that they may be unable to meet the pace of that change, just as in the nineteenth century England was unprepared for the vast social changes produced by the technological revolution that made possible the industrial revolution.

Bertrand Russell wrote that 'technological change, like an army of tanks that has lost its driver, advances blindly, ruthlessly, without goal or purpose'. This is because the humanities have not generally created a culture adjusted to an industrial age. Ireland must be seen in a global context, as Denis Meadows demonstrated in his book *Limits to Growth*. We are using non-renewable natural resources of fossil fuel, stocks of mineral deposits, coal, oil, gas, timber, merely because voracious market forces demand them.

The conventional reply to this is that a technological fix will see us through. This is a Faustian bargain. We shall sell our soul to satisfy immediate market needs and the nuclear option will save posterity when fossil fuels are exhausted. On this basis, posterity will need 24,000 breeder reactors at any one time and plutonium has an estimated radioactive life of 24,000 years. I am quoting Mesarovic, Pecci and Pestel and their arguments have not been answered. Instead of indicative planning on a global scale, many economists are prepared to accept the haphazard consumer society of the unrestrained free market.

At this year's annual meeting of the British Association for the Advancement of Science, there was a strange spectacle of distinguished economists defending currency speculators such as George Soros as 'doing a certain amount of good' and others declaring that in the former Soviet Union today, 'Mafia capitalism was better than no capitalism at all'. I should add that subsequently the *Financial Times* sought to qualify these unfortunate observations with a respectable gloss.

No, we must decide what kind of economic growth we need. Its quality is as important as its size. There is no merit in producing crops that no one wants. Putting invented prices on these crops makes no real addition to our Gross National Product. Economic planning must be revived and adapted to changed circumstances if we are to avoid riding rudderless into a sea of make-believe. This revival must be eventually on a global scale before we enjoy fully its domestic merits. There is, of course, room for a free market economy – but within an environment shaped by human reason and not designed by wild and uncontrolled forces in the name of economic growth at any price.

To counter this dangerous myth of a technological fix for solving our problems, the humanities must come to terms with contemporary industrial and post-industrial society to provide it with a set of appropriate values.

A country's broad culture must combine the most advanced technology and economic development with an awareness by its humanities of the current facts of economic life. T.S. Eliot did this for England but his vision was never fully absorbed in popular culture.

Seamus Heaney is doing it for Ireland, where fortunately the class structure is less rigid. Creative artists must keep us civilised by giving us their vision of our material and social environment. We must not forget Patrick Kavanagh who warned:

> Culture is always something that was,
> Something that pedants can measure
> Skull of bard, thigh of chief
> Depth of dried-up river
> Shall we be thus forever?
> Shall we be thus forever?

DOROTHY AND CECILY

DOROTHY HEATHCOTE *and* CECILY O'NEILL *talk about the value of drama-in-education.*

D.:   Drama-in-education is for me an 'as-if situation'. It is creating a world which will turn out to be truthful – truthful to experience, not truthful in actuality. I have spent my life trying to create the circumstances in which groups of people bring together their experience to deal with decisions. I believe we have disenfranchised children in our schools. We have said, 'When you're grown up, we'll let you do things. Until then, just play around – but we'll stop you if we don't like what you're playing at ...' I can never understand why the curriculum is so split. A child should go out feeling it has learned something it can put together, rather than that it has learned something it can only separate. To do that you need a 'universal joint' – which is the quality of the teacher in keeping their experience together and the quality of the rigour when they are assembling information so the children will see that this fits with that ...

C.:   An American writer once said, 'Teachers are very kind and caring and compassionate but all of that is useless if they don't have courage'. If they have courage there are all kinds of strategies they can adopt which will enable them to be flexible, to invite the children into the learning in a really active way, as the wonderful new primary school curriculum suggests. I recall hearing Dorothy say – twenty-five years ago – that drama is a shared learning experience between teacher and children. All kinds of learning go on in the classroom, but where failure is the main experience of a child it is a real deficit model – having a narrow sterile curriculum based on testing every so often. It is very bad for the morale of both teachers and students. As Jerome Bruner said, 'Teachers are not *just* transmission devices'. You can catch creativity and desire from teachers. Education is about making connections and drama is that 'universal joint' – to use Dorothy's wonderful phrase. It does connect both the interior of the person and their exterior experience. It is by no means a panacea, but it does give access to a way of learning that has been neglected.

D.:   Of course it's not a panacea. I believe very much in the transmission of knowledge but I prefer it to be a transference. The terrible tragedy of splitting the curriculum is that the spirituality is lost. There is a lack of togetherness in our big schools. Children are bussed in. Teachers don't live anywhere near the school. This may sound contradictory but I believe schools need to be made much more attuned to natural living and have a more heightened structural awareness. The world that talks together really learns about itself. When I'm working in drama, my children never stop talking. They are tutoring me. Their needs are causing me to find different languages.

C.:   Peter O'Driscoll said earlier today that education is all about relationship. And it is reciprocal. If the teacher isn't learning as well as the students, education is merely a transmission device.

Someone has said that the last thousand years have been the era of *me* – the individual. It would be nice if the next millennium were the era of *us*.

D.: If you see children as candles, you are a slave to lighting them up all the time. If you see them as jugs, you are a slave to filling them up all the time. If you see them as crucibles, then you are stirring yourself to stir them all the time. The crucible is my model!

THE LAST DAYS

This is the closing part of the script of a radio documentary on my boarding-school days in Patrician College, Ballyfin, Co. Laois. Although written in the third person it is my own story ...

THE LEAVING CERTIFICATE Exam. Boys who had ambled through school up to now suddenly began to rise at 5 a.m. to study ... and to pray.

'O great St Joseph of Cupertino, who by your prayers obtained from God that you be asked at your examination the only proposition you knew ...'

In these final days they were accorded independence. There were no more bounds, no more limitations. Billy Daly caught a pike in the lake and almost the whole class dined royally on it.

On the eve of the Agricultural Science exam (more marks than Commerce, better chance of being called to teacher-training ...) Brother Joseph brought them for a nature walk across the farm and talked of perennial rye-grass and plantain. He no longer seemed to be Brother Joseph, the teacher ...

After all the panic, the exam itself seemed incidental. And then it was all over ... He packed his case, cleared out his locker, said goodbye to his pals – many of whom he would never see again. It was June 1959. A decade was ending. A lifetime beginning. His father came to collect him. The car set off for home. Home. Freedom. No more Latin. No more French – never did French anyway ...

Over the cattle grid. Goodbye, it seemed to sing. Goodbye to porridge ... to the study hall ... to dormitories ... to a sausage on Sunday. Goodbye 'Rosie', Tim, Eddie, Des ... It was over. He was free.

> Two – four – six – eight
> Who do we appreciate?
> B-A-L-L-Y-F-I-N
> Ballyfin!

> He was going home ...
> Ne ambulaveritis in horto, pueri ...
> No more Latin ...
> He was going home ...
> He was happy. But why was he lonely?
> Why – was – he – lonely ...?

A POSTSCRIPT

Well yes, he did get a call to teacher-training (thanks to perennial rye-grass ...). What does he remember fifty years later of the Leaving Cert, 1959? He remembers Brother Joseph ... perennial rye-grass ... Rosie, Tim, Eddie, Des ... and the exotic taste of pike ...

DEEP ECOLOGY

JOHN SEED *argues that we need to overcome the arrogant belief that humans are all that matter on this planet.*

WE ARE NOT aliens on this earth. We are part of its warp and woof. Some thirty years ago Arnie Ness – an emeritus professor at the University of Oslo – coined the phrase 'deep ecology' to describe a way of looking at the world that doesn't see human beings at its centre. Deep ecology asks how is it that such an intelligent species as ourselves could be tearing up the biological fabric out of which our own lives are constructed. As James Lovelock – the British scientist who framed the Gaia hypothesis – put it: 'It is as if the brain decided it was the most important organ and began mining the liver.' A brain like that obviously doesn't have a long-term future! We are like that in the way we treat our life-support systems.

In spite of St Francis and more recently the work of Matthew Fox and Thomas Berry, the Judaeo-Christian tradition has largely led to this incredible arrogance that human beings are at the centre of everything. We are told that only human beings are created in God's image – only human beings have a soul – and basically we can do what we like to the rest of creation. The real action is in heaven and this earth is a kind of moral testing-ground for humans. Because of the deep historical effects of those views, all the institutions of our society are based on that false and pernicious idea.

If, for instance, you look into an economics textbook, you will find among the first principles that nothing has any value until human beings add their labour to it. The earth is seen as just raw materials, resources for human ingenuity, but – as indigenous peoples have always intuited – the world is not a pyramid with humans at the top. The world is a web and we humans are just one strand in that web. Unless we realise that, we will destroy the web and ultimately ourselves.

We have become shallow fictitious selves, disconnected from nature. When we say 'myself', we assume that there is something objective about that, whereas 'self' is socially constructed. For Native Americans, the 'self' extended seven generations into the future, so that when they made decisions, they thought about their children and their children's children. The science of ecology shows us that we need to extend our identity in this way. Arnie Ness says ecological *ideas* are not enough – we need an ecological identity, an ecological *self*.

He further claims that a sense of responsibility is a treacherous basis for conservation, i.e. if we feel responsible or dutiful in protecting nature, that is based on the false notion that nature is something separate from ourselves. Even with our language, when we talk of the environment, it sounds as if it is over there somewhere, and if there is someone good or noble around, he will do something about it. In fact, the environment is no other than our very self and if we want to demonstrate this – just hold your breath for three or four minutes, while you contemplate where the environment begins and where you end! You will quickly realise that the air is as much part of yourself as your brain or your liver – and similarly with the water and the soil. If we could understand this deeply, then it no longer requires duty or responsiblity to do something about 'the environment', but merely our own self-interest. We have self-interest in large supply, but we labour under the delusion that our self ends with our skin ...

LONG LIVE THE CAT!
A personal plea for curiosity ...

As a writer of children's books I am often invited to talk with schoolchildren about books and writing. To be a writer (to be a learner) – I tell them – you need to be curious. It never ceases to amaze me how familiar twenty-first-century children are with the Victorian dictum 'Curiosity killed the cat' ... That – I tell them – is the greatest load of rubbish you will ever be told ...! Listen to what it is saying. Curiosity is *bad*! It could kill you – like the cat! Nonsense. You need to be curious, to ask why. Be a cat, sniffing around, full of curiosity.

A ninth-century Irish scholar-monk felt exactly like this when he wrote about his beloved cat, Pangur Bán ...

I and Pangur Bán, my cat,
'Tis a like task we are at;
Hunting mice is his delight,
Hunting words I sit all night.

Better far than praise of men
'Tis to sit with book and pen;
Pangur bears me no ill will
He too plies his simple skill.

'Tis a merry thing to see
At our tasks how glad are we,
When at home we sit and find
Entertainment to our mind.

'Gainst the wall he sets his eye
Full and fierce and sharp and sly;
'Gainst the wall of knowledge I
All my little wisdom try.

When a mouse darts from its den
O how glad is Pangur then!
O what gladness do I prove
When I solve the doubts I love!

So in peace our tasks we ply
Pangur Bán my cat and I,
In our arts we find our bliss
I have mine and he has his.

Practice every day has made
Pangur perfect in his trade,
I get wisdom day and night
Turning darkness into light.

COME, LET US LIVE WITH OUR CHILDREN

This was the title given to a 1982 documentary marking the bicentenary of the birth of Friedrich Froebel – the originator of the Kindergarten, a radically new concept of early childhood education. Our guide in these excerpts is JOACHIM LIEBSCHNER *of the Froebel Insitute, London.*

FROEBEL LIVED AT a time when it was held that children had not acquired a real personality and therefore needed to be 'filled in'. His work and writing made people aware that children are people in their own right with their own personality, and that such a personality needed to be fostered from an early age. Thus he wrote:

> Let us learn from our children. Let us give heed to the gentle admonitions of their life, to the silent demands of their minds. Come, let us live with our children. Then will the life of our children bring us peace and joy. Then shall we be deemed to grow wise, to be wise ...

Froebel was the son of a pastor. His mother died when Friedrich was an infant and his relationship with his stepmother was unhappy. He spent a lot of time on his own in the garden, exploring and becoming very close to nature. His schooling was unrewarding:

> We repeated our tasks parrotwise, speaking much and knowing nothing, for the teaching had not the very least connection with real life, nor had it any actuality for us.

When he left school at fourteen, he studied forestry and explored his master's big library, so that he was self-educated by the age of eighteen. His observation of nature convinced him of the necessity to care for the young child just as plants are nurtured. He studied science at the University of Jena, but a quirk of fate led him into the world of education. His brother died and Friedrich felt duty-bound to educate his brother's three children. Other nephews joined them and thus began an educational experiment in an old farmhouse. All the activities were done with the children. Whatever was demanded of the children was also demanded of the adults. They lived together as a community. Within five years there were fifty children in his school. There were some complaints about the freedom afforded to the children. An inspector from the Prussian government was sent to investigate and produced a glowing report, which duly resulted in an increase in numbers. In 1826 Froebel published *The Education of Man*.

Froebel realised that he had come too late for older children. They needed to be nurtured at a much younger age. His opportunity came when a Swiss nobleman invited him to set up a school and oversee an orphanage. Now he encountered very young children and he observed how they played and learned. Play was never trivial but serious and deeply significant for the child:

> Play is the highest phase of child development ... It is the purest, most spiritual activity of man at this stage ... It gives joy, freedom, contentment, inner and outer rest, peace with the world. It holds the source of all that is good. ·

For play to be fully beneficial it must be directed and controlled. Froebel devised materials to structure and direct play in a creative way. These he called 'gifts'. If you want to know the great Absolute – the Creator – then you must be creative. Froebel held that there was a great unity between man and God, and that Nature was the mediator of that unity. Just as we nourish and protect seedlings and help them grow, so must it be with children. Thus was born the notion of the Kindergarten where the child would become an active, thinking, feeling person. The first Kindergarten opened in Blankenburg in 1840.

Froebel recognised the importance of women in early childhood education and set up women's associations while on lecture tours. When he told an all-male conference of teachers that women teachers were necessary, the conference collapsed in hilarious laughter. Froebel, however, set up his own training college for women and after his death in 1851 these women carried his philosophy across Europe and set up Kindergartens over the following twenty years. The first Kindergarten in Dublin was set up in 1862.

There is not a Froebel 'method' as such – more a philosophy, a way of looking at children. A century and a half after his death, what is Froebel's legacy? He suggests we:

–   Take children seriously. Respect them as people and recognise their rights and obligations.
–   Tailor education according to individual needs and not to the demands of society. We are going backwards today by trying to fit children economically into society through testing and competition. Cooperation, not competition, should be our goal.
–   The most important thing is to be creative. How else will you know your Creator?
–   Children learn through activity. Talk less to children – do more!

The day before Froebel died, a child brought him some flowers. He took them, kissed the child and gave the flowers to his wife, saying, 'Look after my flowers. Take care of my weeds. I have learned from them both ...'

In a way that sums up his philosophy – all children are in need of careful attention.

THE GAME OF LIFE

Business magnate TONY O'REILLY *argues that the game of rugby was for him a template for life ...*

IN BELVEDERE COLLEGE there was one particularly profound influence on my life, Reverend Father Tom O'Callaghan. He was a mathematician of distinction, a theologian of great merit and probably the best rugby coach that I ever experienced in my entire rugby career. He was a theoretician, a hard taskmaster, a lover of the game – although he had never played it himself – and because I was on what is called the Junior Cup team from the age of twelve, I had his influence for virtually all of the final six years of my rugby career in Belvedere. That was an extraordinary experience, because it brought an intellectual dimension into the game that I think stood by all of us who experienced his training for the rest of our lives.

I have always felt that rugby football was the great tutor, because it is really a template for life. If you don't train, you don't get your rewards. So there's a risk-reward ratio established clearly in your mind at an early stage. If you don't participate collegially with the other boys on the team, you are isolated. One learns about winning with grace and – more importantly – losing with grace. I call to mind Rudyard Kipling's poem, 'If':

> If you can meet with Triumph and Disaster
> And treat those two imposters just the same ...
> Yours is the Earth and everything that's in it,
> And – which is more – you'll be a Man, my son!

My father had given me these lines and he reminded me of them before we went out on the field to play in the Leinster Schools Cup Final. We lost to Blackrock by an intercept in the very last moment, when it looked as if we were about to win. I went behind the line, they took the kick and converted the try. The intercept was achieved by a very brilliant Blackrock player, Tom Cleary, who – funnily enough – had done the same thing the previous year against Clongowes, but this was more mortal, since it was against us. He scored the winning try, the full-time whistle went and the sky was a blizzard of blue-and-white Blackrock scarves. He was festooned with his team-mates and I went over and waited until they disengaged. I shook hands with him. We had lost the cup. My mother had bought a new hat – as she had for the previous nine years – but, yet again, she had no opportunity to present the cup. It was a moment of very acute sadness in my life.

About twenty-eight years later I was president of Heinz and we had a major technical problem which could have led to a product recall and could have cost the company about $30-35 million. It required the support of a company called Del Monte. I flew to California to meet the president of Del Monte, who luxuriated in the extraordinary name of Jim Schmuck. I went to see Mr Schmuck and said to him, 'I'm O'Reilly, president of the Heinz company. We wonder if you could help us in this'. He then related to me a story of how his parish priest in Santa Barbara was a man called Father McCarthy who had been a scholastic at Blackrock College in Dublin when – as Schmuck rather poetically put it – 'you were engaged in the Superbowl while a schoolboy. At the last moment, when you had lost the game, you showed some grace under presssure by shaking hands with an opponent from the side which had won the game. He thought you were a pretty good guy and advises me so. And so the Del Monte company will vote with Heinz on this issue.' That was the famous $35 million handshake.

––––––––

AN INTEREST IN PEOPLE

I remember interviewing Dr GEORGE OTTO SIMMS,
former Primate of Ireland, on a winter afternoon in his Dublin home for
the series 'My Education'. He was such a charming and engrossing man
that our interview ran on into the evening and we ended up barely able to
see each other in the darkened sitting room!
Of course, there had been no need to switch on the light ...

I WAS ALWAYS interested in people – I wanted to know the name of everybody in the school, for instance. My weakness was that I didn't specialise enough. I was so fond of the different subjects that my knowledge of chemistry and physics was a bit shallow at times. We even had a taste of geology and archaeology, as well as Latin and Greek, compositions and writing, verse and translation – all very intensive. I didn't find things like college chapel tedious – I didn't switch off. We worked pretty hard, but I remember how boys came regularly to the voluntary service in Lent, which was a good forty minutes out of their evening which they had to make up somehow. That gave me the kind of support that reassured me that there must be something in this religion – that it is not merely an inherited formal convention.

I came to Trinity College Dublin because I realised that I wanted to spend my life in Ireland. Trinity made a lasting impression on me and I feel I am still there (they very kindly made me an honorary fellow and it is lovely to be there, in the library or occasionally supervising this and that, filling gaps and doing a little talking and instruction). I took my first degree in classics and in political science and history, then I went on to do the Bachelor of Divinity. So, from 1928 to 1935 I was at Trinity College, living in rooms and meeting very interesting people who have often given me more than some of the lecturers. I think it often happens that you learn from those actually sitting beside you in the class. I said to myself, 'I am going to be a librarian. I am not going to drift into the ministry. It seems to be very easy to get into the Church of Ireland – not too demanding'.

I actually tried to do the Bachelor of Divinity before committing myself to ordination, just because that was a demanding examination. I wrote my thesis on monasticism. It was fascinating to learn about Cassian of Marseilles who had visited the Middle East, the home of monasticism and the Senobitic life, and when you actually read from original sources, you do get steeped in the atmosphere. That thrilled me very much and I thought I would like to work at the British Museum. I wasn't quite sure if this would be for life or just for a while, but I went for an interview. Sir George Hill was the director in those days and he was a very interesting person and we got on quite agreeably at the interview. He said, 'If you want to come we will have you, but go away and think about it', and of course that brought me to my decision. When I decided to go on with theology he wrote back and said, 'We would have welcomed you'. At least I knew that there was a choice and that helped me to decide.

There were many people who gave me very good advice. They suggested that – as I was interested in people – it might be that I could give most through the ordained life. If you are ordained, you have an entrée into people's lives, which is very privileged and rather frightening and, of course, full of responsibilities. You are not there as a nosy parker; you are there because you want to share life's possibilities, and ministry really is ultimately that. I still visit the sick – I am privileged to visit old people's homes and celebrate the sacrament with them. I also travel the world to visit leprosy hospitals – these are real people and they have a tremendous amount to teach us.

My first appointment was St Bartholomew's Church in Clyde Road, where they were trying to get an assistant for a vicar who had been there quite a long time. When, after three years, I left St Bartholomew's, tears filled my eyes to be leaving after being so involved in people's lives. However, I left there to teach in a theological college for two years and this laid the foundations for the rest of my ministry. I learned about reading and about discussions. I learned about people who had different ways and to tolerate and understand them and, of course, to benefit from the very differences. Then I was brought back to be a chaplain in Trinity and that seemed to be bliss. I wanted to stay there all my life. People come and go, and if you fail with one lot of students, you know they'll move on and a new lot will come. I was thirteen years there as chaplain, until I was asked to go down to the diocese of Cork to look after the cathedral. I was then asked to be bishop and, eventually, asked back to Dublin to be an archbishop.

My father – although he was in the law and saw the seamy side of life – was very gentle and a man of peace. He wanted to appreciate all that was Gaelic as well as all that was 'plantation' in our history. He left this lesson with me: hear the other side. *Audi alteram partem*. I often remember that.

MUSIC AND THE CHILD

It is May 1994. A seminar on the theme 'Music in the Classroom' is in
progress at the National Concert Hall, Dublin. A distinguished figure comes
to the podium to speak on 'the place of the arts in the life of the child'.
He is the world-renowned violinist ISAAC STERN.
I am fortunate to record his words.

MUSIC FOR ME is the most natural form of the arts. Why does it speak so easily to so many people of differing backgrounds and at different times? The answer is simple (*he raps the lectern in heartbeat rhythm*). While the foetus is still in the womb – the first tempo. And the moment that foetus comes to life – ehhhh! (*he emits a piercing 'baby shriek'*). Sound, sound and tempo – the basis of music, the most natural form of human expression. Every child reacts to it. Sound, the sound of parents' voices. The sound of caressing, of comfort, of strength. This is what all children respond to and there is no such thing as an ungifted child. They *all* react. They are all willing to learn ...

We have reached what I call the 'digitalisation of the world'. You press buttons for preformed thought. You look at television for preformed opinions. And because of short attention spans and the pressure of advertising space, everything is presented in short bites. Anything that has to do with the quality of life takes time for reflection. Children need that time. The arts part of the curriculum is the beginning of the beginning of that process but it must begin early – in the home and in the school. What kind of life surrounds the child at home? Do parents let the child turn on anything they want on radio or television or do they consciously surround the child in some way with what is part of the beautiful stream of man's creativity? Not in order to force it down the child's throat but to make it a natural happenstance of daily living.

Then comes the school. Some of us come from a European background where no child was considered educated if it didn't play, dance, sing, paint – not to *be* a dancer, singer, painter but to know: to know what is beautiful, to know what is possible. As I travel the world I notice a growing lack of respect for teachers in society. They are not the people to whom we give the greatest accolades or income possibilities. And yet I do not know of any well-educated person for whom somehow, somewhere, one teacher didn't turn a light on inside and make that person become what he/she is today.

Teaching – knowledgeable, informed, enthusiastic, dedicated, absolutely passionate teaching. That is one of the keys to the future. And parents – demanding, voting, caring, loving parents. That is another key. Between the two there can be a new world for the next generations. And we have little time. We have already lost one or two generations because the speed of communications has overcome the respect for learning, the idea that a person of the mind is perhaps more important than the person behind the till.

What most children like is to be part of the action – to take part in some artistic effort – painting, singing, marching together. I am a great believer in the Kodaly Method. I remember seeing highly-trained teachers give hand-signals, dictating a melody which was then written on the blackboard by a six-year-old. For the children it was normal – not an occult, strange thing to do. It was what they were there for – to learn. Both Kodaly and Bartok fed on the rich Hungarian folk tradition. They went into the hills and copied down the songs of the people. They transformed the folk songs into children's songs and from these came the children's acquaintance with music in a most natural way. The Kodaly Method makes use of the children's greatest gifts – their voices and their ears. It teaches them about the earth to which they belong. They become not just musicians but the best concert audience you ever saw ...

The main thing about studying the arts is the continuous recognition that it gives to every young mind that there was history that began more than a week ago – that history was written over a long time and has a lot to give us to know about. There has been a great deal of ferment in the United States recently – because of the influx of so many nationalities – about the eurocentricity of artistic training. Eurocentricity – what does that mean?

- that the rest of the world doesn't exist? No!
- that five hundred years of artistic endeavour flourished in Europe? Yes!
- should we be ashamed of it? No!
- should everybody know about it? Yes!
- are we the majority of the world? No!

We are part of a diminishing minority, but do we have to excuse and forgive our background? I don't think so. Genius should be revered because the genius sees with clarity what others dimly feel possible. Genius opens doors. We should not be ashamed of it. Embrace other cultures, yes. But don't give up pride in your own culture.

JAMES JOYCE AND I

Actress FIONNULA FLANAGAN *explains how James Joyce played a very important part in her professional life.*

IT IS VERY hard to say when James Joyce entered my life. In my childhood my parents would say things like, 'Well, Joyce knew that ...' and 'Joyce said ...' and I always assumed they knew him. It was no longer surprising to me when I, too, read his books. Also, coming from the north side of Dublin, many of the shops and small businesses, the streets and the pubs that are named in his books were still there when I was a child. Vestiges of the Edwardian Dublin that Joyce knew were still in existence. My grandmother, who had lived in Portland Row and later in Marino, would hold musical evenings in her house on Sundays and these pale young Irish tenors would bring their sheet music and sing their party pieces, a lot of which were the kind of songs that I was later to encounter in Joyce's work. So the world of Joyce was all around me. When I came to read it, I was just reading about the people I knew. I was reading about a Dublin that still had shadows and echoes in the Dublin of my childhood.

Ultimately, that writing got to me. I had been living in the States and my career was going along quite well. I was doing a lot of television work, but I really wanted to do something that made more of a statement about me and how I think and who I am as a woman. I had been putting together some material for a long time, from the political writings of Rosa Luxembourg to the poetry of Edna St Vincent Millay, with the Joyce fictional women and lots of other things thrown in. I couldn't really find a hook to hang them on in the planning of a one-woman show, other than the fact that they were my favourites.

Then I hit upon the idea of looking at who were the real women in Joyce's life. I had actually met Sylvia Beach when she came to Dublin. My father had been instrumental in helping with that first 'Bloomsday' event when she came to open the Joyce tower. I began to read about her and discovered what a sustaining influence, a great friend and a courageous person she had been, and that is how the show *James Joyce's Women* came about. Burgess Meredith had cast me to play Molly Bloom on Broadway with Zero Mostel in the revival of *Ulysses in Nighttown* in 1973. Forces conspired to make the two things happen – my one-woman show and to work with Zero and Burgess on the Joyce material.

MY FATHER ALWAYS SAID IT NEVER RAINS IN CROKE PARK ...

My own diary of the making of the radio documentary 'Final Day' – a sound picture of the All-Ireland Football Final Day, 1988.

SEPTEMBER 10, 1979
(Yes the date is correct, read on!) A memo to TV producer, Joe Mulholland, outlining a scenario for a *television* documentary on All-Ireland Final Day. (Joe finds it 'interesting' but nothing happens ...)

THE CURIOUS MIND

SEPTEMBER 17, 1987

Meath win the All-Ireland Football title after a gap of twenty years. Sweet! The wonderful atmosphere of the day (especially when your team wins!) rekindles an old interest ... Where's that memo of '79?

AUGUST 1988

Here we go! Here we go! I get clearance for the idea – on radio! And more importantly – a budget – of £350. Move over Cecil B! I discuss the idea with Des Coates, Head of OBS. He's very supportive. Will give me all the help he can but primarily his resources are devoted to the live transmission on the day. Basically the message is – do it yourself! John Egan does a trial recording among fans at the Mayo–Meath semi-final. He is disquieted by the language of the fans (John doesn't go to many matches ...) Also being seated in the Cusack Stand limits movement and therefore variety of voices. Head for the hill, folks.

SEPTEMBER 1988

It's going to be Meath and Cork on the 18th. Ronan Kelly, Aidan Crowley and Dermot Rattigan will be the recordists. Ronan on the Hill, Aidan on the Canal End and Dermot roving around town – Connolly Station, pubs, streets. We need passes for the Hill and the Canal End. Danny Lynch, GAA PRO takes a lot of convincing but finally relents ... On no account will any of us be allowed on the actual field. A pity. We need to record the odd bit of body contact, the kick of a ball, players' comments. What to do? Plan B – we will take a feed of the 'international Sound' (TV sound minus commentary) and record it in studio. (It's going to be fun listening back to that!)

SUNDAY, SEPTEMBER 4, 1988

Hurling Final. Joe Sheridan (Radio OBS) does a trial run and picks up a marvellous piece of conversation between past and present Artane Band leaders. Hell, we'll use it. It's not really cheating.

SEPTEMBER 12–17
Last minute preparations. Beg, borrow and damn near steal stereo mikes and recorders. The organisation has *one* stereo mike for cassette recorder (purchased for this occasion) ... Check the train timetable for arrival of Cork fans. Ronan Kelly will go down to Ashbourne on the Sunday morning – he may even pick up some material at Mass ... Radio OBS will record the TV countdown. Make sure the Weather Forecast after 9 a.m. news will make reference to the All-Ireland Final. Arrange with Radio Sport to get a tape of Mícheál Ó Muircheartaigh's complete commentary ...

THURSDAY, SEPTEMBER 15
Briefing sessions with the Three Recorders. Explain what we're at! Don't get involved in the match! Don't bother with interviews! Don't be noticed! Fly-on-the-wall. Listen out for the 'wits' – the unusual. Move around – if possible! Above all – a clean stereo sound, please. Check settings on the machines, check levels, batteries, tapes. We have only the one shot at it. Go to it!

FRIDAY, SEPTEMBER 16
Pat O'Donovan (Radio Sport) finds me a ticket for the top of the Cusack Stand (and him a Corkman!). Borrow another stereo mike and see what the sound is like from up there.

SUNDAY, SEPTEMBER 18
This is it! Weather ideal for football and – more important – for recording. No wind or rain. (Didn't my father always say it never rains in Croke Park.) Set off for Croke Park at noon. Bump into Dermot Rattigan who is cruising around the pubs – all in the line of duty of course. I record the buzz outside Croke Park. As I walk up the lane to the turnstiles, trying not to look obvious, two Dubs eye me and one exclaims – 'Jaze, the piss-artists are here today alright!' Just let the tape run ... I'm on the second row, top deck, centre of Cusack Stand. Just let the tape run ... The match ends in a draw! (Yes of course WE fixed it!) The real passion is down on the terraces – I can't wait to hear what the lads bring back!

MONDAY, SEPTEMBER 19

The post-mortems ... Ronan has some brilliant stuff from the Meath end. Aidan's stereo quality is excellent but he had problems homing in on Cork fans. (The Canal End is very mixed whereas the Hill is wall-to-wall Meath!)

Dermot's street and pub stuff is very good (mostly Cork) but spoiled by an intermittent fault on the machine. My own stuff is fine before and after the match but I'm a bit far away from the action ... (Artane Boys sound good though). Decisions, decisions! Replay on October 9th. Ronan will go back and 'target' the Cork fans. (*Dear Danny Lynch, you see we had this problem ... I wonder could you spare* ...) Dermot will try again too!

SUNDAY, OCTOBER 9

At least the weather remains the same. (Didn't my father always say ...) The match is quite explosive but we redress the balance with Cork fans – and Dermot's machine works with a marvellous pub sing-song from Cork fans. We have the makings of a documentary – almost ...

WEDNESDAY, OCTOBER 19

In Cork on 'Education Forum' business. Decide to interview Billy Morgan (Cork manager) in his school and Dinny Allen (Cork player) in his office about the drawn match. It's not easy for them as they are still 'down' after the replay but fair play to them – they give of their best.

THURSDAY, DECEMBER 8

Interview Liam Hayes of Meath (the fourth consecutive interview in a two-hour studio session – the other three were concerning the Developing World!) He is – as I expected – very perceptive, full of interesting insights from the players' perspective.

MONDAY, DECEMBER 21

Interview Sean Boylan, Meath manager. I now have all the pieces of the jigsaw. This is what we have: R. Kelly – three hours of tape; D. Rattigan – three hours; A. Crowley – two hours; J. Quinn – two hours;

international sound – three hours; OBS – one and a half hours; interviews – one and a half hours; match commentary – one and a half hours; other (News etc.) – half hour. Total: eighteen hours. So now? LISTEN! LISTEN! LISTEN!

OCTOBER 1988–MARCH 1989
Listen. Listen. Listen. Any time and all times – at work or out for a nightly walk. Make mental notes, make paper notes. Listen, listen, listen – and laugh a lot. The humour and the banter of the fans is a tonic. I bore my colleagues endlessly with quotes. The language is pretty 'raw' but it's 'part of what we are' – when we're in Croke Park ...

MARCH–MAY 1989
Lift the usable extracts onto insert tapes whenever there's a studio session available ... I still end up with sixteen insert tapes. Approach sound technician Mick Bourke, to know if he would work through the project with me. Mick is a man of few words, immense patience and amazing skill. 'Sounds like a lot of pain,' he says. (How little he knew!) He also says 'yes'!

JULY 13, 1989
The first session. Four hours in Studio 7. Three tape machines and a Marantz. Mick procures a portable machine from Studio 12. We will record on to that. No linking commentary. The sounds will tell the story – hopefully ... I have the first seventy inserts 'scripted', beginning with Sean Boylan's summation of Final Day as 'a very special day in Irish life'. The blending of sounds from there on is slow and painstaking. We record a sequence of three or four inserts, repeat that three or four times and then dub that over a master tape. Cross-fading all the time. Does it work? Mick looks at me – 'What d'ye think?' I know by the way he winces slightly that he's not happy. 'Nah,' he says, 'we'll do it again.' I was very ambitious with my seventy inserts. By the end of the session we have reached insert number twenty-one and after four hours we have a total of six minutes on master tape ... But we're on the way.

JULY 20

Session Two. Another four hours. Mick insists on checking a segment we did the last day. It's not in stereo. Do it again. We soldier on. The paper editing doesn't always work. We rearrange the order of inserts. We get another nine minutes in 'master' segments – productivity is improving!

TUESDAY, JULY 25

A marathon session – 4 to 11 p.m. – but a near disastrous one. Things just don't come together, 'segues' don't work. Leave it. We'll come back another day. Now that we have moved inside Croke Park there are all sorts of problems with the different acoustics. Depressed on the way home. Will it work at all?

THURSDAY, AUGUST 3

Session Four. 4 to 11 p.m. Having listened back, I know now what went wrong the last day – and how we can fix it! A very productive session. We're up to insert number 115. Some inserts have to be discarded – levels too low or too much background. In particular we decide to 'ditch' the comments of one Meath fan – 'we're only out for the day – might never see it again'. A pity because it summarises the programme – can't win them all!

THURSDAY, AUGUST 10

Session Five. Four more hours. We finally reach half-time in the match! The international sound is proving invaluable in bridging the acoustic problems ...

TUESDAY, AUGUST 15

Another all-day session – 10 a.m. to 6 p.m. I decide to re-do the half-time sequence – drop Foster & Allen and put in the Artane Boys Band. I get a brainwave – why not end the programme with the 'out for the day' comment but put it On Echo with some filtering. It works – only just – but it works! And it's insert number 180 ...

We now have nineteen master tapes – average duration two and a half minutes each. We do some fine editing – *very* fine editing, as with all that cross-fading, editing is very difficult. I am lost in admiration for Mick Bourke – a total professional and superb craftsman. And people like him are an endangered species in RTÉ. Incredible ... The final session. We take four hours to dub the nineteen tapes onto one final master tape. It comes out at 45 minutes and 30 seconds. Not bad! I listen to it *in toto*. I think it's bloody great!

Monday, September 11
Transmission at 4.02 p.m. At 1 p.m. Mick Bourke suggests we re-do a segment towards the end in order to remove a tiny 'blip'. We do it in half an hour during lunchtime. It really is Mick's programme by now. I'm glad now Joe Mulholland didn't act on my 1979 memo. Radio is after all a much more visual medium than TV ... I dedicate 'Final Day' to my father – who was right.

NOTE
'Final Day' won the gold medal for 'Best Sound Editing' at the New York International Radio Festival, 1990.

WONDERWORLD OR WASTEWORLD?
Fr Tom Berry outlines the stark choices that face the human race.

America was settled by Europeans. When we reflect on what has happened to this magnificent continent – with all its variety and richness of wildlife – it is alarming. We wiped out 60–70 million buffalo in a very short time. Similarly with billions of passenger pigeons. Many sources tell of how it took hours for them to pass overhead and how the sky would be darkened for long periods of time. We wiped them out in a brief while. So when that first European mast appeared over the horizon, every living being on the North American continent must have shuddered in fear. Even the rivers and mountains must have trembled.

There was no sense of the European colonisers joining the community of existence on this land, of listening to the wildlife or learning from the natural phenomena. They were totally autistic to what this continent had to tell them. The Irish, for example, had a spirit-world in the contours of their land and they had a certain rapport with that world. But our colonisers never thought of establishing a human presence that would be acceptable to this continent ... that would be integral with its waterways and its living forms ... that would be compatible with the seasonal sequence ... that would not harm the continent.

Instead of making a pact with the continent, they made a constitution, guaranteeing life, liberty and the pursuit of happiness to *humans* with no rights for the non-humans. That to me is deficient jurisprudence. The indigenous peoples had a rapport with the animal world. The animals were their teachers and guides. The colonisers on the other hand became plunderers. They felled the great white pine – six feet in diameter – to make the masts of ships. They slaughtered the beavers to make their fashionable hats. They assaulted the land. Several writers in the late eighteenth century – including James Fenimore Cooper – tell of the devastation that took place. The colonisers exhausted the land. That was no problem. They just moved on to new land in this vast continent – which they assumed to be inexhaustible. It was a predatory relationship.

I live now in the south-east – in the foothills of the Appalachian mountains. It is considered to be one of the most desirable places to live in. We should have an internal economy but instead we brought in all the industrial giants – huge commercial centres with vast car parks, Walmarts and K-marts with literally miles of aisles stocked with produce from all over the world. When I was a child this place had a population of 15,000 with a good sense of community. Now it has 200,000 people. Great swathes have been cut through the woods to make way for five-lane highways. This whole development process is based on the predatory relationship with the earth and it has evolved into consumerism. We have no rapport with the natural world. We have failed 'to hear the voices'.

The consumerists will hail all this as 'progress', seeing it as entering a wonderworld but more and more we are recognising it as a wasteworld. That, for me, is the tragic dimension of contemporary existence. We are being educated now for continuing and expanding exploitation that has seemingly no limits. There are four establishments that govern everything – the political establishment, the church, the educational establishment and the corporation. Today the corporation controls the other three. Corporations are too acquisitive, religions are too pious, governments are too subservient. It remains for the universities to have some sense! They should have the critical capacity to prepare students for a different world. We cannot trust them anymore to guide us. They taught the economy we have, the agriculture we have, the legal system we have. In science they taught the insights and technologies that are needed to exploit the earth.

The universe is the primary university. The whole 'idea of a university' that Cardinal Newman established is irrelevant to what is happening today. The universities cannot rethink themselves to a significant level. Ours is truly a wonderworld and to assist in bringing us back into this reality is the excitement of this new ecozoic era. Young people need to be oriented towards a new phase of human creativity, to develop their particular competencies to the full. There is no one solution to our problems – not government alone, not education alone, not science alone. The talents of *everybody* are required to assist the planet and the human community into a new phase of its expression.

I call this the ecozoic era. The dream drives the action. We are in this mess now because we dreamed this idea of progress, this wonderworld. Now we need to dream about a more coherent mode of the planet and ourselves on that planet. We need a creative dimension that will be guided by an understanding of what can be done with the resources available to us. That entrancement is the way into the future.

THE CURIOUS MIND

ON HIS HAVING ARRIVED
AT SEVENTY-FIVE

CHARLES HANDY *reflects on life. What was it all about?*

I HAVE ASPIRED to the notion that the important things in life are to live, to love, to learn and to leave a legacy. As for legacy – for a start when I leave this life I want all my books and CDs and tapes burned. There are three long shelves of my books and translations of same at home. They are not important in themselves. What is important is the effect they may have had on people. If I have given people an opportunity to reflect on their lives, their work, their organisations – that is great! That is my legacy.

I will leave behind letters to my children and grandchildren, which I update annually. The greatest legacy I will leave are those children and grandchildren. I once did a 'Thought for the Day' on 'begatting' as in the Bible's ancestry of Jesus of Nazareth. If one of those links were missing, he would not have existed! So the most important thing is to keep the line going.

They say that housewives and writers never retire. It is true in my case. I never had great passions like golf or gardening or wine-making. I just keep on writing because it is what I do. It is not physically demanding. I am sure there is an idea for a book bubbling away somewhere. An old farmer friend said to me, 'I do the same as I always did, only slower. Why would I do anything different? It's what I love'. Retirement is a terrible word anyway. You do move on, of course. I believe in having more than one life in this life and I have tried to do that. One of the most enjoyable books I wrote with my wife Elizabeth was *Reinvented Lives* – about women at sixty who have done something different. They wrote their own stories and the word 'retirement' never occurred in the stories – except for one woman who said she had 'been retired' by her company.

I do have regrets about my youth. Growing up in impoverished Ireland and attending rather bad schools did not help. I didn't do foreign languages. I didn't learn to sail or ski or fish. I probably wouldn't have been any good at them, but I would like to have tried. I didn't travel as young people do today, never campaigned on the streets or joined a protest march. The Greek writer Juvenal quotes a message in the temple of Apollo – 'Know yourself'. That is not easy to do, of course – nor is the corollary – 'Accept yourself'. I could have had a different life if I had a different or more testing youth, but I have to live with what I had – a dull childhood, comfortable and much-loved, but I learned little.

I have been blessed with love. Erich Fromm says, 'Love is the only sane and satisfactory answer to the problem of existence'. So many people have a life without love. I am fortunate to be doing what I love surrounded by those I love. In the end, life is about what Aristotle called *eudaimonia* – doing the best you can at what you are good at, for the good of others. As I look back on life I think, it may not have been much, but still it was worth doing. Voltaire puts it much better: 'How infinitesimal is the importance of anything I do, but how infinitely important it is that I do it.'

THE SATISFACTIONS OF OLDER YEARS

CATHERINE MCCANN *outlines the joys and pleasures to be derived in fully living our later years.*

W.B. YEATS ONCE said: 'Life is an art – an art to be lived.' For me, the older years are the time for the completion of this work of art. It is not necessarily a time for doing a lot of things but for experiencing more deeply what we choose to do – quality living rather than quantity living. It will be different for each individual. Some will live exuberantly; others will take a quieter, more serene path. Recent surveys in Ireland have shown that older people are more satisfied with life than young people. Their expectations are more realistic – I suppose – and happiness is a by-product of that.

There are three ways of achieving satisfaction:

1. Remaining a contributor to society: we must maintain and show a concern for others. Where independence was once deemed a sign of maturity, psychologists tell us that today interconnectedness is the sign. It doesn't require a frenetic pace but – if you'll pardon the cliché – simply being there for others.

2. Developing a heightened use of our senses: this is a time to stand and stare and to *really* see, to *really* hear, to *really* taste, to *really* smell, to *really* touch. I am reminded of Howard Carter's words when he looked into Tutankhamen's tomb – 'I see marvellous things'. Look afresh at things and defamiliarise the familiar. Patrick Kavanagh reminded us that 'ordinary things have lovely wings'. Listen to silence. Acquire new tastes.

3. Exposure to the world of the arts: as well as appreciating the work of others, find creative ways of developing your own talents. It may be in a writing or art workshop but it could also be in gardening or just how we set a table or arrange a living room. I have heard of a project in Cork called 'Creatively Arthritic'! At the age of ninety-three, Pablo Casals said, 'Each day I am reborn. Each day I must begin again'.

Older people who live fuller lives are prophets. They are saying to younger people that life is worth living. Ageing is a time for maturing in wisdom and not for personal diminishment, a time for hope and not despair and above all a time for joy and not for colourless living. Integrity and a certain mellowness would be indicators of wisdom. Letting go of rituals, lifestyles, patterns of thinking, help us along that road. Remember the words of *The Little Prince*: 'What is essential is invisible to the eye. Only the heart understands rightly.'

The person who lives with hope copes with disappointments and challenges and sees possibilities. Hope also eases the pain of remorse and regret. Again, it is about letting go – of bitterness, of what might have been. Aldous Huxley said to his dying wife, 'Let go, let go. Go forward into the light. No memories. No regrets. No looking backwards.

No apprehensive thoughts about your own or anyone else's future. Only light'.

As for joy, the more we seek it, the more it will elude us. It is something that happens us, according to the way we live. If we value life and retain the ability to delight in and wonder at the world about us, we will experience joy. Groucho Marx – who brought joy to many – once said, 'Each morning when I open my eyes I say to myself: "I, not events, have the power to make me happy or unhappy today. I can choose which it shall be. Yesterday is dead. Tomorrow hasn't arrived yet. I have just one day – today – and I am going to be happy in it".'

ROALD MEETS HIS FANS

Children's books author ROALD DAHL *answers questions
from his fans in a Dublin library.*

WHERE DID YOU GET YOUR NAME FROM?
I was called after a hero of my father's – Roald Amundsen, the first man to reach the South Pole. He did this in 1912 and my father was delighted that he beat the wretched Englishman, Scott, to the Pole. So when I was born in 1916 he called me Roald.

DID YOU HAVE A GOOD CHILDHOOD?
Yes. I was lucky. Even though my father died when I was three, my mother brought a large family of us up very well. She took us on a holiday every year. School wasn't much fun. We were whacked a lot but it probably didn't do us much harm.

DID YOU GET SMACKED A LOT AT SCHOOL?
Quite a lot! Even now, if I sit on a hard bench for a couple of hours I can still feel my heart beating along the stripes on my bottom! Boom! Boom! it goes!

WHICH OF YOUR BOOKS HAS SOLD THE MOST?
That's not a fair question, really, because a book like *Charlie and the Chocolate Factory* has been around for twenty-five years while *The BFG* has only been around for five years. In the latest league tables, however, I am told that *The BFG* has knocked Charlie from first place and *The Witches* is now second.

IN YOUR AUTOBIOGRAPHY – *BOY* – DID YOU REALLY PUT THE MOUSE AMONG THE GOBSTOPPERS?
Of course we did – and we got whacked for it too! You tell the truth in an autobiography.

IN *BOY*, DID YOU REALLY PUT GOAT'S POO IN A MAN'S PIPE?
Absolutely. It was the man my sister was going to marry! I was very pleased with that – he thought he was going to die! If any of you have pipe-smoking fathers, it's something you could try. You need very dry goat's poo so that it will crumble well, but remember to put a small bit of tobacco on top!

AS SOON AS YOU FINISH ONE BOOK, DO YOU GO STRAIGHT ON TO ANOTHER ONE?
That's a very intelligent question. You can't go straight on. You have to forget about the first book and wait for the embers to spark on another. I've just finished a book of Silly Rhymes and I have no idea what I will do next. I'm not sure if I want to start another book. I like mooching around, doing nothing.

WHERE DO YOU WRITE YOUR BOOKS?
I always write in a little hut, far away from my house, up in the orchard. A dirty little place, but very comfortable.

DO IDEAS COME EASY AND FLOW ALONG?
No! And anyone who says they do is wrong! Ideas come alright but they seldom flow. You have to dig around quite a lot.

How many books have you written?

I've lost count! About nineteen books for children and five or six collections of short stories for adults.

As a mere adult, I was quite upset when at the end of *The Witches*, the little boy was left as a mouse, even though he had human faculties. Are children harder of heart than adults, in your experience?

There's no question about it! Most adults writing that book would have fallen into the trap that you have fallen into – which is to be corny and have it finish the way everyone is expecting it to finish. They're making a film of *The Witches* with Jim Henson of the Muppets and they are making exactly that mistake. We have all said, 'Don't do it, Jim!' but it's no use. They don't understand that children love the book's ending.

How did you meet the illustrator, Quentin Blake?

About eight books ago, someone suggested he was a jolly good artist and should illustrate my next book. We became good friends. We always meet up and discuss his drawings.

What is your favourite of all your books?

That's a very hard question. If I could only say I have written one book, it would probably be *The BFG* – I think! And then maybe *Danny, the Champion of the World*.

What was your favourite book as a child?

Well for a start we had very few books to choose from – unlike the vast selection available to today's children. Mind you, there wasn't as much rubbish either! I loved *The Secret Garden*, *The Wind in the Willows*, the Beatrix Potter books, and then I graduated on to Captain Marryat books, like *Mr Midshipman Easy*.

A PLAYWRIGHT'S PLAYWRIGHT

HUGH LEONARD *chooses a hero in his life – playwright*
George S. Kaufman.

GEORGE S. KAUFMAN is a hero of mine because he influenced my work
a great deal early in my career, with his structural approach to plays like
The Man Who Came to Dinner and *You Can't Take It With You*. He worked
mostly in collaboration with Moss Hart, who wrote a wonderful portrait
of Kaufman in a book called *Act One* – for me the best book written about
the theatre. Kaufman also worked with Ring Lardner, Alexander
Woollcott and Edna Ferber.

He was a classic theatre figure, the essence of an age. He was a
founding father of the Algonquin Round Table and probably the best wit
of his time. He was most unprepossessing in appearance – very thin
with a shock of black hair, thick glasses and a long Jewish nose. He hated
any kind of sentimentality, effusive greeting or physical contact. He was
a most unlikely lover but had a great reputation with the ladies. On one
occasion he met an ex-girlfriend who was with her latest – and very
wealthy – admirer. She couldn't resist rubbing this in Kaufman's face
and greeted him saying, 'This is Mr Harris and he's in cotton'. Kaufman
instantly replied 'And them that plants it am soon forgotten'. At the
Algonquin Hotel a drunk bumped into his table and said, 'Will you
excuse me?', to which Kaufman replied, 'Certainly. The alternative would
be too dreadful to contemplate'. On another occasion, while playing
bridge, his partner played badly and got Kaufman into all kinds of
trouble. When the partner went to the toilet, Kaufman uttered the
immortal line, 'This will be the first time tonight that we'll know what
he has in his hand ...'

Kaufman started life as a newspaper man. He married Beatrice – a
splendid lady – and began writing plays in the 1920s. A young
playwright called Moss Hart came to him with an idea for a play about
the coming of sound to the film studios. The play – *Once in a Lifetime* –
was a great triumph and Hart and Kaufman became a great team. In the
1930s Kaufman became involved in a great scandal through his liaison

with the actress Mary Astor. She unfortunately kept a diary which her husband found and leaked to the newspapers. Kaufman was subpoenaed as a witness in the divorce proceedings but had himself smuggled out of California, wrapped up like a mummy in an ambulance. His wife stood by 'Public Lover No. 1' – as the press dubbed him – and every time he dated a girl subsequently, his first question to her was, 'Do you keep a diary?' His wife predeceased him and he remarried. In later years he became a broadcaster under the name of 'The Old Curmudgeon', in which he developed a sour, sardonic personality.

As a playwright he had no equal when it came to structure. His collaborators usually came to him with plays that hadn't worked out. He would cut it to the bone and painstakingly rebuild it. You could not stage the Hart-Kaufman plays of the 1930s/40s today because they had huge casts and endless set changes, but they gave unmitigated pleasure in their day. They exuded the warm humour of Kaufman and his great liking for the human race – a liking which never spread into his own personal life. He wrote a few serious plays but hardboiled comedy was his forte.

For myself, I learned a great deal about structure in writing from Kaufman. He was a classic storyteller – knowing when to cut, when to add, when to write ACB instead of ABC in terms of structure. My first play – *The Big Birthday* – was a bad play but I built it painstakingly along Kaufman lines. I read his plays as a schoolboy. The only play of his I ever saw on stage was *The Man Who Came to Dinner*, starring Mícheál MacLiammóir and Danny Cummins. International plays were rarely staged in Dublin so to gain access to them you had to go to the library and read the scripts. In the case of Kaufman I am forever grateful that I did so.

TWENTY-FIRST-CENTURY LEARNING

JOHN ABBOT *outlines a vision of education for the twenty-first century –
based on what we now know about how children learn.*

RIGHT ACROSS THE western world there is no child between the age of
five and eighteen who spends more than 20 per cent of his or her waking
hours in school. Only one hour out of every five. Research in North
America has shown that the influence of the home is four times greater
than that of the school in predicting the child's success at third level and
beyond. Those two facts have enormous implications for learning in the
twenty-first century. The model that we inherited from the nineteenth
century said that the older the child became, the more we could instruct
him. That is why we have a funny regime that gives less money to
primary education than to secondary, and gives more money to
universities than it does to secondary schools. Now we know that it is
not the information that the young child gets that is important, but the
way in which that child grows a brain that can help it learn. If that is
done effectively, the children don't need as much instruction, but more
opportunity to demonstrate the skills they learned when very young and
to build on those. It is nothing more than the old craftsman-apprentice
model. The support was loaded to the earliest years until the craftsman
made himself redundant.

So let us assume that we don't have any more money in total, but that
we redistribute it equally between five-year-olds and eighteen-year-olds.
There are five interconnected steps we then take at primary level:

1. Reduce class size to as low as ten–twelve pupils.
2. Adopt a pedagogy based on the apprenticeship model.
3. Ten per cent of the school budget (minimum) to be spent each
   year on the professional development of teachers.
4. Increase the amount spent on learning resources for children.
5. Educate the community at large that children are their future and
   that every adult should be an informal teacher.

What we call social capital is of crucial importance. We have to make time to create the environment from which children can learn through everyday experience. We need inventive children. Invention comes from thinking the unthinkable and that comes more from playing street games than playing computer games. Learning is not static. In times of change, the learners will inherit the earth, while the learned will find themselves beautifully equipped for a world that no longer exists.

Having returned from a five-year spell in the USA, I am horrified by what is going on in secondary schools in the UK. We are over-schooling students to such an extent that they are highly proficient at passing exams and have no energy left for anything else. They are over-schooled and under-educated. This is a huge issue, but if we can act in the way I have outlined, we have the chance to create people who will have the humanity and the intellect to deal with the enormously complex issues of the twenty-first century.

PARADISE LOST

In the mid-1970s, EILÍS BRADY set about recording
the street games of her neighbourhood – 'The Park' –
an intimate circular estate in the northside of Dublin city.
She published her findings in a delightful book entitled All In! All In!.

'IN OUR HOUSE,' said Eilís, 'we had our own Three Rs – Radio, Reading and Rings.' What learning opportunities were afforded the young Eilís! On the radio the family listened to *Question Time* and the *Sunday Play*. The children read whatever they could lay their hands on. And Rings? Well first you learned the rules and then you learned how to compute your score – your total to date and then what you needed to win. And they were just some of the indoor games ...

There would have been about seventy children in 'The Park' when I was young. After school everyone went out to play on the street or green. They would break up into small groups and play an amazing range of

THE CURIOUS MIND

games – skipping, ball games, make-believe, beds, marbles, chasing or games of just pure devilment! It reminds me of a sentence from the Bible – 'And the streets shall be filled with the sounds of boys and girls playing'.

We played simply for joy. We were never bored and games cost nothing. A piece of rope attached to a lamp post or strung between two gate-posts and you could swing away to your heart's delight. Boys lifted the lid of the water hydrant and it became the mowl into which they pitched buttons or coins. A piece of chalk and an empty shoe-polish tin were all you needed for 'beds' or hopscotch. Just hopping up and down steps became the basis for another game. We used our environment ...

Adults didn't pay (or didn't need to pay) the slightest attention to children's games. This was the only time children were totally without adult supervision. We made our own rules. There were no prizes – just the joy of 'waiting your chance' and maybe occasionally winning a game. When you were 'out' that was it. You accepted that and waited your chance again ...

There was great dexterity involved, whether in keeping three balls juggled or in landing your coin in the 'mowl', or in bowling a hoop all evening long with all the intensity of a rally driver. There was great inventiveness too, especially in the make-believe games of 'Shop', 'House', or 'Mother'. And there was great inclusivity. The little ones were 'minded' – they were encouraged to take part and they were taught the rhymes.

Above all there was great incidental learning. We accumulated a large word store. We were literally streetwise from listening to parents and extended family. And we learned to socialise and accept rules.

It was of course another era, another Dublin, but for me it was Paradise that is lost to today's children ...

REAL LIVES

MAEVE KELLY *traces her emergence and development as a writer to a concern for portraying the real lives of women and to her involvement in the Women's Movement.*

WOMEN HARDLY FEATURED in what I was reading and even when they did feature it was as if they weren't real characters at all. The women I met in my daily life were real people with great humour and strength of character. I wanted to write about ordinary women who had qualities of character that didn't seem to be portrayed by men.

Ultimately, I became involved with the women's movement. I had strong feelings about the way women were discriminated against in law and in society and in particular the way married women seemed to lose all rights when they got married. It was as if, by handing over your name, you handed over your whole person. This was certainly the view of the Church and I was very resistant to it. Married women lost their status and they lost even more status when – having been married – they were deserted. There was a real stigma attached to deserted wives at the time and that was why we started a group to help deserted wives in Limerick.

Initially, my friends used to laugh at me because I would ask questions and I would reject the stereotyped view of women. When I met up with a group of women who were of like mind, I thought it was wonderful. At that time I had been reading Simone de Beauvoir. She was the first and I would say the most important of all the feminist writers. At the time we didn't use the word 'feminist'. She made me realise that what I had been thinking was right, but she put a structure on it and slotted it into a historical perspective, so that I could see how this situation had arisen. It is the case – even today – that women who have really strong views on women's rights are still in the minority, because it is painful for both men and women to have to re-examine something as fundamental as how men and women view one another.

There was a tremendous dynamism about the women's movement in the early 1970s. We were in the middle of a process of change – all of us in the women's movement were actually changing history. We would swap ideas, would argue, would disagree, and would have long arguments about what our priorities should be. Some women didn't want to be called feminists, some women were afraid of not being considered 'feminine', but the real debate was whether one should get involved in practical work – like changing or reforming – or whether one should go into something more radical, like politics.

Eventually, I took the more practical way. I agreed to be committed to helping battered wives, because not only are you helping somebody to a safe place or rescuing somebody from a situation of suffering and danger but you are also changing society. You are saying that it is not proper for men to beat women, it is not proper that women should be raped and that they should be dragged through the courts. There was a need to change the law in its attitude towards abused women and women who are the victims of rape. We were lobbying, with other groups, for changes in the law. We were looking for free legal aid, we were lobbying politicians to introduce family law in Ireland, because there was no such thing at the time. There was a famous court case in Cork that made me nail my colours to the mast. That was the case of criminal conversation which was taken against a woman's lover by the woman's husband. He got compensation for the loss of her company in society and the judge in his summing up said that, in Irish law, a woman is her husband's chattel, like a horse or a cow ...

The experience of meeting abused women in the shelter has been a major influence on my life. I was forty-one and it made me look at life in a different way. It was terribly painful. I always believed that human nature was intrinsically good. I had always had a very optimistic view of life, but for a number of years then I began to believe that human nature was in fact intrinsically bad, because I couldn't come to terms with the kind of abuse that these women suffered. It also made me look at men in a different way. I became much more sceptical of men and less accepting of them. In order to come to terms with that, I had to read a lot and I still read any feminist writers that I think will throw light on what is happening. I suspect it has a lot to do with people who have power being able to abuse people who have no power. There is something even more fundamental underneath it as well. Many men have a fear of women and a fear of women's power over reproduction and I would agree with the feminists who say that this is at the core of a lot of violence against women.

These are questions that men have to ask themselves sooner or later and – fortunately – men are asking those questions today, but they wouldn't have asked them without the women's movement. Certainly, the education of boys until recent times in Ireland left a lot to be desired. They were trained to be suspicious of girls and they had no understanding of sexuality at all. It was loaded with guilt and sin and that must have had a very damaging effect on them and, ultimately, on the women they married. I have always felt that – whatever else about our education with the nuns – we didn't have this sense of guilt. Things were simply not talked about. We were totally ignorant, but in a sense that was its own safeguard, because we were saved the terror of guilt associated with sex.

Some of this thinking began to find expression in my own writing. I was accused of being a propagandist in one of my novels – *Necessary Treasons* – but what I had attempted to do in that book was demonstrate the difficulties of a young woman coming to terms with the women's movement and the confusion and the ignorance that people have to face when they are trying to understand. I would regard my short stories as being, in a way, slightly subversive. On the surface they are stories about rural women and pastoral life, but they are saying something else at the same time. A lot of women who have read them have certainly picked that up so – in a subtle way – my views filter through.

THE CURIOUS MIND

QUESTIONING THE SYSTEM

In the inaugural 'Open Mind' Guest Lecture (1989), ANNE HIGGINS, *a young primary teacher from Limerick, analysed our education system with a barrage of hard-hitting questions. This is part of her lecture.*

PRIMARY EDUCATION NOW

First of all, let's look at primary education. Basically we offer all children a place in a classroom along with thirty-eight others of the same age plus an adult. That's what we offer him or her for the first eight or nine years of their educational journey. Is it fair to ask a child to sit at a desk with so big a crowd for so long? Is it fair to ask one adult to take responsibility for that number of children for five and a half hours per day? In fact, recently two speech therapists from the Mid-Western Health Board went to Mary Immaculate College to talk to the students because so many teachers were going to them with voice troubles. The problem with teachers' voices was because of the large numbers in the classroom, because of the strain placed on a teacher working in that situation. Can the needs of the slow learner, the emotionally disturbed, or the very bright child be met in that environment?

What has happened is that we have given our children over to a system where one adult is entrusted with their education for a year at a time. Parents and other members of the community do not normally interact with this process, except to help with homework. One bright six-year-old I know spends two hours per evening doing his homework. Where is his time for play? Where is his time for his family? Why can't more adults be involved in a looser system? Why have parents become disassociated from the education of their children?

What happens to the child who finishes his or her participation in the system when he or she leaves primary school – maybe often going on to do a six-month or a nine-month course, maybe moving from one course to another, or maybe just dropping out? Is it fair to expect the teacher to organise learning opportunities which are individually appropriate for all thirty-nine children? Is the classroom the only place the child of primary school age can be involved in learning? What about the other areas of the community – the church, the community hall, the fields, the woods, the lakes, the streets? What does a child of that age need to learn? What about the talents and skills of other adults in the community – the storyteller, the gardener, the shopkeeper, the housekeeper, the craftsperson, the cleaning person, the priest, the guard, the farmer, the fisherman – how can they be involved in the education of the children? How can they share their skills and pass on their knowledge? Is the model of thirty-nine children to one adult the best we can offer our children? They are entitled to their heritage – to inherit the knowledge that has been accumulated by their forebears. How can we give them their inheritance with the knowledge that the future of our society is ultimately dependent on our youth? We do not simply inherit the earth from our parents – we guard it for our children.

Let's not allow ourselves to be locked within a system. Why not explore other areas, other ways? I'm not an educational historian, but I believe this rigid classroom model is quite young – yet we seem to have accepted it as if it were sacred and unchangeable. Let's focus on a four or five-year-old child going to school. Yes, I know many of them are happy – many adults say that the children going to school nowadays are much happier than they themselves were – but let's not be satisfied with that alone. I believe that a child needs to develop his or her talents and abilities. Apart from the academic side, the child needs to express himself or herself through crafts and through sports – needs to interact not only with the home and school, but also with the wider environment. A child needs to develop his or her ability to question, to see things from different angles, to be tolerant of differences in people. But most of all a child needs to dream, to explore and to enjoy being a child.

I was talking to a friend recently – an older woman. She was telling me that a neighbour visited her mother the other day and she said, 'The children aren't home from school yet'. And her mother said, 'Ah, they have a while yet, they're grazing home from school'. The amount that they were learning on the way home was very great – and I just wish that every child had that opportunity.

THE CURIOUS MIND

Where is the spark of the individual? A child wears a uniform like all the other children in the school and carries a schoolbag laden down with books produced by publishers who have no knowledge of the life of that child.

Post-Primary education now

What's on offer at second level? There's a points system that discourages cooperation, a rat race to see who the succeeders are, and we reward the succeeders by allowing them to go on to third level if they can afford it, to further run the gauntlet and maybe then what? Emigrate? Is that success? Is our educational system creating and upholding a society in which the most important value is the survival of the fittest? I recently encountered in a book called *The One Straw Revolution* the following:

> Formal schooling has no intrinsic value but becomes necessary when humanity creates a condition in which one needs to become educated to get along.

The technically and academically bright have been awarded money and status by society – by the educational system – yet the person who cares for the old, for the children, for the neighbour, for the land and for the sea, has not been awarded such status. The educational system by its structures, by the way it awards merits to the academic achievers, creates the failures and decides what it is that our society should hold in esteem. It awards payments for different tasks carried out. Yet it is often these academically brilliant people – not all of them, some of them – who have created nuclear power, who explode bombs under the desert, who test their devices to the genetic peril of less powerful cultures. It is also the succeeders who make high-level decisions, decisions to store mountains of food while millions of people die of hunger. Does the race for points help the teenager to be a more responsible, enriched member of society? The education provided by a society reflects the philosophy of that society to a great degree. Therefore when we examine the educational system, we are also looking at that society in which that system is in operation.

I don't think it is possible to suggest changes within an educational system without realising that this means changes within the society. I would like to see a society based on sharing and justice. I would like to see hierarchical power structures – whether they be church or state – replaced by structures where people at grassroots level have more input into the decision-making process.

The clearest example of this phenomenon of second level education I encountered recently on an 'Open Mind' programme. It was a programme where a group of boys from a secondary boarding school were interviewed. They were away from their families and communities; the rules within that very school kept them away from the society in which that building was located. They couldn't actually go down town, they couldn't smoke, they had no opportunity to meet girls. Their day was organised like clockwork, free time was from ten until ten-thirty in the evening, when there was a long queue for the phones, to phone home.

I think that speaks for itself. How were these young men to learn how to relate to young women? How to relate to children? How to relate to the old? How to relate to a newborn baby? How to relate to the sick? Have we placed educational achievement so high in our list of priorities that we allow our young people to be imprisoned away from life in order to attain the desired academic standard, to satisfy the requirements of a third level institution by increasing their points requirements every year? And does the choice of courses taken at third level reflect the personal interests and talents of the individual or does it represent the ever-changing demands of the employment market?

WE DID IT OUR WAY

Although she went to formal school as a child, most of MAIRE
MULLARNEY's *education was acquired at home. When she married and
had eleven children of her own, she and her husband repeated the process,
educating the children at home up to secondary level.*

WHEN I WAS nine, my father had the opportunity to transfer to Gibraltar
and it was there that I had one of many valuable experiences. He didn't
like the idea that I would spend all the summer swimming and fooling
around with my mates, so he insisted that, before I went swimming, I
must spend one hour teaching myself Spanish. When that hour was up,
I was to go down to the garden and pick stones for an hour and throw
them over the wall. He didn't want an undisciplined child and that
worked quite well, because it left me with the feeling that, if you want to
learn something, you go off and do it. I had no resentment and I
thoroughly enjoyed it.

I spent a couple of terms in the national school, which was futile. It
was one long stretch of boredom, because I was reading well by then
anyway. The important thing that my mother was able to do was
something which I now know is called mediation. It is essential that a
mother mediates for small children what life is about. If nobody tells
them that something is beautiful, that music is something worth
listening to, that flowers should be respected, they will miss out and will
be very defective. My mother did all her own gardening, she pumped
water from the well and sawed the wood and so forth – all of which she
was positive about. I remember discovering that, when she chopped a
worm in half with the spade, the two halves would survive, but she
wouldn't have dreamed of chopping a worm in half just to show me.
Worms deserved their share of life as well. My mother – a care-for-nature
countrywoman – wasn't at all unusual among Irish women of her time,
but she certainly gave me her full attention when I was a child, which I
know she enjoyed too. I feel that is probably the most important
background to the rest of my learning.

Karl Popper says that the only things we need to be taught are how to read and write, and even then not everybody needs to be taught – some pick it up for themselves. The kind of thing I learned from my mother was one half of my education and the rest was books. Chesterton and Belloc were part of family life and when my father had me learning Spanish he told me I could buy any books in Spanish that I liked. I had an account with the local stationers. I read a lot of historical fiction, and indeed I went on to read through Spanish literature right up to fairly recent times. In the library, I made a mental rule that for every two Edgar Wallace books, I would read something more solid – if it was in five volumes I felt it was solid! I remember reading the memoirs of Tallyrand, for example. It was quite advanced reading for teenage years. Perhaps the most influential of the lot at that time was a thick, five-volume Boswell. That gave me a feeling that conversation was what life was all about.

I went to school with the Loreto nuns. They did a lot of good, but not a great deal academically. Loreto convents at that time held internal debating competitions between them and that gave me a lot of experience and it was also very good fun.

Eventually I got married and we had eleven children and achieved some fame – I suppose – by teaching our own children. This was due to my husband's habit of picking up second-hand books. We found and read something about Montessori and it sounded very sensible. We also knew we were so far from any school that we weren't likely to be able to send the children until they were quite big, so we decided to have a bash. We started much earlier than the Montessori age. When Barbara was about eight months old, we started doing roughly the kind of things Montessori was offering at two and a half – geometrical insets and so forth. The next boy began to read when he was two and I have done the same sort of thing with the others.

Because of that chance experiment, I was learning all the time. I was watching what they were doing. The first thing I learned was that human beings like learning. That was one reason I was involved in setting up *Reform* – which aimed to get rid of corporal punishment. I was very, very shocked to find that they were actually hitting children in school if they didn't know something. I learned two things. I learned something about comparing methods and experimenting and also to be quite sceptical of authorities. I was already sceptical of the health field and now I am also pretty sceptical of the official educational field.

I enjoyed teaching the children and it took very little time or effort because I did not just sit down with them and tell them things. I showed them how to do something and then they would go and do it themselves. It just seemed so natural. We had a game we played with plants. We would pick several different varieties of leaf in the garden to give to each child and they would have to go and look for a leaf to match it and come back with it. We might just casually talk about which one was spotty and which one was hairy and which was smooth and which was prickly and so on. One of the children turned into a plantswoman and she is now a landscape gardener. She went to the Botanic Gardens and did very well there. Most children – certainly in the primary years – if they are given a chance to follow something of interest, will teach themselves.

THE TRAGIC ANNA

From the series 'My Books, My Friends', EDITH NEWMAN-DEVLIN *gives her appraisal of Tolstoy's* Anna Karenina.

I WAS FOURTEEN when I first read Tolstoy's *War and Peace*. I devoured all three volumes in less than a week. I skipped all the bits about war, Napoleon's invasion of Russia, the Battle of Borodino and the occupation of Moscow ... but I followed the lives of all the characters with passionate interest. I fell in love with Prince Andrey and envied Natasha for being able to sit beside him day after day when he was sick!

The Russian novels which I have continued to read since then have all captivated me in a special way. In them I discovered a new world of amazing people in a spacious snowbound landscape – people who worried about their souls and the meaning of life. This suited my temperament exactly! If you want to know the soul of a people, read its literature, listen to its music, look at its art. The Russian people are deeply poetic and spiritual, whatever may have happened on the political front, and in spite of the fact that until their liberation in 1861, 90 per cent of the population were serfs.

Count Leo Tolstoy (1828–1910) is Russian literature in one sense. Even in translation we recognise that his language is truthful and creative – the mark of a great writer. As a soldier he served in the Crimean War. He became a very unconventional Christian and was excommunicated from the Orthodox Church in 1901. Tolstoy was full of conflicting passions. He had a great lust for life and at the same time a hunger for asceticism. He believed in renouncing property and in the abolition of governments and churches, while believing in God and man. His goal was to make a heaven on earth – hence his rage at injustice. He was a great moral influence in his day and attracted countless pilgrims to his home at Yasnaya Polyana. But he eventually fled from there and died of pneumonia in a railway station at the age of eighty-two.

Anna Karenina was written in 1877. The book opens with the Oblonsky household in turmoil. 'Happy families are all alike; every unhappy family is unhappy in its own way.' No novel sets out so bravely, says Thomas Mann. In the opening pages we get a sense of Stiva – Anna's brother – his gaiety and vivacity. We expect him to be judged as frivolous and immoral, but Tolstoy judges him as innocent. Stiva comes before us, radiant with health and energy, open, generous-hearted, loved by everyone with whom he comes in contact. He feels no sense of sin in his infidelity. He supposes that his worn-out wife Dolly might take an indulgent view of him but she is outraged and humiliated. Dolly is one of the most tenderly presented characters in the book. We are taken into Dolly's heart, into her lack of self-confidence before Anna, into her dreams and disappointments.

Levin, Stiva's friend, occupies a great part of the book. His feelings for Kitty – who is to become his wife – are idealised, romantic, puritan. Tolstoy laughs at his gaucheness but honours his feelings too. Through his soul pass all sorts of thoughts and sensations, as he searches for an understanding of his experience. It is amazing how many different feelings and changes of feeling Tolstoy can express in this regard.

When Anna steps into the book and into our lives, we can never forget her thereafter! She has come to help heal the break between her brother and Dolly. We instantly feel the life within Anna. Her gaiety, charm and energy infect everybody. Then she meets Count Vronsky – who is well acquainted with the opposite sex – and a feeling she never knew existed grips her whole being. We feel the extraordinary power of her beauty and her personality over Vronsky. It is an overwhelming passion, yet she knows 'there is something not quite right in it'. Sunshine and shadow pass over her consciousness, as Tolstoy registers all the changing shifts in her emotions. Her openness to changing feeling is astonishing and moving. Nothing ever seems fixed and final in her life.

The passion of Vronsky and Anna grows over a year of intense and contradictory emotions – joy in each other, shame over the concealment of the life they have to live and the hurt done to others – until, inexorably, the consummation comes. Tolstoy honours this in a way seldom seen in modern novels. He follows the vibrations of Anna's soul with total respect. As a woman of her time, she has to give up everything – reputation, family, friends – for Vronsky. While he gives up his career for her, it is the woman who bears the greater weight of social censure.

Little by little, the burden thrown upon the relationship becomes too much. Without the wider support of family and friends and all the little occupations and distractions of social living which uphold a marriage, the relationship grows tense and strained. This is unbearable to watch. The situation leads her into feelings which are quite foreign to her warm and open nature – guilt, shame, jealousy and finally morbidity. We watch the loss of her proud dignity and independence. Her soul – that best and most beautiful part of her – grows sick, even unto death. She does violence to her deepest innermost feelings. The last act of her sick soul is to punish Vronsky by killing herself. We watch it happen with awe and compassion.

Vronsky is never portrayed as a facile seducer. We feel his physical presence, his male authority. His sufferings after Anna's death are terrible.

There is so much more in this great novel. Suffice to say, literature is here doing its job of making us feel to the full a sense of our common and best humanity.

COLLEGE LIFE AND LOVE

Former Taoiseach GARRET FITZGERALD *very much enjoyed college life in Dublin during the war years.*

MY FATHER WAS a Francophile. I think he spent time in France before he was married and my parents lived in Brittany for almost two years after their marriage in London. He spoke French well and was passionately interested in French literature. He was a friend of French philosophers like Maritain and Gilson – he went to see them occasionally in Paris in the 1930s. We were all sent on exchanges at one time or another. I went to France on exchange in 1938 and I went back in 1939 for another seven weeks in the summer. I was young enough not to be too self-conscious and therefore willing to tackle the proper pronunciation of French. I learned to speak it very quickly and the family I stayed with then are still close friends.

When I started in first year in UCD, I took ten subjects. I dropped economics immediately, because it seemed to me so dull. I intended to do English and French to degree level. My mother had taught me so well that, on entrance into college, I got first place in English and that deluded me into thinking that I could perhaps do well in English. I took it in First Arts, but I only got a Second, and I then realised that your mother may get you a First in the entrance scholarship and a Second in First Arts but she can't get you a good degree at BA level. So I switched and took history instead, with French and Spanish.

It was a wonderful period in my life. The college was smaller then. The war years were a very sheltered period for us. The appalling tragedy happening outside was something we were terribly aware of, and following the events of the war absorbed an enormous amount of my time, but nonetheless we were sheltered from it. It was a very relaxed existence. There was no question of working in the summer holidays – there was no work to be done anyway. We learned to do nothing for three months on end, which I think is a marvellous thing to have experienced for some period of your life. I have never regretted my total idleness for those summers.

College was a marvellous place and I met Joan there quite early on. I proposed to her about the time the War ended and we got married two years later. All the happiness of the rest of my life goes back to that period, meeting and falling in love at that time. Ours has been a very interactive marriage in which everything we have done we have done together. I have been constantly under challenge from her in the positions I have taken up – everything has had to be argued out. Or if I take a wrong turning in some way, I am told so very quickly! So education goes on through life, especially in marriage.

LISTENING TO THE CHILDREN

TROND WAAGE – *Norwegian Ombudsman for Children* – *argues that we are failing our children by not recognising their competence.*

THERE WAS NO concept of childhood in the Middle Ages. At age six or seven the child entered the labour force. Over recent centuries childhood was recognised. Education was provided and legislation was introduced to protect the child. We have now come to the stage where children are more and more excluded from society and are put in 'waiting rooms' – i.e. schools – to keep them away from society. To me, this is a wrong approach. We could do much more for the education of children if they were allowed take responsiblity for their own learning process. They want to do that – to use the competence they have gained. It will be an enormous challenge for us to bring children back into society.

Children are our future. That is not an empty political slogan. They are our greatest resource and we need to invest in them. In school they are controlled and monitored and they emerge often confused about the future and about their own identity. The multinational industries like Coca-Cola, Nokia, Ericsson, have at the same time been doing a lot of research on young people and want them to be active. We look back in nostalgia at our own childhood and think it was the best childhood, but today's children have come through several revolutions – gender, knowledge, technology – into a very different world. We need to communicate with them, learn to trust them, see them as equal human beings. As Ombudsman that is my contract with the child – I am taking him seriously and bringing forward his views. Each day I discover their great competence – not just in technology but in social life and in the knowledge they have gleaned from the media, from each other and from industry. We must not deny that competence in the education system. If we do, we create more and more losers.

Technology and media are invading the nursery. These are multimedia industries that are attacking childhood. Yes, they inform and entertain, but they also impress negative images and information on the child. It is very difficult for the child to tackle these images. They need good supervisors who will guide them rather than 'traditional' parents or teachers from fifty years ago. When we were children our parents gave us a compass and a map for our future. Nowadays you cannot give a map. The only certainty is uncertainty, so the best gift we can give children is a good compass, so that they can keep on course for a positive future.

To be a parent today is a lonely task. Parents need to come together to voice their concerns and stand together in the face of the internet. Just as thirty years ago we had Greenpeace monitoring the environment, perhaps today we need a 'Screenpeace' movement. Unlike TV channels, there is no choice with the internet – you are either on the net or you are off. Parents realise that children need access to the net to search for information, but children need only misspell DISNEY by two letters and they are into pornography. So many children across Europe are now being subjected to these negative images. We cannot control the internet, because it has no borders, but we can encourage the internet service providers (ISP) to take responsibility in order to help parents. In Norway we have asked the ISPs to develop a 'Green Entrance', which is given free of charge to all schools. When you buy a computer in a store, you also receive the 'Green Entrance', which you use in the home.

Today's children are so different to previous generations. They are the 'rights generation' – they know they have rights and they are prepared to accept the responsibliities that go with the rights. They are the 'negotiating generation' – they have extraordinary competence in negotiating agreements. They are the 'institution generation' – they are involved in music, sports etc., and they learn from an early age how grown-ups act towards them. They are the 'generation of individuals' – more and more they are losing the concept of social codes and are depending on themselves as individuals. Again this is fed to them by the media and the multinationals. They are the 'generation of multiple careers', yet the education system prepares them for *a* career.

Today's young people are also creating their own ways of living together – as seen in the TV show *Friends* – another sort of 'waiting-room' for 25–40 year-olds. Above all, they are the 'commercial generation'. It is no longer a question of 'to be or not to be' but 'to have or not to have'. In Norway the 'school uniform' is the trendy gear – jeans, runners etc. The schoolyard is Norway's biggest catwalk. The industries know this and they pay young people to model their wares in the schoolyard.

And then there are 'the others' – the outsiders, the losers who cannot cope with the education system. They end up on the streets, lost. They are 'pushouts' rather than 'dropouts'. In every country we have teachers who should never have been teachers, causing damage to young people. The challenge for all of us is to start integrating children in our lives again. It is astonishing how little parents actually know about their own children's lives. Children are competent individuals who need guidance and communication and who need good role models in adults. It is too easy for parents to look backward and say 'this is how it was for us'. We should not cut all links to the past but neither should we copy everything from the past. Children are simply our greatest resource and we should acknowledge their many competencies.

TO SCHOOL THROUGH POVERTY

Politician MICHAEL D. HIGGINS *remembers a gifted teacher and a poverty-ridden childhood.*

I HAD THE extraordinary fortune of having a marvellous holistic primary teacher in a two-teacher school in Newmarket-on-Fergus, a man by the name of William Clune.

He defeated time because he was going back as well as forward. He knew the names of plants and bushes in Latin and Irish and English and, on sunny days, he used to take the whole school to the top of a hill to show them the history of the local area. He had an integrated approach to everything before that word was invented. He was a man with an extraordinary sense of history in his own life too, because his brother was Conor Clune, the Volunteer who had been shot just before the founding of the State.

He was a man who loved the wonder of children and he had some extraordinary ideas, which I am sure couldn't be proved. He had an idea, for example, that if you tried hard enough and used your concentration, you could go back through not only your own memory but other people's memories to remember an Irish word. He was a Jungian. Everything that I was later to encounter about Jung and consciousness, he was in fact practising in his own way in the school yard. There was not one person who came into his schoolyard from any background, with shoes or without, who wasn't respected as a carrier of wonderment. It was the central value of his pedagogic technique.

We all went barefooted to school at that time, not because we didn't have shoes or boots but because that was what was done. It was before tarmacadam and I remember the sensation of the chippings on your feet as much as I remember the beet dropping off the backs of lorries – beet which we would then eat.

What I don't like is people romanticising these enriching physical sensations to the exclusion of the social side of things. I know the experience of grass between your toes and I know that a fern will cut you and I know where butterflies gather and I know about mosses. I can remember all these sensations very clearly, but I also remember when my aunt and uncle's house was caving in and youngsters going past the house saying, 'We haven't broken windows in our house' and firing stones at the old couple and their nephews who were living inside. I remember the quiet cruelty of it and it is dishonest of people to take the quietness and richness and complexity of natural settings and use them as a mask for the cruel social divisions that prevailed in rural Ireland.

I was very glad to escape from that poverty. It was only after a lot of healing that I was able to reach back through these memories and rediscover again the colour and sensation of a fern or a moss or a grass. I really did not have much time for people who try to perpetuate a kind of pastoral nonsense about rural Ireland.

ON DREAMING

Three views on the importance – the necessity even – of daydreaming.
From TONY BUZAN, JACK BLACK *and* JOHN O'DONOHUE.

HOW MANY OF us remember being reprimanded as children with the words 'Are you daydreaming again? Do you ever listen to me? You're always daydreaming!' Worse still, how many of us have reprimanded our own children or students with those words? Far from being a bad thing, daydreaming is a good and necessary exercise. Tony Buzan – who writes and lectures extensively on memory and learning – puts it quite bluntly:

Daydreaming is a great gymnasium for the mind where the imagination exercises and plays. You *have* to daydream. If you don't, you die ...

Some teachers will find a pupil's daydreaming insulting – a poor reflection on their teaching (which may, of course, be justified!). Rather they should see it as a healthy exercise and explore it as such. We need to be 'imaging' all the time, Buzan claims, because what we understand and remember are images in association. Learning is not linear logic. It is the brain weaving, diverting, connecting. Daydreaming, in fact.

Jack Black – who pioneered the 'Mindstore' approach to personal development – emphasises the power of dream and vision in his work. His own awakening to this reality came when someone asked him: 'When did you stop dreaming – and why?' As children we dream a lot. Why do we stop as adults? The most important gift we can bestow on the child is self-esteem, says Black. If we foster their dreams, we can give them the confidence to learn. There are many examples in the world of sport, none greater than that of Mohammed Ali. Through his mantra 'I am the greatest', Ali dreamed he was the greatest, believed he was the greatest and *became* the greatest. Another great man of vision, Nelson Mandela, said on becoming president of South Africa: 'There's nothing enlightened in thinking small ...'

Giving long rein to our dream is giving way to the wonderful gift of imagination. According to the poet and philosopher John O'Donohue:

> The imagination is always interested in where things break down – failure, resentment, defeat, contradiction, bitterness, darkness, glory, light and possibility – the wild side of ourselves that society would rather forget was there at all. So the imagination mirrors and articulates the subconscious. All we know of ourselves is just a certain little surface. There is a whole under-earth of complexity to us that keeps out of sight. It comes to us through dreams ... It is amazing how many of your needs and hungers and potential and gifts are actually rooted in the subconscious side of your life.

And most of that great plantation of your subconscious seems to have actually happened in the playfields and innocence of childhood ...

So maybe next time we should say to the child: 'Are you daydreaming again? Good!'

I REMEMBER HENRY FORD

Eugene Leonard Clarke, born in Co. Sligo in 1891, recalls how a quirk of historical fate enabled him to become the first native Managing Director of Henry Ford & Son, Cork.

I HAD STUDIED Commerce and Accounting in London, but I became homesick and came home to find employment in Skerries Tuition College in Dublin. At Easter 1916 I went down to visit my girlfriend in Bantry and we had a lovely time cycling around West Cork, unaware of what was going on in Dublin. When I went to return I was told there were no trains running to Dublin as there was 'some serious trouble up there'. I was stranded in Cork but managed to get some temporary employment there, until I heard that Henry Ford was planning to open an automobile plant by the Lee. He had bought Cork racecourse – a site of 150 acres with river frontage – for the purpose. I applied for a job and was fortunate that they needed an accountant to look after payroll, purchasing and so on. I was the second Irishman to be employed at the Cork plant.

> MEMOIR OF HENRY FORD: We chose Ireland for a plant because we wanted to start the country along the road to industry. There was some personal sentiment in it too. My ancestors came from near Cork and that city with its wonderful harbour has an abundance of fine industrial sites. Cork has for many years been a city of casual labour and extreme poverty. We started our plant

there with three men from Detroit in charge of operations and now (1926) we have 1,800 men employed. Eight hours a day five days a week at a minimum of two and threepence an hour. Steady money – something few if any of the men had ever known before.

Within days of my employment there were 300 men on the payroll. For the first two years they were involved in the construction of the plant under the direction of Raymond Brown. Henry Ford had grown up on a farm and was a great agriculturalist as well as being an inventor and his constant ambition was 'to lift farm drudgery off flesh and blood and lay it on steel and motors'. He realised his ambition with the Fordson tractor. When food supplies became scarce during the Great War, Lloyd George appealed for help to Ford and he despatched 5,000 Fordsons to England at a cost price of £150 each.

> MHF: It was these tractors, run mostly by women, that ploughed up old estates and golf courses and let all England be planted, without taking away from fighting manpower or crippling forces in the munitions factories.

After the war, the demand for tractors fell and the Cork plant concentrated on making engines and rear axles for cars. These were shipped to Manchester for assembly. The car in question was of course the famous Model T.

> MHF: I will build a motor car for the great multitude. It will be large enough for the family, but small enough for the individual to run and care for – and so low in price that no man making a good salary will be unable to own one and enjoy, with his family, the blessings of hours of pleasure in God's great open spaces ...

I had many meetings in Detroit with Mr Ford and his son Edsel. He was very simple in his ways and totally devoted to his work. He liked to hear people's opinions even though he rarely changed his mind upon hearing them. If he went for a drive on Sunday, it would be through the huge Detroit plant. He was always interested in Cork. His father William had emigrated with his family from Ballinascarthy, Co. Cork. He headed for the American mid-west and Henry was born on a forty-acre farm near Detroit which he later developed into a huge operation. Later, Henry named his own home 'Fairlane' after a street in Cork which has since disappeared – I tried and failed to find the signboard for Mr Ford. A woman from Fair Lane had helped look after his family. He also gave the name to his private train and to what was probably the best car he designed. Mr Ford had an innate knowledge of everything mechanical.

> MHF: Driving into town, I always had a pocketful of trinkets – nuts, washers and odds and ends of machinery. Often I took a broken watch and tried to put it together. There's an immense amount to be learned simply by tinkering with things. It's not possible to learn from books how everything is made. Machines are to a mechanic what books are to a writer.

In 1926 I was appointed Managing Director in Cork. Everything went very smoothly. We had no disputes of any kind. There was little or no tradition of engineering in Cork before Ford so the system of training was very much that of apprenticeship – the new man was trained by the old hand. Outside the factory the Fordsons soccer team won the 1926 Free State Cup Final, beating Shamrock Rovers 3–2.

Between 1926 and 1930 there were big developments in Cork. We set up our own foundry – the most advanced in Europe – and imported the raw materials, coal and steel. We also began manufacturing tractors and exported them all over the world. We had procured all the equipment from Michigan – five shiploads of it – and installed it in Cork. Our workforce peaked at over five thousand. Eventually Ford opened a plant in Dagenham, England, and our workforce tapered off, but many of the Corkmen moved to Dagenham and trained the workers there. Mr Ford was also keen to help the Russians in developing their industry and sent his best men over to Joe Stalin to advise him.

My outstanding impression of the Cork plant is how well it adjusted to manufacture and assembly at the very highest standard in a city which had no real engineering tradition. My own involvement was a pure quirk of fate – stranded in Cork because of the rebellion in Dublin. In fact I still have that return ticket from Cork ...

THE MAKING OF A WRITER

Joan Lingard *recalls how a Belfast childhood shaped her as a writer.*

I was absolutely crazy about books. They fascinated me. I could never get enough to read and I am sure that is why I ultimately became a writer. The local library was quite far away, so I couldn't go there on my own when I was young. It appeared to me then to be like an old shed, and in fact when I went back there again recently it still looked like that! The books then were very tattered and ancient. They had long since lost their dust jackets and their spines had a greasy feeling about them. The pages were filthy – spattered with egg and tomato ketchup. I hated the feel of those books so much that I used to turn the pages with a postcard and cover the spine with a paper wrapper – but that didn't thwart my love of the books themselves.

I read absolutely everything I was allowed to read in the junior library – you weren't allowed into the senior section until you were fourteen. I read all the books that children have loved for years – the 'Chalet School' books, Enid Blyton, *Just William, Biggles* – and when my mother would ask me what I wanted for Christmas I always demanded a book. One Christmas I got eight books and I had read them all before I went to bed that night! My mother was beginning to despair of keeping me supplied with books and finally one day, when I was moaning, 'I've got nothing to read, I'm bored', she turned to me and said, 'Why don't you go away and write your own books?' That was how I began as a writer, at the age of eleven.

I got some lined foolscap paper, filled my fountain pen with green ink (because I thought that was a very suitable colour for a writer!) and sat down to write my first book. It was about a girl called Gail. It was one of those books in which a telegram arrives calling the parents away to somewhere like Rangoon (*Great Aunt Emily very ill. Come at once*)! Gail was sent to her grandmother in Cornwall where she found a smugglers' cave which led to various secret passages ... Eventually she tracked down the smugglers and was confronted by a villain with scars zig-zagging down his face to the corners of his mouth. It was very unsubtle characterisation – he might as well have had a placard on his chest saying 'I am the villain'! In the end Gail brings the smugglers to justice and – lo and behold – her uncle Bill appears on the scene and he happens to be a detective who has been trying to track the smugglers down for years without success. There were definitely shades of Enid Blyton lurking in the background!

I wasn't happy with my 'book' in loose sheets. I wanted to make a real book, so I copied the whole story out in my best writing in an exercise book (in blue ink this time). I made a dust wrapper, illustrated it and wrote a 'blurb'. I wrote 'Books by Joan Lingard' on the back, then under it 'No. 1 – *Gail*' and at the bottom 'Published by Lingard & Co.' That was my first publication!

Other books were to follow in this series 'Books by Joan Lingard'. I wrote *The Further Adventures of Gail* and another book was *The Strange House on the Moors*. The latter was a story about twin girls of fourteen and it was set on the Yorkshire Moors. I remember painting the twins on the cover. They had long blonde hair in plaits down to the waist. (There was a certain amount of wish fulfilment in that – I had always wanted to grow my hair long but my mother wouldn't allow it, in case I picked up lice in school. She insisted on a pudding-bowl style.) The twins arrived on the moors on a wild stormy night and a big mansion loomed up before them. The door opened and an evil-looking housekeeper invited them in ... I think that by then I would have been reading the Brontës!

I wrote at that time mainly for my own gratification. I showed the books to my best friend and to my mother, but I don't think my father was very interested in them. I doubt if he ever saw them. He liked me to do well at school but that was the limit of his interest. He never came to the prize-giving at school, for example.

I wrote first for adults. My first book – *Liam's Daughter* – was published in 1962. It was set in Northern Ireland and in France but the characters were Irish and they were characters I could understand. My early unpublished 'books' were written from second and third-hand experience and I eventually realised that I would write successfully only if I wrote about the people and the backgrounds that I knew and understood. I wrote six novels in that early phase.

I didn't really consider writing for children until the last of those six were published. It was called *The Lord on Our Side* and it was about Ulster from the 1940s to the 1960s. A friend of mine, Honor Arundel – who was a children's writer – read that book and said, 'Why don't you write a book *for children* about what is happening in Northern Ireland now?' (This was in 1969 when the present troubles were starting up.) I realised then that there was a book waiting inside my head – all I needed was for someone to press the button and say 'Do that' and it happened. I had a Protestant girl called Josie in *The Lord on Our Side*. I changed her into Sadie and I created a Catholic boy called Kevin as a balance to her. They lived very close to one another and I set the story in the days leading up to the twelfth of July. Kevin and Sadie are, of course, on opposite sides until they meet and develop a liking for each other ... In a way, *The Twelfth of July* seemed to write itself. It came very easily to me and I intended to write only that one book. But Kevin and Sadie had got such a hold of my imagination that I couldn't leave them alone. I went on to write *Across the Barricades* and the other three books in the series. I had become a children's writer almost by accident.

When I wrote those five books for children, my aim was to be completely impartial, and my Christian Science upbringing certainly helped me, in that I was detached from both sides. Also, because I had left Belfast I wasn't sucked into it emotionally and therefore I could be more objective about it.

Obviously my childhood has influenced all my writing. I really believe that the first eighteen years lay down almost everything. The more I go on, the more I draw from my childhood. It seems like a well that grows deeper and deeper the more I lower the bucket into it.

REMEMBERING PEG

A personal tribute to a valued mentor.

I HOLD IN my hand a book. A children's classic – *Swiss Family Robinson*. A lovely, hardback illustrated edition. It represents a part of my childhood when our reading diet was confined to classics like this. It feels good and reassuring in my hand. That feeling, however, is not so much engendered by the book but by the name inscribed on the flyleaf – M. Kneeshaw.

Margaret or 'Peg' Kneeshaw was for many years Children's and Schools Librarian for Dublin City and it was in that capacity that I got to know her in the mid-1960s. I was a young enthusiastic teacher in a huge school in the then sprawling new suburb of Finglas West. The school was bursting at the seams within a year or two of its opening. I taught in a room that had been purpose-built as a library but pressure for classroom space meant it was always used as a classroom during my seven years in that school. I fought a running but losing battle to have a properly established library for a school of one thousand pupils but the running joke was 'The library has been shelved again'.

The positive side of the campaign was that I got to know Peg Kneeshaw. The Schools Library Department was on the corner of Wellington Quay – on the fourth floor – and from there Peg and her small dedicated staff serviced the library needs of Dublin City schools. It was an Aladdin's Cave to me – rows and stacks and shelves and jumbles and pyramids of wonderful books. When I failed to make a library out of the school library, Peg allowed me to take a classroom collection – eighty to one hundred books – which I could renew every so often.

I was in heaven – or at least its anteroom – every time I visited that top floor. Here I was introduced to a whole new burgeoning world of children's literature. Here I fumbled my way into the cinema with *Paddington Bear*, went tobogganing with Laura Ingalls of the *Little House on the Prairie*, wept with Granny Conroy as she visited Eilís Dillon's *Island of Horses*, trembled at the advance of Ted Hughes' *Iron Man*. And always the gentle proddings of Peg Kneeshaw guided me. 'Try this one! She's a wonderful writer! ... That's a beautiful story for eight-year-olds.' In my attempts to open new worlds for the children of Finglas, a whole new world was being opened to me by this quiet, gentle and wise woman.

Ten years later the library had at last become a library, but I had moved on. I was now in schools publishing, trying to compile English anthologies for senior primary standards. To whom did I turn? Peg Kneeshaw. Once again I was given the freedom of Wellington Quay to muse and choose, and always at my shoulder the gentle, guiding voice of Peg Kneeshaw – 'Seven to ten is the time when children are introduced to fantasy. There are some books which if children don't get them at this age they will never get them. I'm thinking of a classic like *Alice in Wonderland*. If you don't read that at a certain age, you're always going to be too old or too young for it.'

Another decade later I had moved on once more – to broadcasting. In 1982 I produced a series called 'Children Reading' – a guide for parents to the world of children's books. Once again, I drew on the wisdom and experience of Peg Kneeshaw. Here she is on the thorny subject of Enid Blyton:

> I maintain that Enid Blyton is something that children go through – rather like measles. They catch it and they devour Blyton but they eventually move on. There's no point in getting hung up on Blyton – for some children she may be their introduction to reading and that's good. The trouble is with the child who just won't read anything else – but generally they can be weaned on to other writers at a similar level.

Peg Kneeshaw introduced a whole generation of child readers to exciting new writers like Joan Lingard, Phillipa Pearce and Rosemary Sutcliff. Peg was a gentle and gracious lady who served her public in an unassuming but most dedicated way. To me she was a valued mentor through three different careers. She died just before Christmas 1998. She deserves to be remembered with gratitude and affection – and she is. It pleases me greatly to hold in my hand her copy of *Swiss Family Robinson*.

LEARNING ON THE STREET

Academic and political activist NOAM CHOMSKY *grew up in an extraordinary educational environment on the streets of Philadelphia.*

THE LOCAL AREA was not pleasant. This was the 1930s; we were the only Jewish family in a largely Irish and German Catholic neighbourhood which was fiercely anti-Semitic, rather pro-Nazi in fact. I can even remember beer parties as late as the Fall of Paris. On the other hand, there was an extended family, which was a big influence on me. My father's family, who lived in Baltimore, were very orthodox Jewish. In fact, according to my father, they actually regressed beyond what they had been like in their Eastern European Jewish village community. My mother's family were in New York and they were mostly Jewish working class, which at the time meant mostly unemployed. Many of them had never been to school, but they lived in an atmosphere of quite high culture and also working-class culture, which were not dissociated at that time. They were very active intellectually in every domain.

These were immigrants, usually first-generation immigrants, maybe some early second-generation, working class, largely unemployed. A few had gone on to school, one or two had gotten through college and become teachers. Some had not gotten past fourth grade; they had grown up on the streets. They were very deeply involved in working-class politics of the day, which meant the Communist Party for some and anti-Communist Left for others – every fringe of radical opinion that you could think of. Of course, in those days that political activity didn't just mean having political opinions, it meant a life – it meant everything from the picnics to the summer vacations to concerts to everything else. A large part of their life was what we would nowadays call high culture: there would be debates about Steckel's critique of Freud, discussions about *Ulysses* and Cubist art and the latest concert of the Budapest String Quartet, as well as what was wrong with Lenin's version of Marx and what that implied for politics of the day.

Much of the excitement of this environment was focused for me around one particular uncle who hadn't gotten through elementary school. He happened to be disabled and, as a result, he was able to get a newsstand, which became a very lively intellectual centre in the late 1930s; a lot of European émigrés clustered around it, many of them German PhDs or psychiatrists and so on. I remember going to work on the newsstand in the evening by the time I was twelve or thirteen and it was a very exhilarating experience. I didn't understand much of what was going on, but it was exciting. Nobody bought many newspapers, but there was a lot of discussion.

THE HURRIED CHILD

DAVID ELKIND *makes a plea for children to be allowed develop and grow at their own pace, rather than be robbed of their childhood.*

I WAS FORTUNATE as a clinical psychologist to meet and work with the great Swiss psychologist, Jean Piaget. He believed that children have their own ways of thinking and knowing about the world and we need to support those natural ways of growing. He demonstrated the stages of development through which children develop their intelligence and learn about the external world. For the past twenty years I have been concerned about how we have ignored that process and think instead that we can teach children anything at any time. We now have people training foetuses *in utero*. The fastest-growing software is for infants aged six months to two years. All this is crazy stuff and all of our research shows that this is actually harmful to children. Modern parents feel guilty and want their children to have what they did not have. As our families get smaller and there is less extended family, parents need to be re-educated about early childhood.

With all the societal changes of the past forty years – notably the influence of television – children are not as protected as they once were. Television is insidious. Young children are exposed to murder, violence and tragedy on the news – whether it is a mother drowning her children in South Carolina or bodies dragged down the streets of Mogadishu.

THE CURIOUS MIND

Whereas we used to see children as innocent and in need of protection, we now see them as 'competent' and able to deal with anything. There is no basis for this in research, however. Children are probably more competent than we once gave them credit for, but they are in fact much less competent than we would like them to be – and this is where the hurrying comes in. We *need* children who can be alone through the day, who can deal with divorce or sexual mores etc., such are the societal pressures and the competitive nature of the world. Parents see education as a race and assume that the earlier you start, the better you will finish.

We are biological creatures, not machines. We grow and develop at a natural pace. We need time to reflect, to play, to interact. We are social beings and can be in danger of losing our human-ness to technology. Children need what I call 'beneficent neglect' – time to play and imagine. We need a balance between the demands of our external and our inner worlds. Children need time to know themselves, work out their dilemmas.

It is a busy world and parents are hard-pressed but there are things they can do. Children love and need rituals, so set aside one time a week that is sacred for the family – a meal, a family outing, a chance to talk and deal with issues. Today the traditional nuclear family has been replaced by the permeable family. The old boundaries between public and private lives – between workplace and home – have been eroded. Millions work from home or have children in their workplace. TV programmes like *Oprah* have opened up people's private lives more than we want to know. The value of the nuclear family was togetherness, whereas in the permeable family the overriding notion is autonomy. Each individual's personal lifespace takes precedence over the family, so mealtimes, birthdays etc. often come in second place to the individual. I would hope we would move now to a vital family, which would incorporate the best of both the nuclear and permeable families, putting the needs of children more on a par with the needs of parents.

Children grow up so quickly – sometimes childhood seems to pass like a dream. We need to enjoy our children and help them enjoy life, enjoy the different stages of childhood. I see college students today who feel inauthentic. They are doing what they are told they should be doing. They are often mourning for a lost childhood. You often see them playing on the swings or slides in the children's playground. That is so sad. We can't skip stages in our lives. We can't skip old age. Why should we skip childhood?

ON TELLING THE TRUTH

In an interview about his childhood, the Nobel Laureate, SEAMUS HEANEY, recalled his early attempts at writing while attending primary school.

'YOU WROTE WHAT you were expected to write. You wrote like everybody else ...' Seamus remembered – as will many of his generation – the seemingly interminable workbook exercises, those lists of similes to be completed – 'as black as —', 'as white as —', 'as strong as —' ? The problem was that there was only one 'right' answer. If you didn't write 'as strong as an ox', you were *wrong*! It didn't matter that most of us had little familiarity with the word 'ox'. If you related to the world you knew and wrote 'as strong as Jemmy Toner's plough-horse' you were deemed *wrong* ...

Seamus Heaney also remembered the English Composition – the inevitable 'Day at the Seaside' where, again, you wrote what was expected.

> 'I swam happily in the sea' (I could never swim!)
> 'My mother bought me a bucket and spade ...' (My mother bought me a wooden spoon once and let me foother around in the sand with it before bringing it home for domestic use!)

But that was long ago. Nowadays a more enlightened teacher would take a different and more realistic approach – hopefully. Nowadays, if you were bored out of your mind at the seaside, it would be alright to say so. And it would be alright to use the word 'foother' ...

THE CURIOUS MIND

'I didn't realise you could tell the truth in writing until I was about twenty-one,' says Seamus Heaney, 'and in a way that is why I started writing ...'

VINCENT

In recalling our schooldays, much of our memory is often blurred, but sometimes a singular teacher who had passion and enthusiasm stands out. Actor T.P. McKenna *remembers one such teacher.*

UNQUESTIONABLY, THE BIGGEST influence in my life was Father Vincent Kennedy – now dead, God rest his soul. Looking back, having met many, many eminent people, he was really one of the most sophisticated men I ever met. He was a very stylish man. He was small and dapper and everything he did was very graceful. He had a rather lovely room in Saint Patrick's College, Cavan, with a Bechstein piano and a very nice library.

He used to produce operas. I was a boy soprano. My first appearance on the stage was in *The Yeomen of the Guard*. I had an extraordinarily powerful boy soprano voice – something I inherited from my father. When my voice broke, we used to go up to Father Vincent's room and he would play us a wide variety of music. He also gave us classes in school in general music education and the history of music. He would demonstrate the difference in structure between the work of Beethoven and Chopin, for example, and the development of the piano as an instrument. This was very, very fascinating and unusual for a secondary school. We would listen to the Proms on BBC in his room and follow it with the score. He had a wonderful range as a classical pianist. He could play the Grieg concerto from memory and he had hundreds of scores as well.

We were the chosen few – just three or four of us – like Jean Brodie's *crème de la crème*. We would knock on his door after night prayer and if he was in a good mood he would let us in. We would have coffee and talk and he would play the piano. If he was in a bad mood, he would just sit there and puff smoke into the air very elegantly. I remember one Leitrim fellow saying to him, 'Are you bored, Father?'. There was a long pause. 'Haven't I the right to be bored in my own sitting room?' he replied. We had the good sense to get up and leave.

His influence was all-pervasive at that time. I had moved on from Gilbert & Sullivan and into drama – the plays of Louis D'Alton, for example. I had got the acting bug as young as the age of fifteen. Anew McMaster was visiting Cavan and he had brought his usual repertoire of Shakespeare. We saw *Hamlet* and *Macbeth* and Father Kennedy then brought us backstage to meet McMaster. Myself and another chap decided to go down and talk to him in the Farnham Arms. He was very nice and he bought us tea. He said, 'Don't be an actor, my dear boy, until you are absolutely sure there's nothing else in the world you can do'. I took that very literally, so I decided to set about getting a job when I left school and then maybe get around to the acting sometime later.

GRANNY'S ADVICE

In 1998, in the course of an interview with Paul Wilson – the author of The Little Book of Calm *– I suggested to him that much of the advice he gives in the book to help the reader stay calm and free from stress is the sort of advice a wise granny would impart. Paul was inclined to agree ... We invited listeners to submit the pearls of wisdom they had acquired from granny – or a parent or a teacher or a mentor ... The following is a selection from the many replies.*

GET YOURSELF AN education. It's one thing no one can ever take away from you.

Never mind what's gone. Now mind what's left.

Nothing must be done hastily but the killing of fleas ...

An ounce of breeding is worth a tonne of feeding.

Until you make peace with who you are, you'll never be content with what you have.

Life is lived forwards, understood backwards.

If you have lived a long life, it doesn't mean you have lived a good life, but if you have lived a good life, you have lived long enough ...

Walk easy when your jug is full ...

Broken china is never mended.

If it was meant for you, you'd have got it.

If you love someone, hold tightly with open hands.

Hard work never killed anyone, but long hours murdered the best of horses.

Put yourself totally into whatever you are doing at that time.

Don't sweat on the small stuff – keep your eye on the big picture.

If you like the sound of a particular phrase, don't use it!

If you can't look on the bright side, take out the dark side and polish it up.

Place no expectations on others – then any good thing we receive is a bonus.

Little by little, the bird builds his nest.

Only boring people get bored.

Laugh and the world laughs with you, weep and you weep alone.

The best way to retain friends is to keep them at a distance.

Things without remedy should be without regard.

People who are rearing should be caring.

There's no shame in what's natural.

The richest person is the one who knows what to do with their spare time.

A friendly word, a kindly smile, a helping hand – and life's worthwhile.

Faith can move mountains – but you must provide the spade.

If you never do what you can't, you'll never do what you can!

When the student is ready, the teacher will appear.

Always be ready to live in the age you are born into.

Measure twice and cut once.

The single most important thing to teach the newborn child is the difference between day and night.

Don't put it down – put it away.

Only one life that soon is past: only what's done with love will last.

Tick–tock, tick–tock, tick–tock. Take time, take time, take time.

Follow the boy and he'll fly. Fly and he'll follow ...

Your temper is one of your most valuable possessions. Don't lose it!

Whatever you do, do it with your might. Things done by half are never done right.

If you're only selling a goat, be at the top of the fair.

Be rigid about nothing except flexibility.

If you want to stay sane, plan one (and only one) small thing that is different each day.

Learn to like what you have when you can't have what you like.

Today is the tomorrow you worried about yesterday.

When cleaning a room, if you concentrate on the corners, the middle will take care of itself.

Do the right thing rather than do things right.

A good sex life takes up 5 per cent of your time – a bad sex life takes up all of your time.

It's better to sit idle than to work idle.

Experience is a dear school and fools learn in no other.

Always have the easy word.

NEVER MIND THE ANSWER – ASK THE QUESTION!

Poet BRENDAN KENNELLY *is inspired by a child's questions.*

As FAR BACK as I can remember, my experience of education has been one of questions and answers. In the national school, a man asked a question, and I tried to give what was called 'the right answer'. This continued, with some variations, right up into, and through, university. Always – questions and answers. My purpose here is not to discuss the effects of this format, this question–answer format, on, for example, one's capacity for independent meditation, or on one's love of ideas, or poetry. There is a line from a poem by Patrick Kavanagh, which goes 'There are no answers to any real questions ...' If we meditate on this, we begin to see certain hurtful truths beginning to emerge. Perhaps the question–answer format, far from leading us to knowledge, tends to make us glib in our responses, tends also to give us the conviction, or at least the assumption, that reality itself is composed of questions to which the human mind can find the answers. And perhaps this assumption, underlying so much education, has something to do with the sort of chaotic world we are creating. Perhaps this assumption leads to false certainties, to inflexible dogmatic tyrannies, and worst of all, and most ironically, to the spectre of the closed, complacent mind – the mind cosy with answers.

Which, I wonder, is more important – to ask the question, or to find the answer? I don't know. But, for myself, I would say that any attempt to keep one's mind alive and probing, manifests itself more truly in the impulse to question rather than in the need to answer. Between the question and the answer stretches a whole mental kingdom of possibility. When we lose the impulse to question, we will become satisfied with answers. We will not bother to explore that stretching mental kingdom. Is there anyone more pathetic than a man who believes he has the answers?

Children tend to be questioners. I would like to read you a poem in order to show this. The poem is based on the questions of a child of three, and these questions concern death. I listened to the child's questions, which were so insistent, so concerned, so full of pure desire, so crammed with wonder that I wrote them down. Then I worked at the questions over a period of time. When I had finished the poem (or rather when I decided not to continue shaping it) I looked at it, and knew I had no answers. But the child's questions were more exciting than even if I, the man, had any answers. And I thought – perhaps as a teacher, I'd be more helpful if I could forget about the answers, and try instead to get people to give a precise form to their questionings, however intense or vague. I don't know how well I have succeeded, but I think that sometimes I have lessened the fears and neuroses of those who, under the pressure to find an answer, discovered only that their minds were more unhappy than they needed to be.

Anyway, here is the poem, entitled 'Poem from a Three-Year-Old':

And will the flowers die
And will the people die?

And every day do you grow old, do I
grow old, no I'm not old,
do flowers grow old?

Old things – do you throw them out?

Do you throw old people out?

And how you know a flower that's old?

The petals fall, the petals fall from flowers.
and do the petals fall from people too?
every day more petals fall until the
floor where I would like to play I
want to play is covered with old
flowers and people all the same

together lying there with petals fallen
on the dirty floor I want to play
the floor you come and sweep
with the huge broom.

The dirt you sweep, what happens that,
what happens all the dirt you sweep
from flowers and people, what
happens all the dirt? Is all the
dirt what's left of flowers and
people, all the dirt there in a
heap under the huge broom that
sweeps everything away?

Why you work so hard, why brush
and sweep to make a heap of dirt

And
who will bring new flowers?
And
who will bring new people – Who will
bring new flowers to put in water
where no petals fall on to the
floor where I would like to
play? Who will bring new flowers
that will not hang their heads
like tired old people wanting sleep?
Who will bring new flowers that
do not split and shrivel every
day? And if we have new flowers,
will we have new people too to
keep the flowers alive and give
them water?
And will the new young flowers die?

And will the new young people die?
And why?

THE ODD COUPLE

When a great writer tells you that he grew up in a house with no books, you wonder a lot. Who lit the spark for that writer? Who introduced him to the world of books? In JOHN MCGAHERN *'s case it was two unlikely characters whom many would consider as eccentrics or cranks. But what a debt we as a society owe to the Moroneys ...*

THERE WERE NO books in our house, but I discovered them in the house of friends of my father, a family called Moroney. There is a wonderful portrait of them in that book *Woodbrook,* by David Thompson. Old Mr Moroney was a beekeeper and he was very eccentric. Father and son lived together and they had 180 acres of good limestone land. In fact, David Thompson says they were landless, but in a way they were landless in spirit. They had a farm that they never looked after and in fact they gathered apples and sold them for half a crown a bucketful. I remember being sent to buy a bucketful of apples and falling into conversation with the old man about books. I was interested in books and when I was about eleven he gave me the run of his excellent nineteenth-century library. For about eight or nine years, I would come every fortnight, returning five or six books in my oil-cloth shopping bag and taking five or six more away.

I imagine the Moroneys had once been ruled by women, but at this stage the two boys were on their own. They would run through all the cups and plates and every month they used to have a big washing up. They lived on tea and bread and jam. Willie Moroney was a great beekeeper and he had an enormous beard which was stained with all sorts of colours of food and drink – you could smell him at quite a distance. When he was talking about books and the raspberry jam on his bread fell into his beard, it set off a buzzing noise. Without interrupting his conversation, he extracted three or four bees from his beard, cast them off into the yard and went on with his conversation.

His son was interested in astronomy and so they did practically no work on the land at all. He was also interested in unusual breeds of sheep. I remember going with him in a van with five or six special sheep that they had imported from England to sell at the Dublin market. He wanted to see the stars, so we went out to the top of the Sugar Loaf mountain and were absolutely frozen sleeping in the van. We sold the sheep in the morning and had breakfast in the big hotel at the cattle market. They were both lovely people, so gentle.

SEVEN HANDY PROPOSITIONS

CHARLES HANDY is a social philosopher, a distinguished writer and broadcaster who challenges our thinking on issues such as the nature and role of work in our lives, work-life balance and the purpose of our existence. Here, talking about his book, 'The Hungry Spirit', he offers seven propositions for what he calls 'a school for life and work'.

1. THE DISCOVERY OF ONESELF IS MORE IMPORTANT THAN THE DISCOVERY OF THE WORLD

A school that equips its students with self-confidence, a saleable skill or competence and a high order of social skills has started those students on the road to a full identity.

2. EVERYONE IS GOOD AT SOMETHING

Drawing on Howard Gardner's Theory of Multiple Intelligences, Handy sets out his own list of intelligences (e.g. Spatial Intelligence, Intuitive Intelligence, Interpersonal Intelligence). 'It should be the first duty of a school for life to help the young person build up an "intelligence profile", then to encourage him or her to develop the preferred set of those intelligences and to work out best how to employ them.'

3. LIFE IS A MARATHON, NOT A HORSE RACE

A horse race commits most of the field to being 'also-rans'. 'In life there is no winning and losing, only the taking part and the getting better.'

4. KNOWING WHAT IS NOT AS IMPORTANT AS KNOWING WHERE, HOW AND WHY

'Schools ought not to be force-feeding their students, but teaching them to feed themselves.' This has serious implications for the role of the teacher, moving from the sole repository of knowledge to facilitator and guide.

5. SCHOOL SHOULD BE LIKE WORK AND VICE VERSA

'What would happen if we treated the children as the real workers in an enlightened factory of creativity, with the teachers as the consultants and senior management ...? Work would be organised around tasks to be done ... Learning would then be seen to be the necessary ingredient for better performance on the tasks.'

6. LIFE IS A JOURNEY WHICH STARTS AT HOME

Learning is a lifelong process and it begins with the encouragement of the young child by its parents. 'The best way to learn how to travel is to start travelling ... The natural curiosity of the young is the only fuel needed ...'

7. LEARNING IS EXPERIENCE UNDERSTOOD IN TRANQUILLITY

'The process of education is fundamentally skewed. Most of it comes before, rather than after, experience ... The big danger of a front-loading educational system is that it turns into a one-chance experience. If at first you don't succeed, you don't usually try again ... '

A PROCESS OF UNLEARNING

Writer DENIS JOHNSTON'*s memories of his schooldays are far from idyllic ...*

THE OLDER I get the more I wonder whether schooldays ever end, because looking back on it all, there is as much to unlearn in a lifetime of education as there is to learn. But to confine myself – as I must at the moment – to the days of bare knees and bicycles, I must say that during that halcyon period I was given a good deal of superfluous misinformation from nine in the morning till three in the afternoon, followed usually by Games without Fun for the rest of the afternoon and concluding with about two and a half hours of 'prep' in the evenings, which can hardly be described as an 'eight-hour day'. No liberal lunch hour or overtime with pay as enjoyed by our elders. Yet this was our lot at the Dublin day school that I attended from the age of seven to eighteen, with a brief interlude at a Scottish boarding school from which I was fortunately removed, thanks to the intervention of German submarines and Zeppelin raids.

Looking back on it now without any particular resentment, I realise how little I learnt of any consequence during this important period of life. In Ireland, what they taught us in my school was largely governed by what was called the 'Intermediate Board of Education'. I don't know whether this still exists, but its 'set books' had to be followed from year to year if one ever expected to pass their examinations and the school was to get its grants.

As a result of this outside control, I left school with a knowledge of Shakespeare, for instance, that was confined to a number of plays about various King Henries, beginning with number Four in two parts, then the Fifth ('the gentlemen of England now abed when thou art near' – to the best of my recollection), and finally, Henry the Sixth, believe it or not, in three parts! No mention of course – during my time at any rate – of Romeo – presumably a sexy subject. Or Lear. Or even of Caesar – apart from a celebrated argument between Brutus and Cassius. And as for Cleopatra and her barge – well, I leave that to you, as it was not to be studied by us in Stephen's Green. Believe it or not, I had never even seen *Hamlet* until its glories were first unveiled to me by Mícheál MacLiammóir in the Gate at the age of about twenty-five. Maybe this was a good thing, but it can hardly be called Education.

Then there was this matter of French, which we studied in relation to a large coloured picture, *Le Printemps*. And of course that rather enigmatic song about *Au Clair de la Lune*, quite regardless of the fact that the first things to learn in any foreign language are the cardinal numbers, and the expression '*Ou est la gare*' or '*Wo ist der Bahnhof?*' – with the aid of which you can go anywhere abroad in safety. All that survived from Religious Instruction were the names of the Books of the Bible repeated by rote, while Science, of course, was all before Einstein. Which means that the old stuff is all out of date apart from the angles at the base of an Isosceles Triangle. So what does it matter?

I can't remember a single thing that I learnt at my boarding school in Scotland apart from the unimportance of corporal punishment. I was somewhat frightened of this controversial matter at my civilised Dublin school where it was legal, but seldom administered. In Edinburgh, where it was considered to be essential in 'making a man of you' (to coin a phrase), the headmaster could beat you on the bum for capital offences from larceny to sex, the junior masters for boredom in class and general disorder, the prefects for having grub in your locker, and what was classified inaccurately as 'the sixth' for going around with one's hands in one's pockets in a prohibited way. The fact is that, after a little experience of corporal punishment, one becomes largely indifferent to it – an attitude that in later life one can easily adopt towards the experience of being shelled. So maybe there is some point in it after all. Just as it is probably true to say that the only education that lasts is whatever you teach yourself.

LEARNING IN AND OUT OF SCHOOL

MIKE COOLEY *was born in Tuam, Co. Galway. An engineer by profession,
he is now an internationally respected consultant, writer and broadcaster
whose special concern is human-centred technology. Here he recalls two very
different 'ways of knowing'.*

IN THE TECHNICAL school in Tuam I met an extraordinary teacher, Sean
Cleary. He had worked in England for Vickers Engineering so he could
give you a vision of what engineering and metalwork could be like. He
had a deep sense of quality of workmanship. He would hold up a piece
of material and say 'Isn't that beautiful?' The culture that was
transmitted just by doing that was very powerful. I was very keen to
design and build a steam engine and he was a good enough research
facilitator and teacher to say 'Let's try it!' The only machine-tool we had
was a lathe. We needed close-grain cast-iron for the cylinders and there
was simply none available in Tuam. Now if I was going to be a good civil
servant, I would have learned that you write a report about the material
you want, then you write saying that there is none available and you
conclude that the project can't be done! But we heard of an old sawmill
with an abandoned fly-wheel and we knew that a fly-wheel has to
withstand high centrifugal forces, so it would have been made from good
close-grain cast-iron. So we cut a huge chunk out of the fly-wheel and
built a marvellous steam-engine which I have to this day. It was a very
formative experience ...

Playing hurling taught me more than just the game itself. I think
there were seven roads in the town and each road played against the
others. I was very conscious early on that how you defined a road
determined whether you stood a good chance of winning. If all your best
players were within the precincts of the town, you would try to get an
agreement that it was only the roads up to the edge of the town that
counted. We had a number of players who lived out on the Milltown
Road – excellent players – so we wondered how we could change the
rules. We decided that a road would be defined as a road through which
you went on your way to school, so that gave us a much bigger catchment

area. A lot of my capacity to negotiate in trade union work or in complicated international contracts was established in those childhood games.

THE MAKING OF A REBEL

Peadar O'Donnell *recalls a Donegal childhood.*

I was born in Meenmore, Co. Donegal in 1893. My father worked a small holding in between migrating to Scotland in summer for the harvesting and operating a kiln for the drying of oats in winter. I was one of eleven children so I spent some of my early years living with my grandmother. It was a very noisy townland, full of gaiety and laughter. The houses were quite close together so we all knew each other's business. If we saw a neighbour going the road in his Sunday clothes on a Tuesday, there would be great curiosity about what was taking him to town ...

I went to school at less than three years of age and on my first day one of the older boys, Willie Jim, gave me a rose and told me to fling it at the teacher – which I did! He just smiled at me. School was a primitive affair – mainly because of the indiscipline of lads who had been hired at the hiring fair and had missed a lot of school. I often got into trouble by speaking out against some stupid comments other children made. This was greatly resented of course and I usually suffered on the way home when the fellow that had been humiliated earlier took it out on me in the form of a hammering. I was a bright lad. The teacher always ensured I was present for the inspector's visit. I became a pet of the inspector – he used to give me sixpence. Some of my essays were censored because of the seditious ideas they contained. I wrote an essay about St Patrick's Day in which I expressed regret that the banners being waved were not in defiance of British rule in Ireland. That was censored for the inspector's visit.

My mother was very keen on us going to school. She was a very advanced thinker. Ours was one of the few houses that had a stock of books. I remember A.M. Sullivan's *Stories from Irish History*, *The Wild Rose of Lough Gill* and some Dickens novels. My mother was a supporter of James Larkin and she was the only person in the place who stood up for Patrick McGill's *Children of the Dead End* when that book was published. Times were particularly hard on women in those days. I can remember my mother propping me up against a bundle of sheaves while she sheared a whole field of oats. Life could not have survived along the western seaboard then if women had not carried burdens that no woman should be asked to carry. There were no clocks until the building of the railway. People went by the stars. I remember my mother and other women judging by the stars when to set out on a six-mile walk to a mission. In the evening the women would do the housework and knit woollen socks for a local industry. Again, they would have to walk quite a distance to deliver the socks. It was my mother's influence that led me to dream of rescuing Ireland from British rule one day.

The first time I ever saw a priest was when he came on horseback, collecting money to build a church. He was talking crossly to my mother. I was very young but I picked up some stones and threw them at the horse. He shied away and the priest rode off. My mother picked me up and ran into the house crying. Ironically, when I was older I entered and won an essay competition in the local newspaper. The title was 'What is Your Ambition?'. Mine was to be a missioner. As a young man I had the glimmers of a vocation but you couldn't do that on a few acres of bogland. Much later in life I discussed this with a bishop. If I *had* followed my vocation, I said, I would have gone right to the top and it's not Cardinal McRory would be in Armagh but me! Indeed, the bishop replied, and you would have been just as conservative as your fellow-countyman – Cardinal Logue!

There was a lot of poverty in my childhood and beggars were a common sight going the road looking for a 'shakedown' for the night. For those who could afford it, emigration was the only escape. The American Wake – a goodbye party for the emigrants – was a regular event and it would end with this song:

Lads and lasses as you're passing
Heed these words I'm going to say
How the people from old Ireland
Are moving off to Amerikay

Oh yes they're bound for a foreign nation
For in their home they cannot stand
And as they put their foot on board
They say they're bound for the Yankee land

So hurrah for the darling sons of Ireland
Our fair son is going away
Every day they are emigrating
In thousands off to Amerikay.

After the wake came the convoy, when the whole townland accompanied the emigrants to the railway station. There were very affecting and emotional scenes, as we all knew the emigrants were passing away forever. They would never come home again.

A STATE COMES OF AGE

January 1998. The Irish State is seventy-five years old. Two men who grew up with the State – and who were at the heart of its development – reflect on its growth. They are KEN WHITAKER *and* PATRICK LYNCH.

KW: I would look on the seventy-five years as the coming of age of the State. It started off as a very weak economic entity and spent its first ten years trying to recover from the physical and emotional damage of the civil war. It did very well and now – seventy-five years on – it has come of age economically, culturally and in sporting terms.

PL: After the Treaty we derived benefits that neither the founders of the State nor those who opposed the Treaty ever expected. If Arthur Griffith had his way, he would have an industrial revolution in the new State. For him the agricultural revolution had already occurred with Davitt and Parnell. He didn't live to see the fruition of his ideas but – by a paradox – many decades later, Sean Lemass followed the Sinn Féin views on industry that Griffith had been discussing.

KW: My instinct is that things were so shaky in those early years that any kind of revolutionary policy would have been out of the question. In fact, we were well served by those who bedded down the democratic institutions. They took no risks and this was necessary because there was great doubt about the viability of the State – a doubt that persisted until the 1950s. I say we have come of age *now* because we are able to maintain an increased population at a reasonably high standard; there is no longer any net emigration; we are an open society economically – quite competitive – and therefore we have an independence that will serve us very well for the future.

PL: There is an air of self-confidence among our people today. Of course we have an underclass and more unemployment than we would wish, but there has been a transformation in our economy that would have been unthinkable twenty years ago. The contrast between 1998 and 1956 is extraordinary. To me, 1956 was the nadir of our economy. There seemed to be a death wish abroad. We had very high unemployment and emigration, economic stagnation. We had no belief in our future economically or socially. There was a threat to our political institutions which both Mr Cosgrave and Mr de Valera had stabilised so well in the earlier decades.

KW: One of the great contributing factors to that stability was the widespread ownership of land and dwellings.

THE CURIOUS MIND

PL: It's worth recalling that the first national loan for ten million pounds was floated in 1923 and it was taken up by the Irish people when the Irish banks refused to contribute a penny. This indicated the confidence of the people in themselves.

KW: That would be £330 million in today's money. It was real democracy, and remember, Ireland then was a predominantly rural society. In 1922 there was only one person employed in industry for every eleven employed on the land (and many of the latter were in a state of misery). Now there are three in industry for every one on the land ... We must keep remembering too that Ireland over those seventy-five years was not the world. External influences have been of great importance – changes in world production and trade. For example the Great Depression of the 1930s hit us badly when we had an Economic War here. Then new technology affected transport and communications. Trade has opened up. Protection has been abandoned. So the world has become both a smaller and a more competitive place and much more interdependent.

PL: That interdependence was very evident in 1973 when the first oil crisis took place and economic development here was diverted from its course in a manner from which it took quite a number of years to recover. Going back to an earlier period – 1922 to 1932 – Ireland under people like Gilligan and Costello played a very important role in the evolution of the Commonwealth. They combined particularly with Canada in seeking independence from the old Empire, leading to the Statute of Westminster in 1931 after which Commonwealth members were independent dominions. That independence was recognised by Mr de Valera when he came to construct his new constitution in 1937.

KW: Garret FitzGerald wrote an interesting piece recently when he claimed that the 1937 Constitution legitimised the State for a lot of dissidents from the Treaty days – maybe as much as a third of the population were induced to accept the legitimacy of the State.

PL: As mentioned earlier, the Economic War between Ireland and Britain hit us badly in the 1930s. Again the steadfastness of the people in accepting hardships and supporting the government is quite remarkable. The war ended in 1938 with a satisfactory settlement for both sides – particularly for us with the ending of a number of economic penalties and with the return of the ports which made possible our neutrality in the World War which followed. The manner in which that war was conducted with extraordinary diplomatic skill by de Valera and in which the provision of supplies was handled by Lemass is something worth noting. An important figure here was John Leyden, head of the Department of Supplies – a very practical, hard-headed and enlightened man.

KW: After the war it became clear that protectionism was not going to be the solution to our problems nor was agriculture going to be the foundation of progress, because our exports were going to a consumer-dominated market which meant low prices for us.

PL: Just when we reached that economic nadir in 1956, along came Ken Whitaker and a number of colleagues in the Department of Finance with *Economic Development* – a document that gave us hope by listing the things that could and should be done to lift us out of the morass. The emphasis was on capital investment and this document led to the first and second economic plans which changed our attitudes and began to achieve positive objectives.

KW: It was difficult initially to get the industrial protection dismantled, but Lemass was in the right place at the right time. Like De Gaulle getting out of Algeria, nobody else could have achieved the change so quickly. He was the one man who knew most about how to develop industry in Ireland.

PL: Then in 1965 came the Anglo-Irish Free Trade Agreement, which was the first tangible recognition of an open economy, that protection was giving way to a different economic society.

KW: In the late 1960s we ran into wage inflation, with expectations outrunning our capacity. This was capped by the oil crisis in the 1970s, which raised inflation to unbelievable heights – almost 25 per cent per annum. That set us back and unfortunately we tackled it by borrowing abroad for current domestic needs. So again the economy stagnated between 1970 and 1985 and we were fortunate that there were politicians in place in 1985 to put us on the right track again.

PL: I think it is important to underline the role of politicians who played a prominent and progressive part in the development of the State since its birth. One thinks of 1987 when a combination of McSharry, Dukes and Haughey adopted a financial policy which set the foundation for the kind of economy we have today. Earlier, Patrick Hillery and Donogh O'Malley made an immense contribution by promoting free post-primary education. This with the setting up of regional technological colleges and other advances in third level education laid the foundation for the economic growth we have today.

KW: I endorse that fully. Education has been the key to our success. In a mere ten years the numbers participating at third level have doubled. There is still a low representation of children from poorer families but there are moves afoot to correct that. Overall the average family is three to four times better off than it was in 1922. In our time too there have been great improvements in health. The death rate has been halved, life expectancy has gone up by fifteen years or so and infant mortality – which was 10 per cent in the 1920s – is down to less than a tenth of that today. My generation did feel we were privileged to be the first well-educated generation in the Irish public service and we felt an obligation to serve the State well because of that.

PL: The day we joined the European community in 1973 was one of the most important dates of the past seventy-five years, because our membership of that community has transformed this country intellectually, socially and economically.

KW: I think 'payback time' is possibly coming now, when we will have to accept that we will no longer be beneficiaries of structural and other funding and instead may have to contribute to the community's budget. One other point I would like to make is regarding social change. The family is the social unit that has changed most in our time. Marriage has become a neglected institution. One-third of all first pregnancies today is to unmarried mothers. I am troubled by present trends in morality.

PL: Overall, the great landmarks of the past seventy-five years for me have been the elimination of the squalor of both inner city and rural Ireland and the improvement in material standards for the great majority of our people.

KW: The great economic landmark for me has been the recognition that there had to be a change of policy from inwardness (i.e. protection) to outwardness (free trade, competitive production for export markets). A lot still needs to be done to eliminate inner city poverty which overflows into crime, drug-taking etc.

PL: By and large, we are moving towards a just society, but we are not there yet.

AND FINALLY ...

The closing words from the script of A Letter to Olive *– my wife of thirty-three years, who died suddenly in 2001. This was by far the programme closest to my heart and by far the programme that drew the greatest response in twenty-five years of broadcasting.*

ONLY NOW DO I realise that you were truly and literally my 'other half'. With your going a great part of me has gone too. And I owe you so much and never told you how much. Well, I'm telling you now.

You made me the person that I am. My real date of birth is 1 March 1966 (the day we met in a TB sanatorium) – throat swab-test, vision in a black leather coat, door closed in her face! I look again at your memoriam card. Unreal. I look at the verse –

> Fill my sails, Adonai
> With Thy rhythmical breath
> And blow me
> Wherever Thou wilt
> Over emerald waves.

For someone who loved the sea, worked on the sea, lived by the sea, died in the sea, it seems just right. And I love the notion of freedom – a free spirit wandering where she wills. But don't wander too far. I need you. Now more than ever. So stay very close to me, please, or else I fall apart.

> As I mowed the lawn at sunset
> Did I see you give a little wave
> On returning from your walk?
> Did I see you move about the kitchen
> Making your 'tup of tea'?
> Did I watch you watch the sun set
> From your conservatory chair?
> Did I smile as you gesticulated
> To a friend on the phone?

Did I notice you glide past the window
With a little glass of Muscadet?

And when the dark descended
And I came in, exhausted,
Did I hear you call out
'If you're making a tup of tea,
I wouldn't mind another' ... ?
Of course I did
But when I went to make it,
The dark was all around.

Love you. Miss you. Above all – above all – thank you. *Haec olim meminisse iuvabit.* (One day it will delight us to remember these things.)

And it was lovely then
And you were lovely then
And we were young
And so in love
And it was lovely then
And will be so again
And will be so again.

BIOGRAPHICAL NOTES

ABBOT, JOHN: Former teacher and headmaster who set up the 21st Century Learning Initiative – a transnational association of educationalists. Travels widely as lecturer and advisor on education and learning. His books include *The Unfinished Revolution* and *Learning Makes Sense.*

ARRUDA, MARCOS: Brazilian educator and economist who works with the labour and co-operative movements in his native country.

BAKER, DON: Musician and actor who spent some years of his boyhood in Daingean Reformatory, Co. Offaly.

BARNES, JANE: Author of a comprehensive study of Irish industrial schools – *Saving the Waifs and Strays.*

BERRY, FR TOM: Passionist priest, writer, teacher and activist on man's relationship with his environment. His *New Story* aimed at fostering reverence between humans and the earth.

BINCHY, MAEVE: Bestselling writer of popular novels including *Light a Penny Candle, Circle of Friends* and *Tara Road.*

BLACK, JACK: Founder and Course Director of MindStore – a leading personal development company in the UK.

BOHAN, FR HARRY: Clare-born priest committed to the revitalisation of rural communities through housing projects such as the Rural Housing Organisation. Founder of the Céifin Centre for Values-Led Change.

BOYLAN, CLARE: Former journalist who became a full-time writer with successful novels such as *Holy Pictures* and *Last Resorts*. *d. 2006*.

BOYLAN, SEAN: Herbalist and long-time manager of Meath Gaelic Football team with whom he won four All-Ireland titles. His autobiography – *The Will to Win* – was published in 2006.

BRADY, EILÍS: Folklorist and collector of children's rhymes and street-games, which she published in *All In! All In! d. 2007*.

BRUNER, JEROME: American psychologist whose cognitive approach to his work in childhood learning has made him a key figure in educational reform in the USA and Britain.

BUTLER, DOROTHY: New Zealand-based lecturer and writer on children's books. Her *Babies Need Books* has been an invaluable guide to generations of parents.

BUZAN, TONY: Lecturer and prolific writer on how we learn and remember and how we can 'tap into our natural genius'. His books *Head First* and *Use Your Head* are international bestsellers.

CHILDERS, ERSKINE: Diplomat, writer and broadcaster. Son of the former President of Ireland. Former Senior Advisor to the United Nations. *d. 1996*.

CHOMSKY, NOAM: Philadelphia-born educator and linguist, based at Massachusetts Institute of Technology. Prolific writer on linguistics and politics. Outspoken critic of US foreign policy.

CHUKOVSKY, KORNEI: Russian author of children's books. *From Two to Five* is his classic documentation of his observation of children's acquisition and use of language. *d. 1969.*

CLARKE, EUGENE L.: Accountant employed by Henry Ford and Son Ltd. on the setting up of their Cork plant in 1917. *d. 1987.*

COADY, MICHAEL: Poet and broadcaster. Native of Carrick-on-Suir, Co. Tipperary. Collections include *All Souls, Full Tide* and *One Another.*

COOLAHAN, JOHN: Former Professor of Education at NUI Maynooth. Author of *Irish Education: History and Structure.* Adviser and lecturer on educational issues at many levels.

COOLEY, MIKE: Tuam, Co. Galway-born engineer who is now a writer, broadcaster and consultant on work and technology.

COON COME, MATTHEW: Canadian politician and activist. Leader of the Cree community in Northern Quebec and instrumental in forcing the Quebec government to cancel a major hydro-electric scheme. Former National Chief of the Assembly of First Nations.

COVEY, STEPHEN: Writer, teacher and consultant on leadership and family guidance. One of *Time* magazine's '25 Most Influential Americans', his *Seven Habits of Highly Effective People* was named the 'Most Influential Business Book of the 20th Century'.

CRYSTAL, DAVID: Holyhead, Wales-based writer and lecturer on linguistics. He has broadcast on language extensively on BBC Radio and Television.

CUNNINGHAM, GEORGE: Former teacher. Writer, lecturer and broadcaster on local history and heritage matters. Particularly involved in the heritage of his native Roscrea, Co. Tipperary.

DAHL, ROALD: Internationally acclaimed writer for children. His bestsellers include *The Witches, The BFG, James and the Giant Peach* and *Charlie and the Chocolate Factory. d. 1990.*

DALY, CAHAL: Former Bishop of Down and Connor and Archbishop of Armagh. Appointed Cardinal in 1991. His episcopal career coincided with the Northern Ireland 'Troubles', during which he was an unrelenting critic of violence. Prolific writer on theology and philosophy.

DALY, HERMAN: Former Senior Economist with the World Bank and later professor at the University of Maryland. Now seen as a 'maverick' economist for his views on growth and the environment. Has written extensively on ecological economics.

DE BARRA, EIBHLÍS: Cork-born storyteller and contributor to radio and television. Her memoir – *Bless 'Em All* – is a poignant record of growing up in 'the lanes of Cork'. *d. 2006.*

DE BONO, EDWARD: International authority on conceptual and creative thinking. Prolific writer and lecturer in those areas. Particularly associated with the concept of 'lateral thinking'.

DEENY, JIM: Lurgan, Co. Armagh-born doctor who became Chief Medical Officer to the Department of Health in Dublin in the 1940s. Conducted a major national survey on tuberculosis. Later had a distinguished career with the World Health Organisation. His memoir is entitled *To Cure and To Care. d. 1994.*

DEVLIN, POLLY: Writer and journalist who was born in Ardboe, Co. Tyrone. That landscape provided her with two books – *All of Us There* (a memoir) and *The Far Side of the Lough: Stories from an Irish Childhood.*

DONLON, PATRICIA: Former Director of the Chester Beatty Library and the National Library of Ireland. Respected authority on children's literature. Currently Director of the Tyrone Guthrie Centre, Annaghmakerrig.

DONOGHUE, DENIS: Distinguished critic of English Literature. Formerly lecturer in English at University College Dublin, later holder of the Chair of English at New York University. His memoir – *Warrenpoint* – describes his growing up in Northern Ireland.

DOOLAN, LELIA: Former television producer with RTÉ and artistic director with the Abbey Theatre. Later chairperson of the Irish Film Board. Maintains a continuing interest in film, drama and communications.

DORAN, SEAMUS: Former vocational school principal whose innovative ideas on 'learning for living' led to the founding of *Macra na Tuaithe* – now *Foróige* – a pioneering movement in youth development. *d. 2007*.

ELKIND, DAVID: American child psychologist and author who has written on the dangers of rushing children through childhood in such books as *The Hurried Child, The Power of Play* and *All Grown Up and No Place to Go*.

FINE, ANNE: Award-winning writer for children and adults. Former Children's Laureate. A hugely popular children's author who has been twice voted Children's Writer of the Year.

FITZGERALD, GARRET: Politician, former leader of Fine Gael and former Taoiseach (1981–82 and 1982–87). In retirement, he remained active in writing and contributing to media discussions. His autobiography is entitled *All in a Life. d. 2011*.

FITT, GERRY: Belfast-born politician who grew up amid severe poverty. Prominent in the Civil Rights movement and became a member of the SDLP. Its MP for West Belfast, he was an outspoken critic of the IRA. Later made a peer and took his place in the House of Lords. *d. 2005.*

FLANAGAN, FIONNULA: Distinguished Dublin-born actress on stage and screen. Developed a particular affinity with the work of James Joyce.

FLANAGAN, FRANK: Lecturer in Education at Mary Immaculate College, Limerick. Writer and broadcaster on educational matters.

FRENCH, MARILYN: New York-born feminist writer, influenced by Simone de Beauvoir and Kate Millett. Her debut novel, *The Women's Room*, became a controversial bestseller. Wrote also on patriarchy and the abuse of women. *d. 2009.*

FRIEL, BRIAN: Omagh-born playwright and short story writer. His twenty-plus plays have received universal acclaim, dealing with issues of history, family and memory and creating memorable characters.

GAGEBY, DOUGLAS: Belfast-born journalist and newspaper editor, notably with the *Irish Times. d. 2004.*

GARDNER, HOWARD: Harvard psychologist who came to prominence with his Theory of Multiple Intelligences.

GRAHAM, PADDY: Mullingar-born artist whose expressionist paintings are often inspired by his Co. Westmeath childhood.

GREEVY, BERNADETTE: Dublin-born contralto, internationally renowned as a recording artist and operatic singer. *d. 2008.*

GREGORY, ANNE & CATHERINE: Grand-daughters of Lady Augusta Gregory of Coole. Anne is author of *Me and Nu* – a memoir of childhood at Coole. *Catherine d. 2000, Anne d. 2008.*

HANDY, CHARLES: Writer, broadcaster and social philosopher. His many bestsellers include *The Future of Work*, *The Empty Raincoat*, *The Elephant and the Flea* and his autobiography – *Myself and Other More Important Matters.*

HARGREAVES, ANDY: English-born holder of the Chair of Education at Boston College, USA. Writer and lecturer on culture, change and leadership in education.

HEANEY, SEAMUS: Co. Derry-born poet whose imposing body of work earned him the Nobel Prize for Literature in 1995. Former lecturer at Queen's University, Belfast and Carysfort College, Dublin and Professor of Poetry at Harvard and Oxford. His many collections have won awards worldwide.

HEATHCOTE, DOROTHY: Yorkshire-born teacher, writer and long-time advocate of drama-in-education.

HIGGINS, ANNE: Former teacher and community worker. Founder of the 'Three O'Clock School' – an after-school initiative for parents. Now lectures in third level education.

HIGGINS, MICHAEL D.: Labour Party politician and poet. Former university lecturer in political science and Minister for Arts, Culture and the Gaeltacht (1992–97).

HUGHES, SHIRLEY: Prolific award-winning author and illustrator of children's books for over fifty years.

HUME, JOHN: Early involvement in Civil Rights and Housing issues led to his election as an Independent MP for Derry. Later founded the SDLP, of which he became leader. Won the Nobel Peace Prize with David Trimble (1998).

JOHNSTON, DENIS: Dublin-born playwright and war correspondent during the Second World War. His *Nine Rivers from Jordan* is a philosophical war memoir. *d. 1984.*

KANE, EILEEN: Lecturer, writer and consultant on anthropology. Co-founder of GroundWork – a non-profit organisation specialising in research on education, environment and health issues. Author of *Doing Your Own Research.*

KEANE, MOLLY: Co. Kildare-born novelist and playwright, initially under the pseudonym of M.J. Farrell. The country-house life she grew up in subsequently became the material for books like *Good Behaviour* and *Time After Time. d. 1996.*

KELLY, JOHNNY: Wisest of men from the bogs of Ballivor, Co. Meath. *d. 1998.*

KELLY, MAEVE: Co. Clare-born writer of novels, short stories and poetry. Her particular concern has been the abuse of women and women's issues in general.

KELLY, OISÍN: Distinguished sculptor whose many public installations include the *Children of Lir* in Dublin's Garden of Remembrance. *d. 1981.*

KENNELLY, BRENDAN: Co. Kerry-born poet. Former Professor of Modern Literature at Trinity College Dublin. His prolific poetry output is represented in over twenty collections. Regular contributor to radio and television.

KIELY, BENEDICT: Co. Tyrone-born novelist, short story writer, journalist, broadcaster and lecturer. *d. 2007.*

KING, CECIL: Newspaper magnate, nephew of Lords Northcliffe and Rothermere. Developed the *Daily Mirror* newspaper and became chairman of Daily Mirror Newspapers Ltd. *d. 1987.*

KNEESHAW, MARGARET: Former Children's and Schools Librarian, Dublin City Libraries. *d. 1998.*

KOHN, ALFIE: Writer and lecturer on education and parenting. Books such as *No Contest* and *Punished by Rewards* highlight his criticism of competition and rewards in the classroom. www.alfiekohn.org

LEACH, PENELOPE: London-based writer and broadcaster on child development and parenting. Author of the bestselling *Your Baby and Child*.

LEAHY, ALICE: Former nurse whose work with voluntary groups led her to set up TRUST, which offers practical care and rehabilitation to homeless people.

LEE, JOE: Kerry-born historian, writer and broadcaster on modern Irish history. Former member of Seanad Éireann and Professor of History at University College, Cork.

LEONARD, HUGH: Pseudonym of John Keyes Byrne. Playwright, writer and newspaper columnist. Had a long association with the Dublin Theatre Festival. The largely autobiographical *Da* is his best-known play. *d. 2009.*

LEYDEN, BRIAN: Leitrim-based novelist, short story writer and teacher of creative writing.

LIEBSCHNER, JOACHIM: German-born leading Froebel scholar. Author of two major studies on the work of Friedrich Froebel.

LINDSAY, PATRICK: Former barrister and Master of the High Court. Elected as a Fine Gael TD in 1954 and became the first Minister for the Gaeltacht. Brilliant orator and *raconteur. d. 1993.*

LINGARD, JOAN: Edinburgh-born writer who spent most of her childhood in Belfast. Won acclaim for her quintet of books written against the backdrop of the Northern Ireland conflict.

LYNCH, PATRICK: Former Professor of Political Economy, University College Dublin, chairman of Aer Lingus and deputy chairman of AIB. Frequent consultant and adviser on economics to the Department of Finance, OECD and the Council of Europe. *d. 2001.*

McBRIDE, SEAN: Son of Maud Gonne and Major John McBride. Former Chief of Staff of the IRA. Barrister and politician. As a *Clann na Poblachta* TD he held the post of Minister for External Affairs. Awarded the Nobel Peace Prize in 1974 for his work on Human Rights issues. *d. 1988.*

McCANN, CATHERINE: Former physiotherapist, now counsellor, theologian and writer on caring, stress management and creative living in older years.

MacCURTAIN, MARGARET: Dominican nun (Sr Benvenuta), teacher, lecturer and writer on history, in particular on the role of women.

McGAHERN, JOHN: Former teacher from Co. Leitrim who was dismissed from his job following the banning of his novel, *The Dark.* Subsequently won international acclaim for his novels and short stories. *d. 2006.*

McGinitie, Walter: Professor of Education at the University of Victoria, British Columbia. Former president of the International Reading Association and author of the *Gates-McGinitie Reading Tools*.

McGough, Roger: Liverpool-born poet and humorist. For his services to poetry he has been awarded an OBE and a CBE.

McKenna, T.P.: Distinguished Cavan-born actor on stage, screen and radio.

Milligan, Spike: Comic performer, actor, writer and broadcaster. Member of the famous Goons radio comedy team. *d. 2002*.

Mitchell, Frank: Dublin-born polymath who achieved distinction in zoology, geology and archaeology. Former Professor of Quaternary Studies at Trinity College Dublin. Wrote extensively about the Irish landscape. *d. 1997*.

Mitchell, George: US Senator who played a major role in brokering the Good Friday Agreement in Northern Ireland.

Montanaro, Silvana: Italian medical doctor who is an authority on the life and work of Maria Montessori.

Mooney, Sr Cyril: Bray, Co. Wicklow-born Loreto nun who has spent her career in education in India, particularly devoted to the care of 'street children'.

Moore, Sir Patrick: Astronomer and musician. Presenter of the long-running TV programme *The Sky at Night*.

Mulcahy, Aidan & Síle: Husband and wife teachers who founded their own secondary school in Cloghane, Co. Kerry to meet local needs. *Aidan d. 2006*.

MULLARNEY, MAIRE: Former nurse who with her husband taught all her eleven children at home and wrote about the experience in *Anything School Can Do, You Can Do Better. d. 2008.*

NEWMAN-DEVLIN, EDITH: Dublin-born teacher and lecturer in English literature. Her lectures to and travels with extramural students at Queen's University Belfast for over forty years have become legendary.

NUGENT, WALTER: Professor Emeritus of History at University of Notre Dame, Indiana. Author of several books on American history.

O'BRIEN, EDNA: Co. Clare-born writer who came to prominence with *The Country Girls* and subsequently built a distinguished career with a succession of acclaimed novels.

O'CONNOR, SEAN: Civil servant. Former Secretary to the Department of Education. *d. 1987.*

O'DONNELL, PEADAR: Donegal-born teacher, member of the Old IRA, political activist, novelist and editor of *The Bell* magazine. *d. 1986.*

O'DONOHUE, JOHN: Writer, lecturer and broadcaster on Celtic Spirituality. His books *Anam Chara, Eternal Echoes* and *Benedictus* have been worldwide bestsellers. *d. 2008.*

O'NEILL, CECILY: International authority on drama-in-education. Author and editor of several books on drama.

O'REILLY, TONY: Former rugby star who became chief executive of the Dairy Board at the age of twenty-five. Later he became chief executive of H.J. Heinz and chairman of Independent Newspapers.

PLUNKETT, JAMES: Pseudonym of Dublin-born James Plunkett Kelly, short story writer, novelist and television producer. Best known for his novel *Strumpet City*, set in early twentieth century Dublin. *d. 2003*.

POTTER, MAUREEN: Much-loved Dublin-born actress and comedienne who appeared on stage, film and television over a long career. *d. 2004*.

PUTNAM, ROBERT: Professor of Public Policy at Harvard University. His book *Bowling Alone* highlighted the decline of social capital in the USA.

QUINN, FEARGAL: Businessman. Former owner of the Superquinn supermarket chain. Member of Seanad Éireann.

ROBERTSON, JAMES: Former policy-maker with the British government, latterly an independent writer and thinker who argues for a saner, more humane and more enabling worldview.

SCHUMACHER, DIANA: Daughter-in-law of E.F. Schumacher – author of the seminal book *Small is Beautiful*.

SEED, JOHN: Environmental activist, songwriter and film-maker. Founder and director of the Rainforest Information Centre in Australia.

SEYMOUR, JOHN: Essex-born writer and promoter of self-sufficiency. Spent much of his life in Africa as a farm manager, soldier and traveller. Later settled in Ireland and set up his School of Self-Sufficiency. *d. 2004*.

SHEEHAN, PATRICIA: Southampton-born doctor who specialised in communication and speech disorders. Worked also as a bereavement counsellor and spent time in Nigeria working with disabled Civil War refugees. *d. 1994*.

SHERIDAN, JOHN D.: Humorist, writer and newspaper columnist, very popular in the 1950s and 1960s. *d. 1980.*

SIMMS, GEORGE OTTO: Dublin-born priest of the Church of Ireland. Archbishop of Dublin, 1956-59. Archbishop of Armagh and Primate of All Ireland 1969-80. Deeply interested in Celtic monasticism, he wrote a number of books for young people – *Exploring the Book of Kells, Brendan the Navigator* and *St Patrick. d. 1991.*

STERN, ISAAC: Internationally acclaimed violinist and conductor. *d. 2001.*

SUN, PATRICIA: Californian psychologist, advocate of whole-brain learning.

SUTCLIFF, ROSEMARY: Children's writer who overcame disability to produce a series of acclaimed historical novels. *d. 1992.*

SUZUKI, SHINICHI: Japanese musician and teacher who devised the now worldwide Suzuki Method of teaching music to very young children. *d. 1998.*

USTINOV, SIR PETER: London-born actor, novelist, playwright, film director, opera producer and brilliant *raconteur* and entertainer. *d. 2004.*

VANIER, JEAN: Canadian-born former naval officer who set up a community – *L'Arche* (the Ark) – to help disabled adults who were otherwise excluded from normal life. From that small beginning *L'Arche* has spread worldwide.

WAAGE, TROND: Norwegian Ombudsman for Children.

WHITAKER, KEN: Co. Down-born civil servant whose ideas inspired the writing of *Economic Development* (1958) which marked the opening up of the Irish economy. Former Governor of the Central Bank, member of Seanad Éireann and chancellor of the National University of Ireland.

WILSON, GORDON: Worker for peace and forgiveness who came to prominence following the death of his daughter Marie in the Enniskillen bombing (1987). *d. 1995.*

ZANDER, BEN: Conductor of the Boston Philharmonic Orchestra, professor at the New England Conservatory of Music and writer and lecturer on the *Art of Possibility.*